HUMAN RIGHTS: THEORY AND MEASUREMENT

POLICY STUDIES ORGANIZATION SERIES

General Editor: Stuart S. Nagel, Professor of Political Science, University of Illinois at Urbana-Champaign

David Louis Cingranelli (*editor*)
HUMAN RIGHTS: Theory and Measurement

Sheldon H. Danziger and Kent E. Portney (*editors*)
THE DISTRIBUTIONAL IMPACTS OF PUBLIC POLICIES

Don F. Hadwiger and William P. Browne (*editors*)
PUBLIC POLICY AND AGRICULTURAL TECHNOLOGY:
Adversity despite Achievement

Richard C. Hula (*editor*)
MARKET-BASED PUBLIC POLICY

Rita Mae Kelly (*editor*)
PROMOTING PRODUCTIVITY IN THE PUBLIC SECTOR:
Problems, Strategies and Prospects

Fred Lazin, Samuel Aroni and Yehuda Gradus (*editors*)
THE POLICY IMPACT OF UNIVERSITIES IN DEVELOPING
REGIONS

J. David Roessner (*editor*)
GOVERNMENT INNOVATION POLICY: Design,
Implementation, Evaluation

Human Rights
Theory and Measurement

Edited by

David Louis Cingranelli
Associate Professor,
Department of Political Science
SUNY, Binghamton

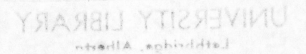
St. Martin's Press in association with the
New York POLICY STUDIES ORGANIZATION

All rights reserved. For information write:
Scholarly and Reference Division,
St. Martin's Press, Inc., 175 Fifth Avenue, New York, N.Y. 10010

First published in the United States of America in 1988

Printed in Hong Kong

ISBN 0–312–01612–3

Library of Congress Cataloging-in-Publication Data
Human rights.
(Policy Studies Organization series)
Includes index.
1. Human rights. 2. Civil rights. I. Cingranelli,
David L. II. Series: Policy Studies Organization
series (New York, N.Y.)
JC571.H7795 1988 323.4 88–4508
ISBN 0–312–01612–3

Contents

List of Tables

List of Figures

Notes on the Contributors

Zehra F. Arat is an Assistant Professor of Political Science at Iona College. She received her BA in political science from Bogazici University in Istanbul, Turkey, and her MA and PhD from the State University of New York at Binghamton. Her speciality is comparative policy analysis, and her current research interests include economic, welfare and human rights policies and their impact on the stability of democratic political systems.

Joyce Aschenbrenner is Professor of Anthropology at Southern Illinois University at Edwardsville. She is Acting Director of Women's Studies at SIUE and teaches a course, 'Women and Social Institutions', with two colleagues. She has conducted fieldwork in South Asia and in black communities in Chicago and Southern Illinois.

David Louis Cingranelli is Associate Professor of Political Science and Acting Associate Dean of the School of Arts and Sciences at the State University of New York at Binghamton. He received his PhD from the University of Pennyslvania in 1977 and is now conducting research on American foreign policy toward the Third World.

M. Glen Johnson is Professor of Political Science and Director of the International Studies Program at Vassar College. He has written on scheduled castes in India and on US foreign policy. His current work deals with human rights and US foreign policy.

James E. Lennertz is an Associate Professor of Government and Law at Lafayette College in Easton, Pennsylvania. His professional interests include the development of tort and property law, apportionment, medical ethics and professional responsibility and water resources and society. He has published articles in *Liberal Education*, the *Journal of Law and Religion*, *The Proceedings of the Western Society for French History* and *Policy Studies Journal*.

Edward C. McDonagh is Professor Emeritus McDonagh and Dean of the College of Social and Behavioral Sciences and Chair of the Department of Sociology at Ohio State University. Previously, he held comparable positions at the University of Southern California, where he received his PhD in sociology in 1942. His research has been in the areas of social stratification and selected social problems.

He is Fellow of the American Sociological Association (Co-Chair of the National Conference Committee 1963 and member of the Budget and Executive Committee 1975–8). He is author (with E. S. Richards) of *Ethnic Relations in the United States* (1953), (with J. E. Nordskog and M. J. Vincent) of *Analyzing Social Problems* (1956, revised 1969), (with Jon E. Simpson) of *Social Problems: Persistent Challenges* (1965, revised 1969). He was Associate Editor of *Sociometry*, 1962–5. He has published in many journals, including *American Sociological Review*, *American Journal of Sociology* and *Social Forces*.

Eileen L. McDonagh is Associate Professor of Political Science at Northeastern University, where she has been teaching since 1975. She received her PhD from Harvard University, Department of Government, in 1972. Her research areas of interest are political participation and women's political issues, and she is engaged in a major project analysing the passage of the Nineteenth Amendment enfranchising women in the context of the progressive reform era. She is the recipient of a Bunting Institute Fellowship, Wellesley Research Center Mellon Fellowship, a NSF Visiting Professorship for Women, and a Murray Research Center, Radcliffe College, Mellon Fellowship. She has published in numerous journals, including the *American Political Science Review* and the *American Journal of Political Science*.

Andrew D. McNitt is Professor of Political Science at Eastern Illinois University. He received his PhD from Michigan State University in 1978.

Thomas E. Pasquarello is Assistant Professor of Political Science at the State University of New York College at Cortland. He is currently extending his research on human rights and US foreign policy.

Kathleen Pritchard is Assistant Professor of Political Science at the University of Wisconsin-Milwaukee, where she teaches in the International Relations Program. Her current research focuses on comparative explanations and measures of human rights.

Alison Dundes Renteln is an Assistant Professor of Political Science at the University of Southern California. Her areas of specialization include international law and international human rights, constitutional law, American politics and political and legal theory.

Robert M. Rosh is Assistant Professor of Government and International Relations at Clark University. His current research interests include Third World militarization and development.

Richard L. Siegel is Professor of Political Science at the University of Nevada, Reno.

Nancy Spalding is an Assistant Professor at East Carolina University. She received her PhD in 1987 from the State University of New York at Binghamton, and has taught at New Mexico State University. Her primary research interests are in development theory and policy, particularly with respect to administration and implementation. Her substantive policy interest is the provision of necessary goods and services, or basic needs, to rural populations. The results discussed in this paper were taken from her dissertation,'The Poverty of Wealth.'

Stephen C. Thomas is Associate Professor of Political Science at the University of Colorado at Denver and Co-Director of CU–Denver's International Affairs Program. He is currently engaged in research on the effects of post-Mao reforms on Chinese social and economic policy outcomes, particularly human rights performances.

Kevin N. Wright is Associate Professor of Criminal Justice with joint appointments in the School of Education and Human Development and the Department of Political Science at the State University of New York at Binghamton. He is Director of the Center for Education and Social Research and is a Kellogg National Fellowship recipient.

Introduction
David Louis Cingranelli

Until recently, the scholarly debate over human rights has been dominated by normative theorists who have asked some very basic and important questions. Do human rights exist? What are they? Are they universal? While there is still considerable difference of opinion, many have answered those questions, at least to their own satisfaction, and would like to move on to others. They want to find ways to measure the extent of respect for human rights around the world. Although statistical measures of human rights practices may seem repugnant to some, measurement is the first step towards objective social science inquiry, towards the development of successful strategies of human rights activism by non-governmental organizations and towards implementation of a well-conceived human rights policy by national governments and multinational agencies. Then they want to develop theories relevant to the human rights practices of nation states from which testable hypotheses may be derived. This volume contains some efforts towards those ends.

Some of the chapters are mainly conceptual and theoretical in orientation. Others attempt to measure particular types of human rights practices within nation states, allowing us to move beyond gross categorizations of national practices as 'good' or 'bad'. About half include tests of hypotheses with measures of human rights practices serving as explanatory or dependent variables. All have something to contribute towards broadly comparative social science research relevant to human rights.

Part I of the book is devoted to selections which take us back to the early, continuing mainstream debate over the existence of human rights. Renteln's chapter is included as the very first, because it provides the best review of key controversies among those who conduct empirical research on human rights. So it is good background for those unfamiliar with existing research on the subject. Her empirical research, using anthropological ethnographies to demonstrate the universality of popular adherence for the principle of retribution, and, by extention, to the right to life, is also innovative and stimulating. Her chapter is an excellent example of the interdisci-

1

plinary focus and the theme of this book – human rights, theory and measurement.

While Renteln argues for the existence of a universal standard of human rights, Johnson, an expert on India and the author of Chapter 2, does not. Instead, he contrasts conceptions of human rights in the USA and India and shows how these alternative conceptions can help explain the different kinds of public policies each nation has developed for dealing with disadvantaged minorities and for the conduct of international relations. Aschenbrenner tries to reconcile the anthropologist's need to avoid ethnocentrism with the need of human rights activists to justify working against some cultural practices such as the repression of women. Cultural, ethnic, and other 'group rights' are difficult for some to incorporate within more common Western conceptions of human rights as belonging to individual human beings, not groups. Siegel, who contributes the last chapter in Part I, examines one group right which has been advanced by many Third World governments in international fora – the right to development.

Although the issue of 'whether human rights exist' is rarely raised in the remaining chapters of this book, most of the authors implicitly have accepted human rights as individual rights and some human rights as universal. Part II of the book addresses the methodological problems of measuring national variations in human rights practices. McNitt's chapter, the first in this part, provides a critical review of past measurement approaches and assesses the future prospects. One of the measurement problems he discusses is the difficulty in obtaining information about the human rights practices of closed societies. The following chapter about China is interesting in this regard, because Thomas uses a broadly comparative measure, the Physical Quality of Life Index, to evaluate the relative provision of and recent changes in the provision of social and economic rights in one such closed society. The final selection in Part II by McDonagh and McDonagh is methodologically innovative, because it reports findings of a study in which content analysis was used to describe the extent of gender-specific language in the USA and some other national constitutions. The authors argue that the absence of gender-specific language is an indicator of the high level of correspondence between espousal of the symbolic value of 'equality' and the even-handedness of actual government treatment of men and women.

Parts III and IV of the book contain examples of the kind of work that will probably become more central to the next phase of research on human rights. Part III includes selections which deal with the question of why rights vary from place to place and over time. Though different types of rights and different measurement procedures are used in each chapter, evidence is presented suggesting that better human rights practices are found in nations with greater levels of national resources (Pritchard; Cingranelli and Wright; and Spalding), with independent judiciaries (Pritchard), and with democratic forms of government (Spalding). Rosh expected to find that economic and social rights would be satisfied best in those third world nations with the lowest levels of militarization, but did not. Both the chapter by Pritchard and the one by Cingranelli and Wright present findings which demonstrate a generally low level of respect for human rights throughout the Third World.

Cingranelli and Wright argue that due process is among the most fundamental of all human rights and attempt to measure the extensiveness and consistency of due process provided by national governments. Lennertz, in the final selection in Part III, analyzes the way in which six developed nations have dealt with the abortion issue. His findings are not easily summarized, since there is little agreement about how the abortion issue fits into the human rights framework (though nearly everyone thinks it does somehow).

While the chapters included in Part III look at some hypothesized explanations of good or bad practices, the two chapters in Part IV examine some consequences of those practices. Arat, in the first selection, argues that, among third world democracies, the achievement of economic progress without corresponding achievement of social rights for citizens will often create political instability, threatening democratic institutions. Pasquarello, after examining the distribution of US foreign aid to African nations, concludes that nations with better human rights records were more likely to receive some economic aid from the US, but not necessarily more economic aid than nations with poorer practices. He also finds little relationship between the human rights practices of African nations and the distribution of US military aid within the region.

Most of the contributors are political scientists. Within that discipline the gap between those who concentrate on normative questions and those who focus on empirical research has, in recent decades, been ever widening. Taken together, the chapters in this book demonstrate the benefits to be derived from bringing normative and empirical concerns closer together. A grant from the Human Rights and Governance Division of the Ford Foundation facilitated communication among the chapter authors and contributed to the quality of this product. We are grateful for their support.

Part I

Theoretical Perspectives

1 A Cross-Cultural Approach to Validating International Human Rights: The Case of Retribution Tied to Proportionality

Alison Dundes Renteln

A comparative analysis of national human rights policies should not proceed without a careful consideration of the philosophical underpinnings of the concept. The unanswered challenge of cultural and ethical relativism has left the universality of international human standards in jeopardy. To determine whether or not specific human rights are universal and can thus be measured cross-culturally, one first needs a comparative analysis of broader moral principles. The central question is whether or not there is any comparable notion, or what has been called the *homeomorphic equivalent*, for human rights in other societies. A study of the principle of retribution may provide a promising starting point for comparative research of this kind. I will show that the principle of retribution tied to proportionality is extremely widespread if not universal. It serves to limit violence and as such may indicate worldwide support for a principled rejection of arbitrary killing. It would be beyond the scope of this study to do more than offer a preliminary discussion of this proposed means of establishing a consensus on particular human rights and of validating international standards.

In this essay I begin by raising some of the problems surrounding the alleged universality of human rights standards. An argument on behalf of cross-cultural research is advanced in the hopes of showing the relevance of empirical data for normative claims. I then take up the case study of the principle of retribution tied to proportionality. The forms of retribution to be investigated include *lex talionis* which follows strict proportionality and the payment of blood money

7

which follows general proportionality. Behavioral manifestations of retribution include such practices as the feud, vendetta, and vengeance killings. While there are differences among these retaliatory actions, they are not important for my purposes. As Hoebel (1976, p. 504) points out, blood revenge and vendetta are vernacular synonyms for the feud. Finally, I attempt to connect this empirical inquiry to international human rights standards.

THE CONCEPT OF HUMAN RIGHTS

There is, indeed, reason to be concerned about the extent to which the concept of human rights is embraced worldwide. There is considerable difference of opinion as to what 'true' human rights are. Some commentators assert that the concept is a Western one, while others insist that it is truly universal (Alston, 1983; Bedau, 1982; Berger, 1977; Berman, 1979; Donnelly, 1982, 1985; Ferguson, 1979; Henkin, 1979; Kleinig, 1981; Manglapus, 1978; Masahiko, 1985; Murphy, 1981; Nickel, 1982; Novak, 1986; Panikkar, 1982; Pappu, 1982; Pollis & Schwab, 1979; Raphael, 1966; Sinha, 1981, 1982; Tomuschat, 1981; Tyagi, 1981). There tends to be a division into two camps, those who advocate civil and political rights and those who champion economic, social and cultural rights. When one considers how voluminous the literature on human rights is and how much divergence there is on the question of human rights, it is startling that relatively little has been written on the subject of its conceptual basis (see the insightful analyses of Alston, 1984; Bilder, 1969; Ramcharan, 1983; Sinha, 1978, 1981, 1982).

It is possible to find analyses of the concept of human rights from various national, ideological, and religious perspectives. But many of these studies are unreliable because the authors are determined to show that their cultures have human rights and thus may be apologists for their traditions. Others dismiss outright the possibility that there may be any notion of human rights in certain societies. There is certainly no comparative treatment of human rights across cultures (except for a few two-country comparisons: Berman, 1979; Kadarkay, 1982) and that is precisely what is needed. Some writers focus on a single right which they assert is the only valid right, e.g. Hart (1979) and the right to liberty, Nickel (1982) and the right to freedom from torture, and Stackhouse (1984) and the right to participate. Much of the literature reflects an ethnocentric bias which

I have discussed elsewhere (Renteln, 1985). Based on the conflicting statements by scholars, it seems difficult to decide one way or the other if the concept of human rights is universal. Instead of assuming that the concept is universal, it would be better to do some empirical investigation.

THE ARGUMENT FROM RELATIVISM

It is not possible to assume a priori that human rights are universally shared moral principles. This is particularly true in light of the unanswered challenge of cultural and ethical relativism. Relativism raises a number of conceptual issues worthy of consideration (see Renteln, 1988), but the scope of this analysis does not permit exploration of them here. Instead of delving into the vast literature on relativism, I focus on one major misconception about relativism. The core idea of relativism is that: 'Evaluations are *relative* to the cultural background out of which they arise' (Herskovits, 1972, p. 14). In a re-evaluation of relativism, Hatch (1983) puts it this way: 'the principles that we may use for judging behavior or anything else are relative to the culture in which we are raised' (p. 3). The implication, according to Benedict (1934, pp. 45–6), is that because cultural relativism recognizes that there is tremendous cultural variability, there are no absolutes.

Many people have misinterpreted the relativist position claiming that it undermines all possibility of making moral criticisms. This is an unfair caricature of relativism. There is no reason why a relativist could not condemn a practice elsewhere on the basis of his own values. A relativist simply recognizes the fact that the object of criticism may be considered moral in its own system. Further, it must be acknowledged that expressing a criticism of this kind is a form of cultural imperialism, i.e., an attempt to impose one's values on another whose values are different. The misunderstanding of relativism stems from a presumption of universal values, and in the case of international human rights provides a classic example of ethnocentrism. One sets forth one's own moral standard as an absolute standard and then judges other systems by it.

The recognition of cultural diversity means that human rights can no longer rely on their traditional sources of justification. Traditionally there have been four sources to which theorists have referred: (1) divine authority, (2) natural law, (3) intuition (that human rights are self-evident), and (4) ratification of international instruments. The first and second are not in vogue and the third is increasingly questioned. Even the claim that because political elites have ratified human rights documents human rights are therefore universal is suspect. There is no guarantee that the elites ratify for reasons other than political expediency. Moreover, it is far from clear that the values of elites correspond to the traditional value systems in the countries they represent. It is, therefore, necessary to try a different strategy to validate human rights standards.

There remains the question of ideals. There may well be a difference between traditional moral ideals and social reality. That is, what societies do may be quite different from what they believe they ought to do. Nevertheless, a comparison of diverse moral ideals is certainly helpful. After all, the universal human rights standards may, in part, be intended to serve as universal aspirations. It would be quite significant if there should happen to be convergence among the many moral systems in the world. Such unanimity might provide a stronger foundation for human rights standards.

The central question then is whether or not other cultures have a concept of human rights, and if they do, whether or not it resembles that of the Universal Declaration of Human Rights along with the Covenants. It is not clear if other societies' moral systems center on rights. Much of the debate has tended to revolve around such linguistic questions. Even if non-Western societies do not express moral concerns in a framework of human rights, they may none the less address them in some other conceptual framework. It becomes necessary to reformulate the basic question: are there any homeomorphic equivalents for human rights in other cultures?

THE RELEVANCE OF EMPIRICAL DATA FOR NORMATIVE INQUIRY

In the quest for structural equivalents for human rights, it is necessary to consider empirical data. This is a difficult undertaking for two reasons. First of all, there is a widespread philosophical objection to combining empirical and normative analyses. To merge them is to risk confusing an 'is' with an 'ought' (Hudson, 1969). Thus it is crucial to establish the relevance of empirical findings for normative theory. Second, it is not obvious what data can provide a means to discovering the 'true' moral standards of a society. Consulting jurisprudential and theological texts will surely paint a picture of moral standards, but they may be only the ideals of the elites; what we are after are native moral categories. This analysis draws on the ethnographic materials pertaining to law, dispute settlement, values, and morality.

In the past there has been some recognition of the relevance of empirical studies for moral claims (Masson-Oursel, 1923, 1951; Russell, 1946; Mabbott, 1946; MacBeath, 1946). Some have tried to demonstrate the interrelationship of anthropology and ethics (Edel, 1962; Edel and Edel, 1968). Others e.g., Danelski (1966, p. 68), are persuaded that empirical study is necessary for human rights. It may not be clear why the descriptions of diverse moral systems should be pertinent. Suppose that all cultures were committed to capital punishment. That might not mean that it was a moral practice. There is a real danger when abstracting from moral systems of assuming that tradition is moral. Just because a type of behavior is conventional hardly makes it right. But having admitted that a simple majority rule principle operating in the international system is not acceptable, it does not follow that a single country ought to set the moral standards for the rest of the world.

It might be the case that one society holds a monopoly of moral knowledge. The United States Constitution writ large in the form of United Nations documents (Henkin, 1979) may reflect true enlightenment. Other cultures may simply lack moral insights. Yet, this cannot be so. Should one say that cultures which have arranged marriages are wrong, just because the practice contravenes international human rights standards (Universal Declaration of Human Rights, Article 16(2); International Covenant of Civil and Political Rights, Article 23; International Covenant of Economic, Social and Cultural Rights, Article 10) even if many cultures accept it? If it turns out to be the case that most cultures do not believe in a moral principle which the Western world embraces, it might be that they are right. It might also be true that most cultures, including Western and non-Western societies, believe in a certain moral idea or value. That there may be evidence that a majority of countries and peoples are committed to a particular moral standard might indicate their willingness to accept a human rights standard which is based on the norm.

There is discussion in the literature of the need to pare down the number of rights from the lengthy, inflated list (Alston, 1984; Nickel, 1982; Pocklington, 1982). Those which should remain on the list are those for which evidence can be marshalled. In the absence of any justification for human rights, other than mere assertions that they are self-evident, inalienable, and other universalistic moral phrases, there is a real need for proof. If one can demonstrate that there is convergence in traditional belief systems with respect to specific moral principles, then there may be hope that one can prove that there is consensus. It may be possible to revive languishing human rights. Although empirical findings may not be automatically relevant to ethical inquiry, in the present case, they are vital. Without evidence of support for the values which underlie human rights standards, any claim to universality will fall flat.

PREVIOUS COMPARATIVE ANALYSES OF MORALITY AND HUMAN RIGHTS

There have been previous attempts to analyze ethical issues on a cross-cultural basis and to evaluate human rights from the viewpoint of specific cultures (Beer, 1984; Claude, 1976; Duchacek, 1973; Stackhouse, 1984). For instance, there exist several comparative studies of freedom (Boas, 1940; D'Angelo, 1973; Haldane, 1940; Nielsen, 1964; Shih, 1940). Much of the existing literature reflects an ethnocentric bias: 'There is extant today no single social accounting scheme that is adequate – both conceptually valid and quantitatively reliable – for monitoring the status of human rights the world over' (Wiseberg and Scoble, 1981, p. 167). The problem is that the measuring tools are culture-bound. Wiseberg and Scoble maintain that the scheme of, for instance, Freedom House 'is so partisan and culture-bound that it would be intellectually and politically dangerous to rely upon it' (pp. 167–8).

Even the book entitled *Comparative Human Rights* (Claude, 1976) fails to avoid cultural bias. First of all, the collection contains essays which compare at most several countries which are all in the Western world. Its greater failure is the lack of any comparative analytic framework within which to study human rights. Nor is there any systematic investigation of any single human right or principle throughout the world. To date there has been negligible progress made in the direction of establishing that human rights are universal or even that certain moral principles are widely shared.

THE PRINCIPLE OF RETRIBUTION: A CASE STUDY

The principle of retribution was selected for comparative study not only because there is available empirical data on this subject but also, and more importantly, because there is reason to believe that this principle may be universal: 'Retribution is a universal phenomenon and experience among primitive as well as among civilized people, in ancient Greek drama, in the Old and New Testaments' (Hall, 1983, p. 294). Herbert Spencer (1900) acknowledges that this principle is widespread: 'The principle requiring "an eye for an eye and a tooth for a tooth", embodies the primitive idea of justice everywhere' (p. 528). Westermarck (1932a) speaks of *'jus talionis*, or rule of equivalence between injury and retaliation, which is characteristic of savage justice' (1932a, p. 95). In his brilliant analysis of the principle of retribution, Kelsen (1946) states that it is the most fundamental principle of social order for 'primitive man' (p. 64). In a 1983 popular work on retribution, *Wild Justice: The Evolution of Revenge*, Jacoby (1983) refers to 'the ineradicable impulse to retaliate when harm is inflicted' (p. 5). Also calling it ineradicable, Westermarck (1924) says: 'The retributive desire is so strong, and appears so natural, that we can neither help obeying it, nor seriously disapprove of its being obeyed' (p. 91). Dautremer (1885), in his analysis of legal revenge in Japan, claims: 'The desire for revenge is indeed a innate sentiment in man, and in all the primitive civilizations we find personal revenge existing as a prescriptive right' (p. 82). Posner (1980) has even claimed that there is a 'vengeful component in our genetic make-up' (p. 79).

Some may wonder about the choice of retribution as a topic for comparative study. One of the three main justifications for punishment (the other two are deterrence and rehabilitation), retribution is generally regarded as the least worthy (Grande, 1983). This is because retribution is viewed basically as another term for the instinct of revenge. In the West there has been a tendency to deny the legitimacy of retribution or revenge (Westermarck, 1898). Some, for example, Percy (1943) have distinguished between revenge (personal gratification) and retribution (impersonal and impartial action). But even retribution has fallen out of favor and has come to be associated with cruel punishment (Poupko, 1975, p. 541). The eminent moral philosopher, Sidgwick (1907), wrote that he had 'an instinctive and strong moral aversion to it [retribution]' and that 'it is gradually passing away from the moral consciousness of educated persons in the most advanced communities' (1907, p. 281). He did admit, however, that 'it is still perhaps the more ordinary view' (1907, p. 281). Even though Western philosophers and theologians may advocate forgiveness in lieu of retribution, their position is not shared by most of the world. There is a deeply rooted belief in the just deserts doctrine that holds that criminals should receive the punishment they deserve (Hall, 1983, p. 294; Rieder, 1984).

A DEFINITION

Retribution means a recompense for, or requital of, evil done; return of evil (OED, 1933, p. 581). The etymological derivation of the word is from the Latin *retribuere*, meaning restored or given back. There is a clear indication that at its root is the idea of compensation (repayment, recompense). This will be important later in the discussion of 'blood money'. There are a few important aspects of retribution worth emphasizing. Retribution makes no sense unless it involves an act taken in response to a first act. It presumes that the original act was wrongly committed (Kelsen, 1946, p. 50). In Japan, for instance, the taking of revenge was moral unless the victim was killed for having committed a crime, i.e., not wrongly killed (Mills, 1976, p. 530). The idea of equivalence or proportionality is central to the principle of retribution. A clear philosophical definition of retribution tied to proportionality is provided by John Rawls (1955): 'What we may call the retributive view is that punishment is justified on the grounds that wrongdoing merits punishment. It is morally fitting that a person who does wrong should suffer in proportion to his guilt, and the severity of the appropriate punishment depends on the depravity of his act' (pp. 4–5).

Often the language of balance and equilibrium is invoked which suggests that there is an underlying reciprocity behind the idea of retribution. Pilling (1957) reports that the Australian aborigines explain the resolution of conflict as 'square now' (p. 241); 'Square' meaning that the dispute is over (pp. 312–17). Boehm (1984, p. 218) describes the feud by reference to the analogy of score-keeping. Kelsen (1946) says that equilibrium is the 'specific function of retribution which balances punishment against wrong and reward against merit, as on scales' (p. 236). The language of balance, equilibrium, and geometry pervade analyses and descriptions of retribution.

Implicit in balance is reciprocity which is frequently expressed in the form of the traditional *lex talionis*,[1] an eye for an eye and a tooth for a tooth. The presumption is that the appropriate social response to a breach of a norm is a response in kind. The determination of what constitutes equivalance between crimes and punishments generally varies cross-culturally. But what is clear is that the principle of retribution is tied to a principle of proportionality. The linking of these two concepts is arguably universal. Even if the proportion is measured differently in various societies, there is a discernible scaling between crime and punishment.

There is a debate in the literature about whether or not *lex talionis* must be interpreted literally. For the purposes of this analysis the outcome of this hermeneutic controversy is not crucial. Proportionality tied to retribution is pervasive. It does not matter if we call it *lex talionis* or not. It turns out, however, that in the case of homicide, there is widespread consensus on the applicability of the *lex talionis* and on the specific punishment that is appropriate. The idea that a life must be paid for with a life is remarkably prevalent throughout the world. Even though the practice of bloodmoney is accepted in many societies, there is still a recognition of the basic norm of equivalence. A retributivist need not insist upon a transcultural and transhistorical system of crimes and punishments. It may be that every society is committed to retribution tied to proportionality but utilizes its own scale.

INTERPRETING ETHNOGRAPHIES

Before examining the ethnographic data, a few warnings about interpretation are in order. Since it is not feasible for any one individual to collect field data on all peoples throughout the world, it is necessary to rely upon the research of others. In the case of anthropological research, there is a danger that the limitations of fieldwork may lead to distortions in the interpretations of aspects of the culture. There is always the question whether the categories and notions used by the investigator are held by the people. There is also the possibility of misinterpretation. For example, when Turnbull (1972) writes about the way of life among the Ik in the *Mountain People*, he describes a systematic plan to starve certain segments of the society to death. The conclusion he draws is that this society is devoid of a moral sense, i.e. is amoral. First of all, his assumption that withholding food from some members of the community demonstrates the absense of morality must be challenged. Among the Eskimo, for instance, infanticide and senilicide are considered moral (Boas, 1888, p. 580). It is by no means clear that the denial of food is universally regarded as immoral. One witnesses the debate in the United States about the subject in the context of euthanisia. Second, Turnbull visited the society during one year. Presumably this was a lean year. It is crucial to know how food is distributed during a year of plenty in order to justify the extreme conclusion that the Ik are an immoral people (Lear, 1984, p. 150).

In the case of retribution there is a particular danger that projection may occur. The scholars who write about retribution tend to think, naturally enough, in retributive terms. It must be admitted that there may be a possibility that by seeking out the principle of retribution and the *lex talionis*, the anthropologist, through this determination, may make sure to find it. Kelsen, in a discussion of vengeance among animals, recounts an extraordinary example of projection. It is Westermarck citing the following case from Palgrave's report of a journey through central and eastern Arabia as proof of 'animal revenge':

> One passion alone he [the camel] posseses, namely revenge, of which he furnishes many a hideous example, while in carrying it out he shows an unexpected degree of far-thoughted malice, united meanwhile with all the cold stupidity of his usual character. One instance of this I well remember. It occurred hard by a small town in the plain of Ba'albec, where I was at the time residing. A lad of about fourteen had conducted a large camel, laden with wood, from that very village to another at half an hour's distance or so. As the animal loitered or turned out of the way, its conductor struck it repeatedly, and harder than it seems to have thought he had a right to do. But not finding the occasion favourable for taking immediate quits, it 'bode its time'; nor was that time long in coming. A few days later the same lad had to reconduct the beast, but unladen, to his own village. When they were about half-way on the road, and at some distance from any habitation, the camel suddenly stopped, looked deliberately round in every direction to assure itself that no one was within sight, and, finding the road far and near clear of passers-by, made a step forward, seized the unlucky boy's head in its monstrous mouth, and lifting him up in the air flung him down again on the earth with the upper

part of skull completely torn off, and his brains scattered on the ground. Having thus satisfied its revenge, the brute quietly resumed its pace towards the village as though nothing were the matter, till some men who had observed the whole, though unfortunately at too great a distance to be able to afford timely help, came up and killed it (Kelsen, 1946, pp. 51–2).

Kelsen wonders whether to be more amazed by the camel with its sense of justice and its clever cautiousness or by the men who were so far away that they could not come to the boy's rescue but could watch the strange behavior of the camel and observe its motives and intentions exactly. There is the same danger that in interpreting human behavior the anthropologist may project unjustifiably the principle of retribution on the societies he or she is studying.

THE ETHNOGRAPHIC MATERIAL

Considerable ethnographic data exists which shows that the *lex talionis* is extremely widespread.[2] After a consideration of some of the ethnographic material on the *lex talionis*, I will present evidence of its existence in some of the major religious texts of the world. Following this demonstration of the geographical distribution of the *lex talionis* formulation will be an analysis of the feud as a logical development of it. The feud, it will be argued, occurs wherever there is a lack of agreement about proportionality. Then I will take up the case of blood money in order to show how retribution with general proportionality operates. Finally, I will try to suggest how the principle of retribution may provide support for certain international human rights.

There are very few cross-cultural studies of retribution (Kelsen, 1946; Posner, 1980; Westermarck, 1924). The most brilliant analysis of the principle of retribution is found in Kelsen's book, *Society and Nature: A Sociological Inquiry* (1946). I have drawn from his impressive work and have provided additional examples.

Among the most noteworthy examples recorded of *lex talionis* is the account of the Maori of New Zealand: 'The great principle of justice upon which the New Zealanders acted was an eye for an eye and a tooth for a tooth, and the object of their punishments was to obtain compensation for injuries, not to prevent crimes' (Thomson, 1970, Vol. I, pp. 98–9). Of the American Indians it has been said:

'There never was any set of people, who pursued the Mosaic law of *retaliation* with such a fixt eagerness as these Americans' (Adair, 1930, p. 157).

Possibly the most precise formulation is found in Karsten's (1923) monograph *Blood Revenge, War, and Victory Feasts among the Jibaro Indians of Eastern Ecuador*:

> The Jibaro Indian is wholly penetrated by the idea of retaliation; his desire for revenge is an expression of his sense of justice. This principle is an eye for an eye, tooth for tooth, life for life. If one reprehends a Jibaro because he has killed an enemy, his answer is generally: 'He has killed himself' . . . When a murder committed by an own tribesman is to be avenged, the social morals of the Jibaros require that the punishment shall be meted out with justice, insofar that for one life which has been taken only one life should be taken in retaliation. Thereupon, the blood guilt is atoned (*tumashi akerkama*) and the offended family is satisfied. Consequently, if a Jibaro Indian wishes to revenge a murder of his brother, it may well happen that he, in case the slayer himself cannot be caught and punished, will assassinate his brother or father instead of him, but he does not take the life of more than one member of the family, even if he has an opportunity of killing more (pp. 10, 11, 13).

Karsten presents evidence of the *lex talionis* formulation, collective responsibility, and the clearly understood limit to the retaliatory act. It is permissible among many peoples to take revenge not necessarily on the offender but on any member of his family or clan. Although this may strike Westerners as strange, this surely provides a deterrent to violence. What is most important to understand is that the practice of vengeance killing is not comparable to uncontrolled warfare. The principle of *lex talionis* as expressed here provides a limit to action. Karsten elaborates on this point: 'This principle, which requires that there shall be justice in the retaliation so that life is weighed against life, of course, in itself has a tendency to limit blood revenge' (p. 13).

In Japan a victim could be avenged only once (Mills, 1976, p. 534). Retribution in China also conformed to the principle of a life for a life (Meijer, 1980, pp. 203, 214). Among the Bedouin of Cyrenaica (now part of Eastern Libya), Peters (1967) reports that the *lex talionis* is found: 'A life had been taken for a life and the way is now open for the restoration of normal peaceful relationships' (p. 265).

Evidently, it is a common practice among this people to hold a peace meeting at which time 'it is accepted that the killings have cancelled each other out' (p. 265). This notion of cancelling out the original wrong is perhaps what makes the *lex talionis* so widely appealing.

The idea of equivalence is of central importance in understanding retribution in many societies. Some people observe the rule of equivalance strictly. For example, the Quianganes of Luzon, an island of the Philippines, must retaliate by killing someone of exactly the same status. They will even wait years until someone becomes a noble of the correct status (Blumentritt, 1891, p. 390). The need to take revenge on a person of precisely the appropriate status may justifiably delay the vengeance killing. One imagines that this must discourage aspirations to higher social status in some societies. Equivalence may refer not only to status but also to gender and age (Nadel, 1947, p. 151). These sorts of strict requirements are customary among many peoples. Even the cannibalistic natives of British New Guinea did not kill or eat their victims indiscriminately: 'in spite of the pleasure to be derived from a cannibal feast it was clear that commonly prisoners would only be tortured and killed in such numbers that their deaths made the score even between their community and that of their captors' (Seligman, 1910, Part 2, pp. 569–70).

Even cannibals do not exceed the bounds of equivalence. This suggests that the commitment to one for one may be shared on an extremely wide basis.

RETRIBUTION IN MAJOR WORLD RELIGIONS

It may appear that the only examples cited are from smaller-scale societies. One might be in doubt as to the applicability of the principle of retribution in so-called modern societies. But since the major religions of the world whose influence extends thoughout the globe contain provisions for *lex talionis*, there is reason to believe that the principle of retribution is shared by countries which follow these religious tenets as well.

The Judaeo-Christian religious traditions take much from the Bible. There are numerous places in the Old Testament where *lex talionis* is mentioned (Genesis, 4:10, 9:6; Leviticus, 24:17; Deuteronomy, 19:21; for analysis see Daube, 1969). One of the most famous texts on retribution tied to equivalence appears in Chapter 21 of Exodus which has been extremely influential for both Christian and Jewish law: 'And if any mischief follows, then thou shalt give life for life, Eye for Eye, tooth for tooth, hand for hand, foot for foot, Burning for burning, wound for wound, stripe for stripe' (Exodus, 21:23–5, *Holy Bible*, King James, 1952).

Islam also makes provision for the right of retaliation in the *Qur'an* in Surah V (49):

Therein have We prescribed [as a law] for them: 'A life for a life, an eye for an eye, a nose for a nose, an ear for an ear, a tooth for a tooth, and wounds are [an occasion for] retaliation'; so if anyone remit it as a gift, it is an expiation for him, but whoever does not judge by what Allah hath sent down – they are wrong doers (Bell, 1960, Vol. I p. 100; see also Surah II:173,175, Surah XVII:35).

ANCIENT LAW

In ancient law there is evidence of the pre-Biblical importance of *lex talionis* and of blood money (Alt, 1934; Blau, 1916; Cohn, 1971; Daube, 1969; Diamond, 1957; Dembitz, 1895; Doron, 1969; DuCros, 1926; Finkelstein, 1936; Frymer-Kensky, 1980; Harris, 1924; Kugelmass, 1981; LaGrange, 1916; MacCormack, 1973; Tower, 1984; Weingreen, 1976). Some have claimed that the *talion* is cited and applied literally in the Mesopotamian law codes of Eshnunna (c.2000 BC), Lipit-Ishtar (c.1860 BC) and Hammurabi (c.1700 BC). There is fragmentary evidence in the Code of Hammurabi that a life paid for a life:

(229) If a builder has built a house for a man and has not made his work sound, and the house which he has built has fallen down and so caused the death of the householder, the builder shall be put to death.
(230) If it causes the death of the householder's son, they shall put the builder's son to death (Driver and Miles, 1956, Vol. II, p. 83).

These are clearly examples of *lex talionis* and there are others in the Code. This indicates acceptance of strict proportionality. In ancient law we also find evidence for the acceptance of general proportionality, for the practice of blood money. For example, the Laws of Eshnunna provided that for all personal injuries short of death the sanctions were pecuniary (Sections 42–8; Diamond, 1957, p. 151). Section 42 states that: 'If a man bites the nose of another man and severs it, he shall pay one mina of silver. For an eye, one mina; for a tooth $\frac{1}{2}$ mina; for a slap in the face ten shekels of silver' (Fisher, 1982, p. 583). The existence of both revenge and compensation suggests that stage theories claiming that restitution is historically later than physical punishment are not correct (see Daube, 1969; Diamond, 1957; MacCormack, 1973; Posner, 1980). Daube (1969) extrapolates from the data on punishment and compensation, concluding that they are fundamental to any social order: 'The two notions are so frequent, they appear in sources so different in all other respects, they underlie terms so ancient . . . and, it may be added, they are of so universal a nature, occurring in the ancient and modern literatures of all nations, that we must assume their existence right from the beginnings of any social life' (p. 146).

THE FEUD

The existence of *lex talionis* in many of the world's traditions is clearly found in the preceding ethnographic and religious data. In addition, this principle can be shown to underlie several major social processes. Although there is debate about the differences between these processes, they are not important for my purposes. Pospisil (1978) defines the feud according to the following characteristics: prolonged and intermittent hostilities, that the two groups fighting each other must be related, and that it is 'extra-legal' (p. 389). The main point is that a single fight cannot be defined as a feud. There must be more than two acts of violence. In effect, the feud begins after the two killings when both sides do not perceive an equivalance. This means the feud depends on the failure to satisfy *lex talionis*. Consequently, I take the feud to be evidence for a commitment to the principle of *lex talionis*.

In Europe the feud exists in Turkey (Stirling, 1960), Montenegro (Boehm, 1984), Albania (Elezi, 1966; Ellenberger, 1981; Hasluck, 1967), Corsica (Busquet, 1920; Ellenberger, 1981), and Sardinia (Di Bella, 1980). It was well established in what is now France, Germany, and Italy (Bloch, 1961, p. 127). In Africa the custom of blood revenge has been studied among the Lendu, a Congolese people (Southall, 1956, p. 160), the Bedouin of Libya (Peters, 1967), the Acioli of Uganda (Boccassino, 1962), the Nuer of Sudan (Evans-

Pritchard, 1963), the Nuba of Sudan (Nadel, 1947), the Tonga of Northern Rhodesia (Colson, 1953), natives of Central Africa (Kelsen, 1946, p. 56), the Kabyles of Algeria and the Jbala of Northern Morocco (Westermarck, 1924, Vol. I, p. 484; Lewis, 1961), the Moundang of Chad (Adler, 1980), the Massa and Moussey of Chad and Cameroun (Garine, 1980), the Bulsa of Northern Ghana (Schott, 1980), the Kabiye of Togo (Verdier, 1980), the Beti of Cameroun (LaBurthe-Tolra, 1980), and the Damara mountain hunters of Southwest Africa (Thurnwald, 1930). In Asia retaliatory killings have been documented in Japan (Dautremer, 1885; Mills, 1976), in China (Dalby, 1981; Meijer, 1980), in Islamic South Asia (Dupree 1980 – specifically in Afghanistan and Pakistan). Studies on feuding in the Middle East and in the Mediterranean exist (Barth, 1953; Black-Michaud, 1975; Chelhod, 1980, Hardy, 1963). Other societies in which the principle of retribution operates include the Australian aborigines (Hoebel, 1954, pp. 302–303; Pilling, 1957), the Huli of New Guinea (Glass, 1959), the Tauade of New Guinea (Hallpike, 1977), the Kutubu of Papau (Williams, 1941; Kelsen, 1946, p. 61), the Kalingas of the Philippine Islands (Gluckman, 1966, p. 22), the Quianganes of Luzon (Kelsen, 1946), the Maori of New Zealand (Kelsen, 1946), the Brazilian aborigines (Westermarck, 1924, Vol. I, p. 478), the Chorti Indians of Guatemala (Wisdom, 1940), the Jibaro Indians (Karsten, 1923), the Eskimo (Boas, 1884–5), the Hindus of India (Kelsen, 1946), the Chukchi, Papago, Tallensi, Tlingit, Jivaro and Marshall Islander (Anon., 1970, p. 945), the Kandhs of India and the Feloops bordering on the Gambia (Westermarck, 1924, Vol. I, pp. 480–1; n. 10).

The feud also existed in the United States in the recent past (Anon., 1970; Ayres, 1984; MacClintock, 1901; McCoy, 1976; Mutzenberg, 1916, Sonnichsen, 1971), e.g., that of the Hatfields and McCoys. Thus, it appears that the feud is not an exotic custom practiced only in remote lands. The feud is often, and perhaps wrongly, associated with 'primitive societies'. The Otterbein (1965) study, 'An Eye for an Eye, A Tooth for a Tooth: A Cross-Cultural Study of Feuding' challenges the proposition that societies with a high degree of political complexity lack feuding. Utilizing ethnographic materials from the Human Relations Area Files (HRAF) (1965, p. 476), they found no support for this hypothesis (see also Hoebel, 1976).

It is interesting to see how the attempt to deny legal status to institutions in non-Western societies serves to denigrate their way of life. The presumption that only 'primitive' societies have retribution, revenge, and feuds is reflected in the debate about the legal status of the feud. Many anthropologists claim that the feud lies outside of law (Hoebel, 1949, p. 3; Radcliffe-Brown, 1940, p. xx; Pospisil, 1956). Their explanations of the feud may be inaccurate. Just because such action is considered 'lawless' does not necessarily mean that the carefully controlled mechanism of the feud may not represent a legal system to peoples who do not have a centralized political authority.

BLOOD MONEY

Whereas the feud is an example of strict proportionality, the practice of paying blood money is an instance of general proportionality. The idea is that the punishment need not fit the crime identically. An equivalent penalty is considered sufficient to achieve retribution.

Blood money is known to exist in the Middle East (Hardy, 1963), in such countries as Somalia (Contini, 1971), the Tonga of Northern Rhodesia (Colson, 1953, p. 202), the Bedouin of Libya (Peters, 1967, pp. 265–6), in Europe in Montenegro (Simic, 1967, p. 91), in Albania (Hasluck, 1967, p. 395), among the Australian aborigines (Pilling, 1957, pp. 148–9), among the Tauade (Hallpike, 1977, pp. 190, 212–30), and Huli (Glasse, 1959, pp. 277) of New Guinea, the natives of New Caledonia (Leenhardt, 1930, p. 46), and the Jibaro Indians of Eastern Ecuador (Karsten, 1923, p. 11). The Indians of Western Washington and North-Western Oregon recognize the principle of life for life but still opt for material damages in some cases. Among the Tlingit a certain number of blankets will atone for the murder of a relative (Westermarck, 1924, Vol. I, pp. 477–96). The practice of paying blood-money presumably exists elsewhere but may have not been studied.

For many peoples there is often a choice between blood revenge and blood money. But among some peoples blood money is considered dishonorable, e.g., in Albania (Hasluck, 1967, p. 395); among the Konso of Ethiopia (Hallpike, 1975, pp. 114–15); among those peoples explored by Westermarck (1924, Vol. I, p. 487); and in Montenegro (Boehm, 1984, pp. 106–7). Generally there is a scale for determining the payment of blood money. Among the Nuer of Sudan forty to fifty head of cattle are paid, at least in theory (Evans-Pritchard, 1963,

p. 153). The Mae Enga of the central New Guinea highlands place the value of life at forty pigs (Boehm, 1984, p. 213).

Another noteworthy proportionality concerns the value of woman as compared with man. In some societies the value of the female is precisely half that of the male (Albania, Hasluck, 1967, p. 395; Middle East, Hardy, 1963, p. 39; Libya, Peters, 1967, p. 270). At the same time that proportionality is affected by gender, it remains, in some places, unaffected by age. Payment for an eighty-five-year-old man and a young man were the same in Albania (Hasluck, 1967, p. 395).

There are some practices which differ from the standard payment of blood money. For instance, among the Berbers of Southern Morocco, a person who commits a murder must flee to another tribe and place himself under its protection. His relatives pay blood money to the family of the victim to insure that the offended party does not take revenge on them. This does not, however, entitle the murderer to return. If he does, he is liable to be killed (Westermarck, 1924, Vol. I, p. 488).

Occasionally the payment takes the form of a person. Sometimes the murderer instead of being killed is adopted as a member of the family of his victim. In another variation the murderer will persuade the victim's clan not to retaliate by giving the avenger his sister or daughter in marriage. Among the Nuba of Sudan one finds the institution called *nmar*. The kin group avoids blood revenge by offering one of its own members to the victim's clan to take the victim's place. The person surrendered has to correspond in sex and age to the victim (Nadel, 1947, p. 152). If the exchanged man is married, he must leave his wife and family for good. Among certain North American Indians the feelings of a desolate mother whose son had been brutally murdered were assuaged by adopting the murderer in place of her slain son (Krappe, 1944, p. 183). According to one account, a widow whose husband had been murdered might be consoled by marrying the murderer (Krappe, 1944, p. 183). Among the Habe hill-men of the French Sudan a murderer is expected to supply the family of the victim with a woman from his own family. When she bears a son, he is given the name of the murdered man; and then the two families 'are once more on the best of terms' (Krappe, 1944, p. 184). Sometimes the offender's family gives slaves to the relatives of the slain to atone, i.e. to compensate for the guilt (Westermarck, 1924, Vol. I, p. 484).

Retribution, according to Kelsen (1946, p. 60), means punishment and reward. So restitution is one form of retribution and as shown above is tied to a principle of proportionality. Although in theory retribution is distinguished from restitution because it is the offender oriented whereas restitution is victim oriented, restitution is retributive. Therefore, blood revenge is both restitutive and retributive.

THREE MISCONCEPTIONS

In this section I will respond to three objections to my analysis. It is crucial to understand the doctrine of collective responsibility. Otherwise some might mistakenly be under the impression that retribution, as it is practiced in the cultures considered, undermines the presumption of innocence which is held in high esteem in the West. From the point of view of other societies the entire group is considered guilty or responsible. It is important to acknowledge this different understanding of responsibility. The vengeance killing is not, therefore, regarded as arbitrary so long as it is accepted that the first offense was actually committed by a member of the group which must suffer the retaliatory killing. Thus, since the membership of the offender's group is not innocent, this way of looking at responsibility, as exemplified by Hall (1983, pp. 290–1), must be considered ethnocentric.

It is quite possible that collective responsibility not only satisfies the need for revenge but also provides an immensely powerful deterrent to violence. The group will try to restrain its own members in order to avoid retaliatory action. If a person harms someone in another group, he may put his entire community in jeopardy. If the person engages in this sort of action frequently, he may eventually be ostracized. The group forswears responsibility for his sporadic, violent acts. Collective responsibility serves to limit the extent to which individuals become embroiled in violent activities.

One of the most important features of retribution, which is often overlooked, is its function as a limit to violence. In fact, *lex talionis* ensures that one life is taken for one life (Margolin, 1933–4, p. 758; Posner, 1980, p. 82). Blau (1916) interprets the *lex talionis* in this 'limiting sense of "*only one* life for a life" – no more; "*only one* eye for an eye" – no more (p. 8) (see also Fisher, 1982, p. 583; Oesterreicher, 1980, p. 16). The original intention behind the talion was 'to limit the escalating cycle of the practice of blood vengeance clans and families' (Fisher, 1982, p. 583).

The feud attempts to achieve *lex talionis*, which is a limit. The feud is a device for preventing violence. One should recall the important point made earlier which is that when both sides perceive the first killing and counter-killing as cancelling each other out, violence ceases. The feud exists and continues only so long as the parties involved fail to achieve mutual agreement that the principle of *lex talionis* has been observed.

The feud discourages violence because it drives parties to seek peace (Boehm, 1984, pp. 140, 207), and collective responsibility creates a deterrent (Simic, 1967, p. 91). Evans-Pritchard (1963, p. 150) says that the fear of incurring a blood feud is the most important legal sanction within a tribe and the main guarantee of an individual's life and property. Feuds are highly structured, rule-based conflicts and are, therefore, not unlimited. A consideration of several procedures should reveal the limitations inherent in the feud. There are rules providing that certain persons are exempt from retaliatory killings, e.g. guests (Boehm, 1984, p. 153) and women (Ellenberger, 1981, p. 126). There are often rules about who specifically may avenge the death of the victim, e.g., the father or older brother (Mills, 1976, p. 536; Hasluck, 1967, p. 382). In some societies the avenger had to request permission, as in Japan (Mills, 1976, p. 536). Sometimes there is a requirement that the revenge be taken within a certain time period (Pilling, 1957, p. 105; Di Bella, 1980, p. 41; Hasluck, 1967, p. 389).

Not only is blood revenge viewed as a sacred duty, but it is part of filial piety. Moreover, the process of taking revenge, in fact, leads to mutual forgiveness. Colson (1953, p. 204) observes that the point is not to punish but to restore harmony. Furthermore, it is specifically retaliation which makes forgiveness possible. Admittedly, the standard meaning of forgiveness implies forgiving the act just committed without retaliating (as in turning the other cheek). But forgiveness in other social contexts requires action.

Even if the process of taking revenge strikes one as abhorrent, it is undeniably an effective mechanism for restoring social cohesion. Among the Nuba of Sudan it is only when the same number of individuals has been killed that 'the account is squared on both sides'. At that point in time, the balance is considered to have been reached and the feud lapses. Until then the two clans cannot drink beer together, in their homes or elsewhere, lest leprosy befall them (Nadel, 1947, p. 151). Those who believe that the feud is simply spontaneous violence are misinformed. Virtually every scholar who has investigated the feud comments on the specific formalities, procedures, and rules which govern the feud. Boehm (1984) maintains that 'revenge killing is controlled as carefully as possible' (p. 229).

The third misconception concerns the interpretation of blood money. It is arbitrary to insist that compensation is conceptually distinct from punishment. Restitution is a form of retribution. The practice of blood money does not show that *lex talionis* has been discredited historically or otherwise. The empirical data reveal that the decision to apply the *lex talionis* or to require the payment of blood money depends on the context. When the case involves unintentional homicide, quite often compensation is regarded as sufficient. When the two sides grow weary of battle, even where *lex talionis* is the norm, the agreement to accept blood money or wound money is appropriate to achieve reconciliation. So, there is no necessary dichotomy between the *lex talionis* and blood money. Both are forms of retribution tied to proportionality, strict proportionality for *lex talionis* and general proportionality for blood money.

THE PRINCIPLE OF RETRIBUTION AND RESPECT FOR HUMAN LIFE

Some might take the view that the feud, vendetta, vengeance killing, and other retaliatory killings reflect a lack of respect for human life. This is perhaps not the correct interpretation of these practices. One could just as well advance the argument that it is precisely because human life is sacred that a group has the duty to avenge the death of one of its members. If life were not valued highly, then there would be little reason to bother with revenge. Some might try to refute this contention by arguing that it is purely fear which motivates the group to retaliate. Although there may be some kernel of truth to this claim, it does not refute the original proposition that human life is sacred. If the group taking revenge were only interested in terrorizing the other group to ensure that it is does not attack again, it would have no reason to limit the counter-act to one life. The context is not warfare but the feud. It should be noted that even in warfare among some peoples there must be an exact balance in the numbers of dead on each side. Peace cannot be restored until compensation is paid to even the score. The application of the *lex talionis* of a life for a life is not a bloodthirsty rule. It epitomizes the supreme value of life. Moore (1972) has astutely remarked that all societies have doctrines of restraint. They have clear limits on violence: 'I have no doubt that there is some form of restraining doctrine in all societies. Even in self-help systems, there are clear limitations on sanctioned violence. One must not harm except to right a wrong, or even a score, and then only in prescribed ways and circumstances' (p. 67).

Although her analysis is devoted to distinctions among different types of legal liability, she is generally persuaded that violence is not the creed of any society. Tylor (1873) remarked that 'no known tribe, however low and ferocious, has ever admitted that men may kill one another indiscriminately' (p. 714). Pollis and Schwab (1979) also believe that no cultural or ideological system condones 'arbitrary and indiscriminate destruction of life or incarceration' (p. 15). If the interpretation of the data is accepted and the views of these eminent social theorists are compelling, then there is reason to believe that most peoples in the world reject arbitrary, indiscriminate killing.

Westermarck (1924) provides an interesting twist to the discussion. When comparing the punishments of 'civilized' and 'savage' peoples, one finds, says Westermarck, that 'Wanton cruelty is not a general characteristic of their [savage] public justice' (Vol. I, p. 188). He notes that among several 'uncivilized' peoples capital punishment is unknown or almost so (Vol. I, p. 189). To support this claim, he presents ethnographic materials on a number of cultures. If anyone has violated *lex talionis*, it is the 'civilized' peoples: 'We find that among various semi-civilized and civilized peoples the criminal law has assumed a severity which far surpasses the rigour of the *lex talionis*' (Vol. I, p. 186). While few crimes are punishable by the death penalty among the 'savages', in Europe numerous offences were capital. In nineteenth century England many crimes were punishable by death such as pick-pocketing, sheep-stealing, forgery, arson, and sodomy (Vol. I, pp. 4–8). The Maoris were horrified by the English method of executing criminals, first telling them they are to die and then letting them lie for days and nights in prison until finally leading them slowly to gallows. 'If a man commits a crime worthy of death', they said, 'we shoot him, or chop off his head; but we do not tell him first that we are going to do so' (Vol. I, p. 190).

It seems that all cultures have mechanisms which are intended to limit violence and to prevent needless killing. But if any comparison is to be drawn, then it is the 'modern' societies which have tended to have more repressive punishments than the 'savages'. Westermarck's data contradict the historical stage theory put forward by such scholars as Diamond and Durkheim. In fact, small-scale societies are much more likely to accept restitution for a crime that could bring the death penalty than are larger nation-states.

RETRIBUTION AS NEGATIVE RECIPROCITY

Some have claimed that reciprocity is a fundamental characteristic of all societies (Malinowski, 1949; Mauss, 1954; Becker, 1956; Hobhouse, 1915; Simmell, 1950), and some have argued that retribution is negative reciprocity (Brown, 1986; Hallpike, 1975, p. 117; Kelsen, 1946, p. 63; De Waal 1982, p. 205). In a classic article on reciprocity as a moral norm and one of the universal principle components of all moral codes, Gouldner (1960, p. 172) distinguishes between two types of reciprocity. Heteromorphic reciprocity means that the things exchanged may be concretely different but should be equal in value. Homeomorphic reciprocity means that exchanges should be concretely alike or identical in form. Gouldner's two types of reciprocity may be applied to blood money and *lex talionis*, respectively. In fact, he identifies homeomorphic reciprocity with the talionic formulation: 'Historically, the most important expression of homeomorphic reciprocity is found in the *negative* norm of reciprocity, that is, in sentiments of retaliation where the emphasis is placed not on the return of benefits but on the return of injuries, and is best exemplified by the *lex talionis*' (p. 172).

In an intriguing article on the idea of justice, Krappe (1944) also remarks on the relationship between *lex talionis* and reciprocity: 'In the main . . . the *ius talionis* is merely the expression of the same conception as absolute reciprocity' (p. 184). He further notes that a striking example of the reciprocity he associates with justice is furnished by intertribal slayings (p. 182). Finally, he suggests that reciprocity is the essential ingredient of justice: 'we may recall that the symbol of justice is the balance, a form of symbolism which may or may not be older than the rise of trade in the great river valleys. At all events, it expresses the idea of reciprocity and seems to indicate that reciprocity is an essential, perhaps the most essential, element in the complicated concept of justice' (pp. 180–1; see also Kelsen, 1941, p. 537).

CONCLUSION

Some may ask what the precise relationship is between principles and rights. There is no necessary connection. My claim is that where it is possible to demonstrate acceptance of a moral principle or value by all cultures it will be feasible to erect human rights standards. The reality of universality depends on marshalling cross-cultural data.

The question remains as to which specific human rights can be derived from the apparently universal principle of retribution. If my interpretation of the principle is accepted, namely that cultures are committed to limits on arbitrary killing and violence, then what are the practical implications for universal human rights standards? I am not claiming that the principle will clarify all moral debates about killings. For instance, the principle will not resolve the arguments about infanticide and abortion because some societies view these acts as arbitrary, unjustified killings while others will take the opposite view.

Nevertheless, the demonstration of a principle is not an empty gesture. I maintain that worldwide support for the principle indicates that were we to hold a global referendum on international human rights, all societies, if they were to vote according to their own ideals, would unanimously favor certain standards. In particular, they would endorse the principle that 'No one shall be arbitrarily deprived of his life' (Article 6(1), International Covenant of Civil and Political Rights; this is not to say that they would subscribe to the other provisions of this article, e.g., the inherent right to life.) It would follow that they would also agree with Article 6(3) of the Covenant and the Convention on the Prevention and Punishment of the Crime of Genocide, both of which condemn the arbitrary deprivation of life that is genocide.

The use of the term 'arbitrary' in international documents may strike some as unhelpful for the simple reason that different societies will have different ideas about what constitutes arbitrariness. None the less, in some instances cultures will share an understanding that specific acts are arbitrary. When it comes to genocide, this is universally regarded as wrong. No society believes in the *ideal* of genocide.

Any form of killing which lacks justification, e.g. summary executions, would be contrary to the universal principle of retribution. The principle depends on the notion that an act occurs in response to a prior wrongful act. In the absence of the prior wrong, no society tolerates killing. I would go so far as to argue that some forms of arbitrary violence might also be contrary to the principle of retribution inasmuch as they lack justification. Retribution does not apply to killings only. The infliction of punishment for no crime, e.g., torture, would arguably violate the notion of retribution.[3]

According to the principle of retribution, a victim has the right to seek redress of grievance whether the perpetrator of the act is a private citizen or the state. Since the principle requires that wrongful acts be punished, this entails punishment for officials of the state who commit crimes. That is, in cases where the state causes individuals to vanish or uses torture as a method to extract information, punishment should be imposed. A universal right to retribution would strengthen the demand by citizens that dictators suffer the consequences for harming innocents. Of course some governments may try to manipulate statutes which classify virtually anyone as an enemy of the state. But generally speaking, those who disappear have not committed an act that the society to which they belong would consider a crime. Just because political elites use transparent and retroactive laws to justify their ruthless means, this does not undercut the power of a right to retribution. Those responsible for the actions of the state should be punished according to the right to retribution.

Ultimately the search for cross-cultural universals must be realistic. Even the discovery of a moral principle embraced on a universal basis may not be translated easily into particular human rights. But this approach offers the possibility of grounding international human rights in reality instead of naturalistic abstractions. By identifying principles that are shared, we can construct standards which could be implemented because they are based on values meaningful in all cultural contexts. So, while infanticide remains debatable, the plight of the disappeared, the victims of death squads, and so on, can be the legitimate focus of international concern. Despite striking cultural diversity, there are some areas of moral agreement.

I have argued that retribution tied to proportionality in its various forms serves two main purposes. It constitutes an essential ingredient in most peoples' conceptions of justice and as such is ubiquitous. I have also tried to show that these social processes, if properly interpreted, reflect a profound commitment to a limitation on violence. If there is universal support for a principle based on the idea that arbitrary, indiscriminate killing is indefensible, then this may provide a foundation for human rights, in particular those against torture and arbitrary killing. It also suggests that there may be hope that cross-cultural empirical research may reveal other universally shared moral principles.

Notes

1. There is an intriguing discussion in the *Rivista Internazionale di Filosofia Diritto* (Mitias, 1983; Primorac, 1979, 1984) about the question of whether or not a retributive theory of punishment necessarily requires the *lex talionis*. The debate is confused because the writers have wrongly equated *lex talionis* with the principle of proportionality (see Renteln, 1987).
2. Three writers claim to have found societies which lack *lex talionis*: the Huli (Glasse, 1959), the Gamo of Ethiopia (Bureau, 1979), and some parts of Albania (Hasluck, 1967). These apparent counterexamples, I contend, are simply misinterpretations of the cultural practices in question (for a more complete discussion, see Renteln, 1987).
3. There are other provisions in the international instruments which might win universal approval. Among those which all might support are: Article 9 of the Universal Declaration of Human Rights; 'No one shall be subjected to arbitrary arrest, detention or exile'; some version of Article 12: 'No one shall be subjected to arbitrary interference with his privacy, family, home or correspondence, nor to attacks upon his honour and reputation'. Although the phraseology might have to be modified, the underlying notion that arbitrary acts against individuals or groups are wrong and, therefore, contrary to law might be embraced by all peoples.

References

ADAIR, J. (1930) *Adair's History of the American Indians* (S. C. Williams, ed.) (Johnson City, Tennessee: The Watauga Press.) (Original work published 1775.)

ADLER, A. (1980) 'La Vengeance du Sang chez les Moundang du Chad', in R. Verdier (ed.), *La Vengeance*, Vol. 1, pp. 75–89 (Paris: Editions Cujas).

ALSTON, P. (1983) 'The Universal Declaration at 35: Western and Passe or Alive and Universal?' *International Commission of Jurists Review*, 31: 60–70.

ALSTON, P. (1984) 'Conjuring Up New Human Rights: A Proposal for Quality Control', *American Journal of International Law*, 78: 607–721.

ALT, A. (1934) 'Zur Talionsformel', *Zeitschrift fur die Alttestamentliche Wissenschaft*, 52: 303–305.

ANON. (1970) 'Vendetta', *Encyclopedia Brittannica*, 22: 944–5 (Chicago: William Benton).

AYERS, E. L. (1984) *Vengeance and Justice. Crime and Punishment in the 19th-Century South* (New York and Oxford: Oxford University Press).

BARTH, F. (1953) *Principles of Social Organization in Southern Kurdistan.* Universitets Etnografiske Museum Bulletin No. 7. (Oslo: Brodene Jorgensen A/s Boktrykkeri).

BECKER, H. (1956) *Man in Reciprocity* (New York: Praeger).

BEDAU, H. A. (1982) 'International Human Rights', in T. Regan and D. V. DeVeer (eds.) *And Justice for All*, pp. 287–308 (Totowa, NJ: Rowman & Littlefield).

BEER, L. W. (1984) *Freedom of Expression in Japan. A Study in Comparative Law, Politics and Society* (Tokyo, New York and San Francisco: Kodansha International Ltd).

BELL, R. (1960) *The Qur'an.* Translated with a critical re-arrangement of the Surahs, Vols. 1–2 (Edinburgh: T. & T. Clark). (Original work published 1937.)

BENEDICT, R. (1934) *Patterns of Culture* (Boston: Houghton Mifflin).

BERGER, P. (1977) 'Are Human Rights Universal?' *Commentary*, 64: 60–3.

BERMAN, H. (1984) 'Are Human Rights Universal?' *Interculture*, 17(2): 53–60.

BERMAN, H. J. (1979) 'American and Soviet Perspectives on Human Rights', *Worldview*, 22(11): 15–21.

BILDER, R. B. (1969) 'Rethinking International Human Rights: Some Basic Questions', *Human Rights Journal*, 2: 557–608.

BLACK-MICHAUD, J. (1975) *Cohesive Force: Feud in the Meditteranean and the Middle East* (New York: St Martin's Press).

BLAU, J. (1916) *Lex Talionis* (New York: Central Conference of American Rabbis).

BLOCH, M. (1961) *Feudal Society* (Chicago: University of Chicago Press).

BLUMENTRITT, F. (1891) 'The Quinganes of Luzon', *Popular Science Monthly*, 39: 388–93.

BOAS, F. (1888) 'The Central Eskimo, in US Bureau of Ethnology, *Sixth Annual Report, 1884–1885* (578–582). (Washington, DC: Government Printing Office).

BOAS, F. (1940) 'Liberty Among Primitive People', in R. N. Anshen (ed.), *Freedom: Its Meaning*, pp. 375–80 (New York: Harcourt Brace).

BOCCASSINO, D. R. (1962) 'La vendetta del sangue praticata dagli Acioli dell'Uganda; riti e cannibalismo guerreschi', *Anthropos*, 57: 357–73.

BOEHM, C. (1984) *Blood Revenge: The Anthropology of Feuding in Montenegro and Other Tribal Societies* (Lawrence, Kansas: University Press of Kansas).

BROWN, D. (1986) 'Toward a Universal Ethnography'. Unpublished manuscript.

BUREAU, J. (1979) 'Une Societe Sans Vengeance? Les Gamo D'Ethiopie', *L'Ethnographie*, 79: 93–104.

BUSQUET, J. (1920) *Le Droit de la Vendetta et les Paci Corses*, These de Droit, Lyon (Paris: Pedone).

CHELHOD, J. (1980) 'Equilibre et Parite dans la Vengeance du Sang chez les Bedouins de Jordanie', in R. Verdier (ed.), *La Vengeance*, Vol. I, pp. 125–43 (Paris: Editions Cujas).

CLAUDE, R. (ed.) (1976) *Comparative Human Rights* (Baltimore and London: Johns Hopkins University Press).

COHN, H. (1971) 'Talion', *Encyclopedia Judaica*, 15: 741.

COLSON, E. (1953) 'Social Control and Vengeance in Plateau Tonga Society', *Africa*, 23: 199–212.

CONTINI, P. (1971) 'The Evolution of Blood-Money for Homicide in Somalia', *Journal of African Law*, 15: 77–84.

DALBY, M. (1981) 'Revenge and the Law in Traditional China', *American Journal of Legal History*, 25: 267–307.

DANELSKI, D. J. (1966) 'A Behavioral Conception of Human Rights', *Law in Transition Quarterly*, 3: 63–73.

D'ANGELO, E. (1973) A Comparative Concept of Freedom. International Congress of Philosophy, 15th Varna, Bulgaria. *Proceedings of the XVth World Congress of Philosophy*, 4: 47–50.

DAUBE, D. (1969) *Studies in Biblical Law* (New York: Ktav Publishing House).

DAUTREMER, J. (1885) 'The Vendetta or Legal Revenge in Japan', *Transactions of the Asiatic Society of Japan*, 13: 82–9.

DEMBITZ, L. (1901) 'Retaliation', in I. Singer (ed.), *Jewish Encyclopedia*, Vol. 10, pp. 385–6) (New York: Ktav Publishing House).

De WAAL, F. (1982) *Chimpanzee Politics* (New York: Harper & Row).

DIAMOND, A. S. (1957) 'An Eye for An Eye', *Iraq*, 19: 151–5.

Di BELLA, M. P. (1980) 'Le Code de la Vengeance en Barbagia (Sardaigne) Selon A.Pigliaru', *Production Pastorale et Societe*, 7: 37–42.

DONNELLY, J. (1982) 'Human Rights and Human Dignity: An Analytic Critique of Non-Western Conceptions of Human Rights', *American Political Science Review*, 76: 303–16.

DONNELLY, J. (1985) *The Concept of Human Rights* (New York: St Martin's Press).

DORON, P. (1969) 'A New Look at an Old Lex', *Journal of the Ancient Near Eastern Society of Columbia University*, 1: 21–7.

DRIVER, G. R. and MILES, J. C. (1956a) *The Babylonian Laws. Legal Commentary*, Vol. I (Oxford: The Clarendon Press).

DRIVER, G. R. and MILES, J. C. (1956b) *The Babylonian Laws: Transliterated Text, Translations, Philological Notes, Glossary*,' Vol. II (Oxford: The Clarendon Press).

DUCHACEK, I. D. (1973) *Rights and Liberties in the World Today: Constitutional Promise and Reality* (Santa Barbara, California and Oxford, England: ABC-Clio).

DuCROS, P. (1926) 'De la Vendetta a la Loi du Tailon', *Revue d'Histoire et de Philosophie Religieuses*, 6: 350–65.

DUPREE, L. (1980) 'Militant Islam and Traditional Warfare in Islamic South Asia', *American Universities Field Staff Reports*, 1980/21 Asia, 1–12.

EDEL, A. (1962) 'Anthropology and Ethics in Common Focus', *Journal of the Royal Anthropological Institute*, 92: 55–72.

EDEL, A. and EDEL, M. (1968) *Anthropology and Ethics: The Quest for Moral Understanding* (Cleveland: The Press of Case Western Reserve University).

ELEZI, I. (1966) 'Sur la Vendetta en Albanie', *Studia Albanica*, 3: 305–18.
ELLENBERGER, H. F. (1981) 'La Vendetta', *Revue Internationale de Criminologie et de Police Technique*, 34: 125–42.
EVANS-PRITCHARD, E. E. (1963) *The Nuer* (Oxford: Clarendon Press).
FERGUSON, C. C. (1979) 'Global Human Rights: Challenges and Prospects', *Denver Journal of International Law and Policy*, 8: 367–77.
FINKELSTEIN, J. J. (1936) 'An Eye for an Eye', *The Menorah Journal*, 24: 207–18.
FISHER, E. F. (1982) 'Explorations and Responses: *Lex Talionis* in the Bible and Rabbinic Tradition', *Journal of Ecumenical Studies*, 19: 582–7.
FRYMER-KENSKY, T. (1980) 'Tit for Tat: The Principle of Equal Retribution in Near Eastern and Biblical Law, *Biblical Archeologist*, 43: 230–4.
GARINE, I. D. (1980) 'Les Etrangers, la Vengeance et les Parents chez les Massa et les Moussey (Tchad et Cameroun)', in R. Verdier (ed.), *La Vengeance*, Vol. I, pp. 91–124 (Paris: Editions Cujas).
GLASSE, R. M. (1959) 'Revenge and Redress Among the Huli: A Preliminary Account', *Mankind*, 5: 273–89.
GLUCKMAN, M. (1966) 'The Peace in Feud', in M. Gluckman (ed.), *Custom and Conflict in Africa*, pp. 1–26 (Oxford: Basil Blackwell).
GOULDNER, A. W. (1960) 'The Norm of Reciprocity: A Preliminary Statement', *American Sociological Review*, 25: 161–78.
GRANDE, F. (1983) 'Tolerancia Versus Ley Del Talion', *Cuadernos Hispanoamericanos*, 395: 203–11.
HAAS, E. B. (1978) *Global Evangelism Rides Again: How to Protect Human Rights Without Really Trying* (Berkeley, California: Institute for International Studies).
HALDANE, J. B. S. (1940) 'A Comparative Study of Freedom', in R. N. Anshen (ed.), *Freedom: Its Meaning*, pp. 447–72 (New York: Harcourt, Brace).
HALL, J. (1983) 'Biblical Atonement and Modern Criminal Law', *Journal of Law and Religion*, 1: 279–95.
HALLPIKE, C. R. (1975) 'Two Types of Reciprocity', *Comparative Studies in Society and History*, 17: 113–19.
HALLPIKE, C. R. (1977) *Bloodshed and Vengeance in the Papuan Mountains* (Oxford: Clarendon Press).
HARDY, M. J. L. (1963) *Blood Feuds and the Payment of Blood Money in the Middle East* (Beirut).
HARRIS, J. S. (1924) *Lex Talionis and the Jewish Law of Mercy* (London: Pelican Press).
HART, H. L. A. (1979) 'Are There Any Natural Rights?' in D. Lyons (ed.), *Rights*, pp. 1–25 (Belmont, California: Wadsworth Publishing).
HASLUCK, M. (1967) 'The Albanian Blood Feud', in P. Bohannan (ed.), *Law and Warfare*, pp. 381–408 (Garden City, New York: The Natural History Press).
HATCH, E. (1983) *Culture and Morality: The Relativity of Values in Anthropology* (New York: Columbia University Press).
HENKIN, L. (1979) 'Rights: American and Human', *Columbian Law Review*, 79: 406–25.

HERSKOVITS, M. (1972) *Cultural Relativism: Perspectives in Cultural Pluralism* (New York: Random House).

HOBHOUSE, L. T. (1915) *Morals in Evolution. A Study of Comparative Ethics* (London: Chapman & Hall).

HOEBEL, E. A. (1949) 'Review of Man and His Works by Herskovits', *American Anthropologist*, 51: 471–4.

HOEBEL, E. A. (1954) *The Law of Primitive Man* (Cambridge, Massachusetts: Harvard University Press).

HOEBEL, E. A. (1976) 'Feud: Concept, Reality and Method in the Study of Primitive Law', in A. R. Desai (ed.), *Essays on Modernization of Underdeveloped Societies*, Vol. I, pp. 500–13 (Atlantic Highlands, NJ: Humanities Press).

HUDSON, W. D. (ed.) (1969) *The Is/Ought Question* (New York: St Martin's Press).

JACOBY, S. (1983) *Wild Justice: The Evolution of Revenge* (New York: Harper & Row).

KADARKAY, A. (1982) *Human Rights in American and Russian Political Thought* (Washington, DC: University Press of America).

KARSTEN, R. (1923) *Blood Revenge, War, and Victory Feasts among the Jibaro Indians of Eastern Ecuador*. Bureau of American Ethnology Bulletin 79 (Washington DC: Government Printing Office).

KELSEN, H. (1946) *Society and Nature: A Sociological Inquiry* (London: Kegan Paul, Trench, Trubner).

KELSEN, H. (1941) 'Causality and Retribution'. *Philosophy of Science*, 8:533–56.

KLEINIG, J. (1981) 'Cultural Relativism and Human Rights', in A. E. Tay (ed.), *Teaching Human Rights*, pp. 111–18 (Canberra: Australian Governmental Publishing Service).

KRAPPE, A. H. (1944) 'Observations on the Origin and Development of the Idea of Justice', *University of Chicago Law Review*, 12: 179–97.

KUGELMASS, H. J. (1981) *Lex Talionis in the Old Testament*. Unpublished thesis, Theology. University of Montreal.

LaBURTHE-TOLRA P. (1980) 'Note sur la Vengeance chez les Beti', in R. Verdier (ed.), *La Vengeance*, Vol. I, pp. 157–66 (Paris: Editions Cujas).

LaGRANGE, F. M. J. (1916) 'L'Homicide D'Apres le Code de Hammourabi et D'Apres la Bible', *Revue Biblique*, 13: 440–71.

LEAR, J. (1984) 'Moral Objectivity', in S. C. Brown (ed.), *Objectivity and Cultural Divergence*, pp. 135–70 (Cambridge: Cambridge University Press).

LEENHARDT, M. (1930) *Note d'Ethnologie Neo-Caleodonienne*. Universite de Paris, Travaux et Memoires de l'Institut d'Ethnologie, 8.

LEWIS, W. H. (1961) 'Feuding and Social Change in Morocco', *Journal of Conflict Resolution*, 5: 43–54.

MABBOTT, J. D. (1946) 'Is Anthropology Relevant to Ethics?' *Aristotelian Society*, Supp., 22: 85–93.

MacBEATH, A. M. (1946) 'Is Anthropology Relevant to Ethics?' *Aristotelian Society*, Supp., 22: 94–21.

MacCLINTOCK, S. S. (1901) 'Kentucky Mountaineers and Their Feuds', *American Journal of Sociology*, 7: 171–87.

MacCORMACK, G. (1973) 'Revenge and Compensation in Early Law', *American Journal of Comparative Law*, 21, 69–85.

MALINOWSKI, B. (1949) *Crime and Custom in Savage Society* (London: Routledge & Kegan Paul).

MANGLAPUS, R. S. (1978) 'Human Rights Are Not a Western Discovery', *Worldview*, 21(10): 4–6.

MARGOLIN, A. (1933–4) 'The Element of Vengeance in Punishment', *Journal of Criminal Law, Criminology, and Police Science*, 24: 755–67.

MASAHIKO, K. (1985) 'Asian Perspective – Human Rights – A Western Standard? *Japan Christian Quarterly*, 51(2): 110–12.

MASSON-OURSEL, P. (1923) *La Philosophie Comparee* (Paris: Librairie Felix Alcan).

MASSON-OURSEL, P. (1951) True Philosophy is Comparative Philosophy. *Philosophy East and West*, 1: 6–9.

MAUSS, M. (1954) *The Gift* (London: Cohen & West).

McCOY, T. W. (1976) *The McCoys: Their Story as Told to the Author by Eye Witnesses and Descendants* (Pikeville Kentucky: Preservation Council Press of the Preservation Council of Pike County).

MEIJER, M. J. (1980) 'An Aspect of Retribution in Traditional Chinese Law', *T'oung Pao*, 66: 199–216.

MILLS, D. E. (1976) 'Kataki-uchi: The Practice of Blood-Revenge in Pre-Modern Japan', *Modern Asian Studies*, 10: 525–42.

MITIAS, M. H. (1983) 'Is Retribution Inconsistent Without *lex talionis*?' *Rivista Internazionale di Filosofia del Diritto*, 56: 43–60.

MOORE, S. F. (1972) 'Legal Liability and Evolutionary Interpretation: Some Aspects of Strict Liability, Self-help and Collective Responsibility', in M. Gluckman (ed.), *The Allocation of Responsibility*, pp. 51–107 (Manchester: Manchester University Press).

MURPHY, C. (1981) 'Objections to Western Conceptions of Human Rights', *Hofstra Law Review*, 9: 433–47.

MUTZENBERG, C. G. (1917) *Kentucky's Famous Feuds and Tragedies* (R. F. Fenno).

NADEL, S. F. (1947) *The Nuba* (London: Oxford University Press).

NICKEL, J. W. (1982) 'Are Human Rights Utopian?' *Philosophy and Public Affairs*, 11: 246–64.

NIELSEN, N. C., Jr. (1964) Freedom as a Transcultural Value. *International Congress of Philosophy, Proceedings*, 13th, 7 (Mexico): 359–67.

NOVAK, M. (1986) *Human Rights and the New Realism* (New York: Freedom House).

OESTERREICHER, J. M. (1980) 'Christianity, Judaism and the Law of Retaliation' (Letter to the editor); *New York Times*, 21 December, p. 16.

OTTERBEIN, K. F. and OTTERBEIN, C. W. (1965) 'An Eye for an Eye, A Tooth for a Tooth: A Cross-Cultural Study of Feuding', *American Anthropologist*, 67: 1470–82.

PANIKKAR, R. (1982) 'Is the Notion of Human Rights a Western Concept?' *Diogenes*, 120: 75–102.

PAPPU, S. S. R. R. (1982) 'Human Rights and Human Obligations: An East–West Perspective', *Philosophy and Social Action*, 8: 15–28.

PERCY, J. D. (1943) 'Revenge and Retribution', *London Quarterly and Holborn Review*, 168: 69–71.

PETERS, E. L. (1967) 'Some Structural Aspects of the Feud among the Camel-Herding Bedouin of Cyrenaica', *Africa*, 37: 261–82.

PILLING, A. R. (1957) 'Law and Feud in an Aboriginal Society of North Australia'. Doctoral dissertation, University of California, Berkeley.

POCKLINGTON, T. C. (1982) 'Against Inflating Human Rights', *Windsor Yearbook of Access to Justice*, 2: 77–86.

POLLIS, A. and SCHWAB, P. (eds). (1979) *Human Rights: Cultural and Ideological Perspectives* (New York: Praeger).

POSNER, R. A. (1980) 'Retribution and Related Concepts of Punishment', *Journal of Legal Studies*, 10: 71–92.

POSPISIL, L. (1956) 'The Nature of Law', *New York Academy of Sciences Transactions*, 18: 746–55.

POSPISIL, L. (1968) 'Feud', *International Encyclopedia of the Social Sciences*, 5: 389–93 (New York: Macmillan and The Free Press.

POUPKO, C. K. (1975) 'The Religious Basis of the Retributive Approach to Punishment', *The Thomist*, 39: 528–41.

PRIMORAC, I. (1979) 'On Some Arguments against the Retributive Theory of Punishment', *Rivista Internazionale di Filosofia del Diritto*, 56: 43–60.

PRIMORAC, I. (1984) 'On Retributivism and the *Lex Talionis*', *Rivista Internazionale di Filosofia del Diritto*, 61: 83–94.

RADCLIFFE-BROWN, A. R. (1940) 'Preface', in M. Fortes and E. E. Evans-Pritchard (eds), *African Political Systems*, pp. xi–xxiii (Oxford: Oxford University Press).

RAMCHARAN, B. G. (1983) 'The Concept of Human Rights in Contemporary International Law', *Canadian Human Rights Yearbook*, 267–81.

RAPHAEL, D. D. (1966) 'The Liberal Western Tradition of Human Rights', *International Social Science Journal* 18: 22–30.

RAWLS, J. (1955) 'Two Concepts of Rules', *Philosophical Review*, 64: 3–32.

RENTELN, A. D. (1985) 'The Unanswered Challenge of Relativism and the Consequences for Human Rights', *Human Rights Quarterly*, 7: 514–40.

RENTELN, A. D. (1987) *a Conceptual Analysis of International Rights: Universalism versus Relativism*. Doctoral dissertation, Jurisprudence and Social Policy. University of California, Berkeley.

RENTELN, A. D. (1988) 'Relativism and the Search for Human Rights', *American Anthropologist*, Vol. 90, 56–72.

RIEDER, J. (1984) The Social Organization of Vengeance. In D. Black (ed.) *Toward a General Theory of Social Control*, Vol. I, pp. 131–62 (Orlando, Florida: Academic Press).

ROSHWALD, M. (1958–9) 'The Concept of Human Rights', *Philosophy and Phenomenological Research*, 19: 354–79.

RUSSELL, L. J. (1946) 'Is Anthropology Relevant to Ethics?' *Aristotelian Society*, Supp., 22, 61–84.

SCHOTT, R. (1980) 'Vengeance and Violence among the Bulsa of Northern Ghana', in R. Verdier (ed.), *La Vengeance*, Vol. I, pp. 167–99 (Paris: Editions Cujas).

SELIGMAN, C. G. (1910) *The Melanesians of British New Guinea* (Cambridge: The University Press).

SHIH, H. (1940) 'The Modernization of China and Japan: A Comparative Study in Cultural Conflict and a Consideration of Freedom', in R. N. Anshen (ed.), *Freedom: Its Meaning*, pp. 14–22 (New York: Harcourt, Brace).

SIDGWICK, H. (1922) *The Methods of Ethics* (7th edn) (London: Macmillan).

SIMIC, A. (1967) 'The Blood Feud in Montenegro. Essays in Balkan Ethnology', *Kroeber Anthropological Society*, Special Publications, No. 1.

SIMMEL, G. (1950) *The Sociology of Georg Simmel* (K. H. Wolff, trans, & ed.) (Glencoe, Illinois: The Free Press).

SINHA, S. P. (1978) 'Human Rights Philosophically', *Indian Journal of International Law*, 18: 139–59.

SINHA, S. P. (1981) 'Human Rights: A Non-Western Viewpoint', *Archiv fur Rechts- und Sozialphilosophie*, 67: 76–91.

SINHA, S. P. (1982) 'Why and How Human Rights', *International Journal of Legal Information*, 10: 308–19.

SONNICHSEN, C. L. (1971) *Ten Texas Feuds* (Albuquerque, New Mexico: University of New Mexico Press).

SOUTHALL, A. W. (1956) *Alur Society: A Study in Processes and Types of Domination* (Cambridge, England: W. Heffner).

SPENCER, H. (1900) *The Principles of Sociology*, Vol. II (New York: D. Appleton).

STACKHOUSE, M. L. (1984) *Creeds, Society and Human Rights: A Study in Three Cultures* (Grand Rapids, Michigan: William B. Eerdmans Publishing).

STIRLING, A. P. (1960) 'A Death and a Youth Club: Feuding in a Turkish Village', *Anthropological Quarterly*, 33:51–75.

THOMSON, A. S. (1970) *The Story of New Zealand* (New York: Praeger). (First published 1859).

THURNWALD, R. (1930) 'Blood Vengeance Feud', *Encyclopedia of the Social Sciences*, Vol. II, pp. 598–9) (New York: Macmillan).

TOMUSCHAT, C. (1981) 'Is Universality of Human Rights Standards an Outdated and Utopian Concept? in R. Bieber and D. Nickel (eds), *Das Europa der zweiten Generation: Gedachtnisschrift fur Christoph Sasse*, Vol. 2, pp. 585–609 (Strassburg: Engel Verlag, Kehl am Rhein).

TOWER, M. (1984) 'Popular Misconceptions: A Note on the *Lex Talionis*', *Law and Justice*, Vol. 80–1, pp. 21–7.

TURNBULL, C. M. (1972) *The Mountain People* (New York: Touchstone Book, Simon & Schuster).

TYAGI, Y. K. (1981) 'Third World Response to Human Rights', *Indian Journal of International Law*, 21: 119–40.

TYLOR E. B. (1873) 'Primitive Society', *Contemporary Review*, 21: 701–18.

VERDIER, R. (1980) *La Vengeance*, Vol. I (Paris: Editions Cujas).

VERDIER, R. (1984) *La Vengeance*, Vol. III (Paris: Editions Cujas).

VERDIER, R. (1984) *La Vengeance*, Vol. IV (Paris: Editions Cujas).

WEINGREEN, J. (1976) 'The Concepts of Retaliation and Compensation in Biblical Law', *Royal Irish Academy, Proceedings*, 76, Section C, 510.1; 1–11.

WESTERMARCK, E. (1898) 'The Essence of Revenge', *Mind*, 7: 289–310.

WESTERMARCK, E. (1924) *The Origin and Development of Moral Ideas* (London: Macmillan).

WESTERMARCK, E. (1932a) *Early Beliefs and their Social Influence* (London: Macmillan).

WESTERMARCK, E. (1932b) *Ethical Relativity* (New York: Harcourt, Brace & Co.).

WILLIAMS, F. E. (1941) 'Group Sentiment and Primitive Justice', *American Anthropologist*, 43: 523–39.

WISDOM, C. (1940) *The Chorti Indians of Guatemala* (Chicago: University of Chicago Press).

WISEBERG, L. and SCOBLE, H. (1981) 'Problems of Comparative Research on Human Rights', in V. P. Nanda, J. R. Scarritt and G. W. Shepherd, Jr. (eds), *Global Human Rights: Public Policies, Comparative Measures, and NGO Strategies*, pp. 147–71) (Boulder, Col.: Westview Press).

2 Human Rights in Divergent Conceptual Settings: How Do Ideas Influence Policy Choices?

M. Glen Johnson

When divergent human rights policies are observed in different countries, analysts usually turn to ideological commitment or forms of government for explanations, contrasting democratic support for human rights with violations by authoritarian regimes of the left and right. There is validity to this analysis up to a point. But divergent human rights policies may be observed even when these variables are held relatively constant. The argument of this paper is that human rights policies can be understood most fully by incorporating cultural and philosophical variables into the analysis. The argument has broad applicability but the Indian and American cases are used illustratively in order to hold forms of government and ideological commitments relatively constant.

Whenever India and the United States are discussed, it is inevitably said early on that these are the two largest democracies in the world, as if this should tell us something about the nature of their political systems and policy frameworks. Yet on those matters which are the very core of democracy – human rights policies – there are some sharp differences between the two societies. In the international arena, India is a party to the major UN Human Rights Covenants, the United States is not; India supports a New International Economic Order as a human rights policy, the United States objects to it; the United States condemns the denial of civil and political rights in Marxist states, India is silent. In the domestic realm, there are similarities of openess in political debate, freedom of political participation and protections of judicial due process but there is also an elaborate structure of preferential treatment for disadvantaged Indian minorities while, in the United States, arguments over equality threaten even modest affirmative action programs. These differences cannot be explained by different forms of government or types of

41

political system, but they are congruent with different philosophical assumptions about human rights.

HUMAN RIGHTS: UNIVERSAL OR CULTURALLY RELATIVE?

Theorists have long debated the true meaning of human rights. That debate has taken on a new scope and intensity since the Second World War, in part because newly independent non-Western countries have joined it – often adopting alternative policies and concepts justified by assertions of cultural differences. One response to these developments has been to dismiss claims of cultural relativism in the human rights area as nothing more than rationalizations for violations by regimes pursuing other goals (Donnelly, 1982). And sometimes this seems clearly the case.

In a more subtle approach, however, some analysts (Renteln, 1985) discuss human rights in broad comparative terms, asking such provocative questions as: To what extent, if at all, does a concept of human rights exist in traditional non-Western cultures and political philosophies? Are non-Western ideas of rights compatible with classical liberal Western notions of rights? Does the traditional Western notion of human rights or any part of it have universal validity?

Differing conceptions of human rights can be compared along five separate but related dimensions:

1. whether rights claims are based on status as an *individual* human being or status as a member of some *community or group* of persons;
2. the extent to which differential treatment of persons is permitted on grounds of *achievement* or *ascription*;
3. the emphasis on *rights* compared to *duties* or obligations and the extent to which rights and duties are thought to be interdependent;
4. the emphasis on so-called *economic and social rights* compared to the emphasis on *civil and political rights*, sometimes conceived as a difference between the *positive rights* of governmental obligation to provide economic and social well-being and the *negative rights* of governmental obligation to refrain from abridging political and civil rights;

5. the extent to which rights are viewed as *absolute* or *relative*.

The boundaries between these categories are far from rigid. But they provide a useful analytical framework for comparing philosophical systems. In theory, every philosophical system – whether traditional or modern, formal or informal, synthetic or 'pure' – could be compared using these categories. In general, the classical Western liberal notion of human rights emphasizes absolute individual political and civil rights while most non-Western, Third World traditions place greater emphasis on the community basis of rights and duties, on economic and social rights and on the relative character of human rights. Marxist/socialist ideas highlight economic and social rights and duties absolutely grounded in collectivist principles.

The cultural diversity reflected in these categories has proved a vexing issue for those approaching human rights in a global comparative framework. How can one evaluate rights claims in the face of such diversity? How can a global framework for human rights be developed? Is it possible to develop effective international human rights instruments in the face of culturally specific concepts of human rights? Not surprisingly, analysts have given sharply divergent answers to these questions. In general, however, recent discussions seem to take one of the following positions:

1. traditions other than Western liberalism lack concepts of human rights; the Western liberal tradition is either the *only* or the *most legitimate* concept of human rights;
2. non-Western ideas about human rights are not only comparable but compatible with the ideals of Western liberalism;
3. non-Western traditions may differ even to the point of incompatibility but it is possible to reconcile various views;
4. human rights concepts differ and cultural relativism means that no particular view can be held more valid than others.

Jack Donnelly is illustrative of the first approach. Although he accepts Third World and Marxist notions of group based economic and social 'rights' as possibly desirable goals, the fundamental thrust of his argument is to defend the purity of Western liberal ideals from the encumbering dilution of other, lesser principles. Contrasting the array of ideas rising out of other cultures with classic Western liberal values, Donnelly (1982, p. 315) concludes that 'the distinctly valuable aspects of a human rights approach are seriously eroded [by giving credence to non-Western or Marxist ideas]. Human rights are thus attacked through their apparent advocacy in a covert linguistic operation which is not only particularly difficult to handle but which frustrates rather than encourages the discussion demanded by issues of such importance.' Non-Western claims about the content of human rights become, for Donnelly, not only incompatible with Western notions but positively threatening to the 'true' ideal of human rights, i.e. the classical Western liberal ideal. Indeed, the thrust of Donnelly's work is to urge upon theorists the need to resist the threat.

A second, essentially opposite view is exemplified by Raul Manglapus (1978, pp. 4–6). Without elaborating a full philosophical argument, Manglapus asserts that non-Western cultures have the same ideals of 'respect for the dignity of the individual, absence of arbitrariness, availability of remedies against despotic rule' (p. 5) which evolved over several centuries into the specifics currently enshrined in Western constitutions and international human rights instruments. Recognizing that evolutionary development has led to greater refinement of these ideas in the West than in Third World countries, Manglapus suggests that the experience of colonial rule, far from bringing Western notions of human rights to peoples who had no such concepts in their indigenous cultures, may have instead retarded the development of human rights by interrupting indigenious evolution from basic ideas very much like those which undergird contemporary Western formulations of human rights.

A third approach – the attempt to reconcile divergent views even while recognizing their theoretical incompatibility – is exemplified in the work of Adamantia Pollis and Peter Schwab (1979). They hold that Western liberal ideas evolved out of the peculiarities of Western political experience and have no claim to superior validity or special relevance to Third World situations. Noting that the Universal Declaration of Human Rights embodies essentially Western notions at variance with the 'cultural patterns, ideological underpinings, and developmental goals of non-Western and socialist states', Pollis and Schwab (1979, p. 14) charge that 'efforts to impose the Declaration as it currently stands not only reflect a moral chauvinism and ethnocentric bias but are also bound to fail'. Nevertheless, they argue for a rethinking of the concept of human rights drawing on common threads in varied traditions. They find the seeds of a reconciled concept of human rights in broad ideals of political participation, restraints on the use of force and violence and sanctions against violators. Using these themes as building blocks, Pollis and Schwab

(1979, pp. 15–16) urge a priority effort to construct a reconciled concept of human rights. Pappu (1982) and Murphy (1981) have argued along similar lines. Speaking specifically to the Indian context, Ralph Buultjens (1980, p. 121) expresses a similar belief (or hope?) that the traditional synthesizing and absorptive character of Indian culture may provide a vehicle for reconciling divergent views of human rights.

Finally, some analysts have moved in yet another direction. They have found some validity in a wide variety of divergent views and have sometimes seemed to argue that the cause of human rights will be advanced more readily by greater understanding of different approaches than by attempts to impose or develop a common approach. William Bradley (1980) displays characteristics of this approach when he discovers varied themes in the Western cultural tradition some of which relate to themes found in other cultural traditions and conflict with certain other themes in the Western tradition. At times Kenneth Thompson (1980, p. 241) also seems to reflect this view when he suggests with approval that one option for US foreign policy would be to 'accept cultural diversity and moral disunity as conditions of international politics for the immediate future'. At other times, however, Thompson (1980, p. 242) extolls the superiority of the Western liberal notion by urging resistance to efforts to incorporate economic and social goals in the concept of human rights.

The discussion thus far has focused on broad categories of cultural differences as they are applicable to human rights considerations. Before we can examine the relationship between theory and policy at the more specific level of India and the United States, it will be necessary to examine the ways in which the operative philosophical system of each of these national entities fits the schema outlined above.

HUMAN RIGHTS PHILOSOPHIES IN INDIA AND THE UNITED STATES

The United States has its own unique variant of the classical Western liberal notion (Hartz, 1955) while India places its special imprint on an otherwise generally Third World approach. Growing out of strong and vital roots in philosophical Hinduism, modern Indian political philosophy has absorbed overlays of both the classical liberal and

Marxist traditions of the West. While it gives less formal attention to what Westerners call human rights, the Indian tradition – and here, as throughout the paper, I speak of the predominant Hindu tradition – does have a good deal to say about the categories which structure the international human rights debate.

Individualism

The United States is noted for its celebration of individualism raising that ideal to a level remarkable even within Western liberalism. In fact, so firm and full is the American commitment to individualism that little legitimacy is granted to community or group based claims in struggles for human rights (Johnson, 1980b).

In the classical Indian tradition, by contrast, individuals have social meaning only as part of a group defined by birth. Membership determines relationships within and outside the group – work options, marriage possibilities, indeed, identity itself. To be an outcast – literally to be cast out from one's *jati* or sub-caste – is to be rootless and unrelated to the society. However much Hindu reformers have decried the more discriminatory features of the caste system, most have agreed that it properly defines the groups which are the basis of individual identity and, hence, individual rights. The distinction between the individual and the group as the basic unit of social organization is one of the most fundamental contrasts between Indian philosophy and that of Western liberalism (Pye, 1985, pp. 26–8).

The group basis of identity leads to what one student of Indian philosophy has called 'the corporate nature of human rights' in India (Panikkar, 1982, pp. 90–1). 'Nothing', he suggests,

> could be more important than to underscore and defend the *dignity of the human person*. But the person should be distinguished from the individual. The individual is just an abstraction, i.e., a selection of a few aspects of the person for practical purposes. My *person*, on the other hand, is also 'my' parents, children, friends, foes, ancestors and successors . . . If you hurt 'me,' you are equally damaging my whole clan, and possibly yourself as well. Rights cannot be individualized in this way . . . One individual is an isolated knot; a person is the entire fabric around that knot, woven from the total fabric of the real . . . Certainly without the knots the net would collapse; but without the net, the knots would not even exist.

To aggressively defend my individual rights, for instance, may have negative, i.e., unjust, repercussions on others and perhaps even on myself. The need for consensus in many traditions – instead of majority opinion – is based precisely on the corporate nature of human rights.

Equality

Building on a devotion to individualism, American philosophy also prizes principles of equality of opportunity and equality before the law. To Americans, it follows logically that individuals as the basic and fundamental units of society deserve differential treatment only as a result of individual activities and achievements, not from a status over which the individual has no control.

But in India, where group identity is the basis of social organization, differential treatment is mandated on the basis of different stations in life. The Indian concept is imbedded in the fabric of Hindu philosophy and culture, a fabric which clothes what Louis Dumont (1972) has labeled *Homo Hierarchicus*. Human rights, in traditional Indian terms, do not require the kind of equality of opportunity for achievement so prized in Western ideal culture; in general, Indian conceptions involve differential treatment based on ascribed status.

Panikkar (1982, p. 86) notes that this conceptual framework has certain implications for defining the subjects of rights. 'Human rights were known long ago', he says, 'but only for the nobleman, or the free citizen, or for whites or Christians, or males, etc., and when they were hastily applied to "human beings" it was often defined just which group belonging to the race could properly be styled "human"'. Since Hindu philosophy assigns a different meaning to equality, such definitional gymnastics are less necessary.

Duties

Another feature of American political theory is the separation of rights from duties or obligations. Duties do not fall in the same category as rights. In American thinking, the emphasis is on rights which can be asserted, primarily against governmental authority. There is no comparable duty toward governmental authority. Moreover, governmental duty is essentially negative – to refrain from abridging the 'rights' of citizens. Government is not generally thought to have duties of positive action.

The corporate sense of person-hood in India means that as one claims rights based on group identity, so one correspondingly has duties which flow from that same identity. Indeed the thrust of classical Hindu law and philosophy is an emphasis on obligation defined in terms of relationships within groups, especially caste and family groups (Sinha, 1981, pp. 87–8; Pappu, 1982).

Economic and Social Rights

The emphasis on individualism and equality leads Americans to identify human rights almost exclusively with civil and political rights. Broader definitions which incorporate a recognition of economic and social rights have been resisted (Johnson, 1987, pp. 34–8). American political thinkers have debated the wisdom of accepting social and economic well-being as an important goal of governmental policy but few have asserted that Americans have a right to government guarantees of economic and social well-being in the same sense that they have a right to guarantees that the government will not abridge their civil and political rights. Economic and social well-being may or may not be desirable governmental policy but it certainly is not 'a right' in any sense in which Americans have understood that term.

Modern India has borrowed both the concept of individual civil and political rights and that of economic and social rights largely from the West – the latter from Western Marxist traditions and the former from classical Western liberalism. Although these ideas are not deeply imbedded in classical Indian philosophy and law, they none the less seem to be sinking tenacious roots into modern Indian political culture, albeit with nuances and emphases which reflect the influence of traditional Indian philosophical principles.

Relativism

Finally, Americans tend to emphasize the absolute character of rights. This is facilitated by a view of rights focused on the civil and political arena and restraining only the actions of government.

The absorptive, eclectic character of Hinduism involves a less absolutist tradition. Hinduism lacks the dichotomous perspective of Western philosophy – both Marxist and non-Marxist. The opposition between good and evil is melded into a holistic conception in which good and evil coexist within the whole and the various parts of the whole. Things (people, organizations, policies, events) are not good or evil in themselves but possess elements of both good and evil. Policy judgements, then, cannot be absolutist and human rights must be considered relative because 'they are relationships among entities' (Panikkar, 1982, p. 99).

To summarize to this point, the United States has evolved a philosophical conception of human righs which draws heavily on classical Western liberal ideas and emphasizes absolute principles of civil and political rights based on individualism and equality of opportunity. The philosophical underpinnings of modern India, by contrast, rest on group based rights and duties of a relative and differential nature with a substantial emphasis on economic and social rights as well as civil and political rights.

Conceptions of human rights are not fixed for all time any more than they are universal to all societies. They evolve and change; otherwise we would still be subject to the divine right of kings! An absorptive philosophical system like Hinduism can be expected to draw on a variety of traditional indigenous and modern imported sources as its own conception of human rights evolves (cf. Rudolph and Rudolph, 1967). And, indeed, even Western societies seem to be moving toward a gradual – and sometimes grudging – acceptance of a collective basis for rights and the inclusion of some form of economic and social rights in human rights concepts (Van Boven, 1982, pp. 51–7). Conceptual changes derive in part from policy demands and debates even as those concepts help frame policy debates and shape policy choices. It is to the latter process that we now turn.

HUMAN RIGHTS AND PUBLIC POLICY

Does the discussion of underlying philosophical assumptions help us grapple with the differential policy choices mentioned at the outset? If there is a relationship between the two, we should now be in a position to examine policy choices more closely in the framework of a comparative assessment of philosophical assumptions. Divergent policy choices which may appear confusing when viewed against the backdrop of similar political systems are better understood in terms of their congruity with divergent philosophical assumptions. Space does not permit detailed treatment of policies here; it is only possible to highlight the general characteristics of policies which demonstrate congruence with human rights norms embedded in the culture.

Domestic Policy

The policies of the United States and India for dealing with disadvantaged minorities have often been compared, especially US policies dealing with blacks and Indian policies dealing with ex-untouchables (Johnson and Johnson, 1974; Verba, Ahmed and Bhatt, 1971). For our purposes, it is important to see how these policy debates and their outcomes are different in the two societies in ways which reflect differing philosophical traditions.

In an attempt to redress centuries of discrimination against ex-untouchables, independent India constructed an elaborate system of constitutional and legal protections coupled with structures of compensatory discrimination (Galanter, 1984). Constitutional protections are embodied in several provisions which appear remarkably familiar to Western readers for the Indian Constitution, like many Third World constitutions, is based on a Western model. Thus provisions guaranteeing various fundamental rights (Constitution of India, Articles 12–28; Gajendragadkar, 1969, pp. 23–55) are congruent with Western liberal notions of individualism, political and civil rights, and equality.

Elsewhere in the Constitution, provisions more consistent with traditional Indian conceptions are incorporated. A unique section on the Directive Principles of State Policy (Constitution of India, Articles 36–51; Agarwal, 1983, pp. 149–50; Gajendragadkar, 1969, pp. 12–22) – a kind of constitutionally-mandated policy directive – provides for group-based policies, an emphasis on obligations of both government and people, and goals of economic and social well-being. However, the Directive Principles were made explicitly unenforceable through the Courts.

In other provisions of the Constitution, congruence with the Indian tradition is even more evident. Provision is made (Constitution of India, Articles 330, 332) for a significant number of seats in the Indian Parliament and in the State Assemblies to be reserved for members of the ex-untouchable castes and certain 'disadvantaged' tribal groups. Implementing Directive Principles and Article 335 of the Constitution, the Indian Government soon expanded the reservation system to public employment and broad sectors of education. Preferential treatment has also been provided for a wide-range of other backward classes and ethnic groups (Galanter, 1984; Weiner and Katzenstein, 1981).

This policy structure is varied and complex in its character and implementation but it has certain clearly discernible features which 'fit' remarkably well with the mix of Indian philosophical traditions. In the first place, constitutional protections from discrimination are clearly based on Western notions of human rights. The Untouchability Offenses Act of 1955 with Amendments reflects a mixed philosophical heritage; it includes the group basis of treatment characteristic of Hindu thought while adhering to non-discriminatory protection characteristic of ideas borrowed from Western liberal thought.[1] Constitutional and statutory provisions for preferential discrimination in favor of 'disadvantaged' groups in employment and education are congruent with more traditional ideals and sharply at odds with Western liberal principles. Here policies are quite explicitly group based and discriminatory.

Mixed policies set in a mixed philosophical tradition could not but elicit some opposition from those who sought policies based on 'purer' commitments to one tradition or another. A major court challenge grounded in Western liberal notions of individualism, equality and non-discrimination was quickly settled by a constitutional amendment explicitly embodying provisions for group-based preferential discrimination (Hardgrave, 1976). Although much litigation continues to flow from various provisions for preferential treatment, the controversies tend to revolve around issues other than fundamental questions of group-based preferential treatment (Galanter, 1984, pp. 498–513).

In recent years, India's preferential policies have sparked often bitter organized protests in some parts of India (Bose, 1981; Desai, 1981) and a spate of articles attacking the system and offering recommendations for changes (for example, Arora, 1984; Desai, 1984; Shah, 1985; Baxi, 1985). Interestingly, few of these commentaries attack the principle of preferential discrimination; they typically accept the principle while recommending changes in the particular set of policies currently in place, some challenging the use of caste as the sole basis of preference.

In the United States, policy choices have seemed more consistent since the philosophical underpinnings are less mixed than in the Indian case. Here the argument has not been over what constitutes a legitimate basis for policy – on that there is widespread agreement. Rather the controversies have revolved around whether or not specific policy choices step over that line.

Historically, a variety of philosophical and constitutional circumlocutions were employed to facilitate policies of systematic discrimination against American blacks in employment, education, housing, political participation, etc. In the 1960s, when circumstances of protest and conscience finally successfully challenged these policies, civil rights legislation developed at the federal level was cast largely in the traditional American framework. Discrimination was prohibited against individual persons by the state or its agents, increasingly defined to include private individuals acting under state license or regulations. Separate facilities were unacceptable on the grounds that they could never be made psychologically equal. Only in the Voting Rights Act were these principles modified to any appreciable extent and then only to compare the proportions of blacks among registered voters with general population figures to determine a prime facie case for dispatching federal registrars to insure non-discriminatory application of the laws.

These approaches were accepted with remarkable ease by most Americans precisely because they were so congruent with the American philosophy of rights. However, their implementation did not lead to the removal of differential representation of blacks and whites in various parts of the American social system – in quality education, in employment at all levels, in the professions, in poverty, etc. Pressure for other policy choices developed. Affirmative action programs responded to these pressures.

In their original form, affirmative action programs were consistent with underlying American philosophical principles. They were based on ideals of non-discrimination and equality of judgement of individual merit. Programs were to involve special efforts to seek out and train members of target groups so that their chances of success would be enhanced when they came to be judged without preference or prejudice. Controversy arises over whether such programs have evolved into schemes of preferential discrimination in favor of certain groups.

Critics charge that they have become ways of imposing group quotas in hiring and training (Reagan, 1986). Defenders aver that such programs involve only goals or targets for those hiring minorities on the basis of individual merit (Edwards, 1986).

Interestingly neither the critics nor the defenders of affirmative action argue that special preferential quotas *should* be provided, only whether it has in fact come to that. By contrast, in India, proponents of anti-discrimination policies argue for policies of preferential discrimination and the opponents generally accept this principle while arguing against specific Indian programs on grounds of costs, the basis of group definition, etc. Indian culture makes it easier to argue for and justify compensatory discrimination programs. American political ideals require either more elaborate and therefore less persuasive justifications or denial that the programs constitute compensatory discrimination.[2]

Foreign Policy

In the foreign policy agendas of both the United States and India, national security and economic interests outrank human rights by substantial margins. Nevertheless, human rights have become significant foreign policy issues. And it has been noted in both India and the United States that these two democracies often fail to see such issues from the same vantage point. Traditional reasons of international politics are often advanced to explain differences. Without doubt, intruding pressures of the international and domestic situations of both countries do explain a good deal of their different approaches to international human rights issues. But are there foreign policy insights to be gained from examining what relationships, if any, exist betweeen underlying conceptions of human rights and policy choices on human rights questions?

The United States was among the early vigorous participants in the international human rights effort. A substantial part of the initial impetus for the original United Nations human rights mandate, the Universal Declaration and the UN Covenants came from the United States (Henkin, 1978, pp. 115–18; Johnson, 1987). Even before that Americans had conceived of themselves as having special claims to superior human rights commitments and, from time to time, had debated ways in which such a commitment should be incorporated into foreign policy (Johnson, 1980a; Schlesinger, 1979; Tarcov, 1984). After initial leadership in the UN sponsored effort to erect an international structure to protect human rights, the United States, for all practical purposes, withdrew from the multilateral effort in the 1950s and never really returned to it. When the US again placed global human rights high on its foreign policy agenda in the 1970s, it chose unilateral and bilateral approaches rather than the multilateral approach it had led in the 1940s.

Several factors contributed to these policy choices, among them a developing awareness that the American conception of human rights was not fully shared by other countries, especially by many of the countries which were gradually becoming independent and joining the United Nations. As it became clear that it would be harder with every passing year to insure that the US conception of human rights was the one embodied in international agreements, American enthusiasm for the effort waned. The specific points on which American concern centered were the rising insistence that positive economic and social rights be incorporated into the human rights framework and that duties be addressed along side rights.

These ideas were foreshadowed in the Universal Declaration of 1948, strengthened in the Covenant on Economic and Social Rights approved by the General Assembly in 1966 and by later UN resolutions. The United States endorsed the Universal Declaration with enthusiasm albeit with some expressed interpretive reservations. It opposed drafting the Covenant on Economic, Social and Cultural Rights and, once it was adopted by the General Assembly, refused to sign until 1977 when President Carter submitted it to the Senate for advice and consent. In signing and submitting the Covenant, however, the Carter administration attached so many reservations some observers thought the overall effect would be detrimental to the Covenant (see Lawyers Committee for International Human Rights, 1980; Agarwal, 1983, p. 144). In any case, the Senate has not yet consented to ratification of the Covenant (or the Covenant on Civil and Political Rights for that matter) and there is no significant public or governmental pressure to do so. The United States vigorously and regularly dissents from other attempts by the UN majority to strengthen commitments to economic and social rights. Thus the American withdrawal from *multilateral* human rights efforts coincided with the increasing emphasis on economic and social rights and duties, positions which were antithetical to fundamental postulates of the American conception of human rights.

When the United States rediscovered international human rights in the 1970s, its policy choice was for bilateral and unilateral methods which could be made congruent with American philosophical presuppositions more easily. American administrations were prepared to use economic tools – bilateral aid and American influence in multilateral lending institutions – in human rights policy but the rights which elicited concern were almost always the civil and political rights fully congruent with the traditional American conceptions. The Carter administration briefly broadened the official definition to include certain economic rights (Department of State, 1980, p. 2) but the Reagan administration quickly reverted to a conceptual framework more familiar in the American setting (Department of State, 1985, p. 2).

Both during the Indian independence struggle and through the first fifteen years of independence, Jawaharlal Nehru, India's first Prime Minister, dominated foreign policy. He set the tone and articulated policies which were to describe India's foreign policy with minor variations down to the present day. The themes he emphasized drew heavily on the philosophical presuppositions of Indian political culture with its overlay of imports from the West. These themes included non-violence and moralism, anti-colonialism and anti-racialism, and non-alignment (Chawla, 1976, pp. 47–53).

Non-alignment was based on the political realities of a militarily weak power struggling to exercise some influence in a world dominated by two superpowers and their allies. But it was also philosophically congenial to the Hindu tradition emphasizing the mixed character of events and actors which embody both good and evil. No actor or alliance was seen to be the main source of evil in the world. Non-alignment, then, espoused a policy of judging each event or policy independently on the basis of a moral standard while avoiding prior commitments based on moral principles. This posture made India reluctant to judge the human rights performances of other countries or to instruct them about human rights policies – except on the issues of colonialism and racism.

As a prominent member of the United Nations from the start, India was represented in the drafting of the Universal Declaration and the UN Covenants. As a leader of the so-called Group of 77, India played a leading role in broadening UN definitions of rights to include economic rights and obligations. India became a party to the two main UN Covenants in 1979 through an instrument of accession which stipulated a handful of reservations notably that the right of self-determination be understood to apply to those seeking independence from colonial rule but not those trying to secede from a unified independent state (Agarwal, 1983, pp. 95–6, 140–4, 204–5). India did not fully implement the Covenants, however; required reports to the Human Rights Committee were not submitted and constitutional adjustments were not made (Agarwal, 1983, pp. 158–61).

At the international policy level, India has pursued a policy supporting the proposals for a New International Economic Order and has joined other Third World countries in relating this proposal to human rights considerations as embodied in UN General Assembly

Resolution 32/130 adopted 16 December 1977 (United Nations, 1978, p. 68). Thus, the Indian approach to human rights in foreign policy has been very different from that of the United States. India has been much more involved with the international efforts in recent years, much less judgemental on a bilateral level except on issues on colonialism and racism and much more concerned with economic and social rights. All of these positions are congruent with the philosophical conceptions of rights which inform Indian political culture.

CONCLUSION

Sharply different conceptions of human rights exist in various parts of the world. Understanding these conceptions facilitates an understanding of differential policy choices on rights issues, both domestic and foreign. Further study of such differences – both of policy and philosophy – should contribute to a more sophisticated understanding of human rights in varied cultural settings. This in turn may open national debates over human rights policies to new possibilities and permit broader concepts of human rights to evolve, both of which are essential if truly universal notions of human rights are to be developed.

Notes

1. It should be noted that none of these provisions – Constitutional or statutory – sought to abolish the categories of group identity within the caste system. Untouchability was outlawed and made an offense in the sense of certain forms of discriminatory behavior based on caste identity but the identity itself was left untouched. Indeed by reserving seats and maintaining an official schedule of eligible groups, government policy may have actually strengthened the group basis of identity. The Indian legal system does not outlaw caste, only certain types of discrimination based on caste.
2. Some theorists have begun to address the question of the justice of reverse or preferential discrimination in less culture bound terms (see Nagel, 1977) although the policy debate still tends to rest on assumptions characteristic of the American conception of human rights.

References

AGARWAL, H. O. (1983) *Implementation of Human Rights Covenants with Special Reference to India* (Allahabad: Kitab Mahal).

ARORA, V. N. (1984) 'Special Inputs for the Backward', *Seminar*, 296: 24–8.

BAXI, U. (1985) 'Caste, Class and Reservations', *Economic and Political Weekly*, 20: 426–8.

BOSE, P. K. (1981) 'Social Mobility and Caste Violence: A Study of the Gujarat Riots', *Economic and Political Weekly*, 19: 713–16.

BRADLEY, W. L. (1980) 'The Cultural Factor Reappraised', in K. W. Thompson (ed.), *The Moral Imperatives of Human Rights: A World Survey*, pp. 229–36 (Washington: University Press of America).

BUULTJENS, R. (1980) 'Human Rights in Indian Political Culture', in K. W. Thompson (ed.), *The Moral Imperatives of Human Rights: A World Survey*, pp. 109–22 (Washington, DC: University Press of America).

CHAWLA, S. (1976) *The Foreign Relations of India* (Encino, California: Dickenson Publishing Company).

DEPARTMENT OF STATE, UNITED STATES OF AMERICA (1980) *Country Reports on Human Rights Practices for 1979* (Washington, DC: US Government Printing Office).

DEPARTMENT OF STATE, UNITED STATES OF AMERICA (1985) *Country Reports on Human Rights Practices for 1984* (Washington, DC: US Government Printing Office).

DESAI, I. P. (1981) 'Anti-Reservation Agitation and Structure of Gujarat Society'. *Economic and Political Weekly*, 16: 819–23.

DESAI, I. P. (1984) 'Should "Caste" be the Basis for Recognising Backwardness?' *Economic and Political Weekly*, 19: 1106–16.

DONNELLY, J. (1982) 'Human Rights and Human Dignity: An Analytical Critique of Non-Western Conceptions of Human Rights', *American Political Science Review*, 76: 303–16.

DUMONT, L. (1972) *Homo Hierarchicus* (London: Granada Publishing).

EDWARDS, D. (1986) 'Keep Affirmative Action', *The New York Times*, 13 February, p. A31.

GAJENDRAGADKAR, P. B. (1969) *The Constitution of India: Its Philosophy and Basic Postulates* (London: Oxford University Press).

GALANTER, M. (1984) *Competing Equalities: Law and the Backward Classes in India* (Berkeley: University of California Press).

HARDGRAVE, R. L., Jr. (1976) 'DeFunis and Dorairajan: "Protective Discrimination" in the United States and India'. Paper prepared for delivery at the annual meeting of the American Political Science Association.

HARTZ, L. (1955) *The Liberal Tradition in America: An Interpretation of American Political Thought Since the Revolution* (New York: Harcourt, Brace & World).

HENKIN, L. (1978) *The Rights of Man Today* (Boulder, Co.: Westview Press).

JOHNSON, M. G. and JOHNSON, S. B. (1974) 'Anti-Discrimination

Policies in the United States and India'. Paper prepared for delivery at the annual meeting of the American Political Science Association.

JOHNSON, M. G. (1980a) 'Historical Perspectives on Human Rights and U.S. Foreign Policy', *Universal Human Rights*, 2(3): 1–18.

JOHNSON, M. G. (1980b) 'The United States and the Quest for International Social Justice', *Indian Journal of American Studies*, 2: 32–47.

JOHNSON, M. G. (1987) 'The Contributions of Eleanor and Franklin Roosevelt to the Development of International Protections for Human Rights', *Human Rights Quarterly*, 9: 19–48.

LAWYERS COMMITTEE FOR INTERNATIONAL HUMAN RIGHTS (1980) 'Critique of Reservations to the International Human Rights Covenants Proposed by the US Department of State', in *International Human Rights Treaties*, pp. 48–54. Hearings Before the Committee on Foreign Relations, United States Senate, Ninety-Sixth Congress, First Session (Washington, DC: US Government Printing Office).

MANGLAPUS, R. S. (1978) 'Human Rights Are Not a Western Discovery', *Worldview*, 21(10): 4–6.

MURPHY, C. F., Jr. (1981) 'Objections to Western Conceptions of Human Rights', *Hofstra Law Review*, 9: 433–47.

NAGEL, T. (1977) 'Equal Treatment and Compensatory Discrimination', in M. Cohen, T. Nagel and T. Scanlon (eds), *Equality and Preferential Treatment*, pp. 3–18 (Princeton: Princeton University Press).

PANIKKAR, R. (1982) 'Is the Notion of Human Rights a Western Concept?' *Diogenes*, 120: 75–102.

PAPPU, S. S. R. R. (1982) 'Human Rights and Human Obligations: An East–West Perspective', *Philosophy and Social Action*, 8: 15–27.

POLLIS, A. and SCHWAB, P. (1979) 'Human Rights: A Western Construct with Limited Applicability', in A. Pollis and P. Schwab (eds), *Human Rights: Cultural and Ideological Perspectives*, pp. 1–18 (New York: Praeger).

PYE, L. W. (1985) *Asian Power and Politics: The Cultural Dimensions of Authority* (Cambridge: Harvard University Press).

REAGAN, R. (1986) 'President's News Conference on Foreign and Domestic Issues', *The New York Times*, 12 February, p. A12.

RENTELN, A. D. (1985) 'The Unanswered Challenge of Relativism and the Consequences for Human Rights', *Human Rights Quarterly*, 7: 514–40.

RUDOLPH, L. I. and RUDOLPH, S. H. (1967) *The Modernity of Tradition: Political Development in India* (Chicago: University of Chicago Press).

SCHLESINGER, A. M., Jr. (1979) 'Human Rights and the American Tradition', *Foreign Affairs*, 57: 503–26.

SHAH, G. (1985) 'Caste, Class and Reservation', *Economic and Political Weekly*, 20: 132–6.

SINHA, S. P. (1981) 'Human Rights: A Non-Western Viewpoint', *Archiv fur Rechts – und Sozialphilosophie*, 67: 76–91.

TARCOV, N. (1984) 'Principle and Prudence in Foreign Policy: The Founder's Perspective', *The Public Interest*, 76: 45–60.

THOMPSON, K. W. (1980) 'Implications for American Foreign Policy', in K. W. Thompson (ed.), *The Moral Imperatives of Human Rights: A*

World Survey, pp. 237–46 (Washington: University Press of America).
UNITED NATIONS (1978) *Monthly Chronicle* (Asian edn), 15(1): 68.
VAN BOVEN, T. C. (1982) 'Distinguishing Criteria of Human Rights', in
  K. Vasak (general ed.), and P. Ashton (English ed.), *The International
  Dimensions of Human Rights*, Vol. I, pp. 43–59 (Paris and Westport,
  Conn.: UNESCO and Greenwood Press).
VERBA, S., AHMED, B., and BHATT, A. (1971) *Caste, Race, and Politics:
  A Comparative Study of India and the United States* (Beverly Hills, Cal.:
  Sage Publications).
WEINER, M. and KATZENSTEIN, M. F. with RAO, K. V. N. (1981)
  *India's Preferential Policies: Migrants, the Middle Classes and Ethnic
  Equality* (Chicago: University of Chicago Press).

3 Human Rights and Culture Change

Joyce Aschenbrenner

THEORIES OF CULTURE CHANGE AND HUMAN RIGHTS OF WOMEN

A historical bias toward cultural relativism has led to a general unwillingness by anthropologists to deal with questions of human rights. A descriptive science, anthropology is concerned with the various lifeways of humans, eschewing value judgements. Thus, anthropologists face something of a dilemma in developing a concept of universal morality. Some attention has been given to possible moral universals, such as the incest taboo and strictures on in-group assault and homicide. While these moral precepts approach universality, incest and homicide receive positive sanction in specific situations in societies. Likewise, while rape, for example, is one of the most heavily sanctioned crimes cross-culturally (Brown, 1952), institutionalized rape is not uncommon as a punitive or ritual cultural practice (Webster, 1979).

Some anthropologists have questioned the claim of cultural relativity, pointing out that by professing a neutral stance, anthropologists have in many instances aligned themselves with forces of oppression; profiting by the disenfranchisement of peoples they have studied – often colonized or formerly colonized peoples – they have, in effect, these critics claim, upheld systems which continue to exploit the people they are studying (Marriotti and Magubane, 1978; Maquet, 1964). The structural-functionalist view of society, which still influences much anthropological writing, is critically viewed by these writers; it is held that the idea of each element contributing to the functioning of the whole has resulted in a static orientation in which the sufferings of people are ignored for the benefit of the existing order. A paternalism that encourages the continuation of what are termed regressive practices, rendering peoples less open to social and economic progress, is also condemned by these writers (see e.g. Bonfil Batalla, 1966).

On the other side of the issue, examples abound in literature on

60

applied anthropology of misguided attempts to assist people by introducing technology and social and economic practices which are not appropriate to their way of life (see Bodley, 1982). One solution to this dilemma – that is, seemingly callous non-involvement and neutrality, on the one hand, and on the other, inappropriate cultural intrusion – that has emerged among activist-oriented anthropologists is to concentrate on cases of actual or cultural genocide and the oppression of minority cultural groups by the governments of their respective nations. Two organizations, the Anthropology Resource Center (1975–) and Cultural Survival (1972–), which produce various publications, focus on research, applied projects and dissemination of information on endangered indigenous peoples. The goal of these organizations is to promote the survival of these minorities as cultural entities; hence the focus is on preservation rather than change.

CULTURE CHANGE: THEORETICAL PERSPECTIVES

Anthropologists have come to terms individually with ethical dilemmas of the field in various ways; however, few have attempted to develop a view of culture on which a policy of human rights can be based. Some efforts have been made to go beyond criticism to develop perspectives to meet the challenges of contemporary national and social movements (see e.g. Harris, 1979). Sékou Touré, President of the Republic of Guinea, an avowed Marxist and a trained anthropologist, presents a dynamic view of culture as the creation and collective property of a people, 'the means for the mastery of nature, the source and the surest defender of people's power' (Touré, 1973, p. 19); his view is that culture represents the preoccupations, struggles, successes and setbacks of a people at a particular time, while the ultimate goal is the 'universalization of the content of culture interpreting the aspirations of all peoples' which will accompany the 'revolutionization of industrial relations' through the world (p. 7).

Touré has difficulty reconciling his Marxism with his anthropology, since to the Marxist, cultural differences are essentially the result of a 'false consciousness' which divides people and distorts their true class interests. Perhaps the most penetrating critique of both Marxist and structural-functional theories is that of British sociologist Dahrendorf; adopting a view influenced by Marxian thought, he substitutes 'interest group' for 'class', since the latter exist as organized, articulate groups in only a minority of cases (Dahrendorf, 1959, p. 163). He offers a view of society in which the functional modes of stability, integration, functional maintenance and value consensus are balanced by a conflict model characterized by change, conflict, disintegration, and coercion. Whichever analysis applies in a given instance depends on the situation, since a society exhibits all of these characteristics. According to Dahrendorf, conflict between different interest groups, i.e. those in different social positions, remains latent until a concatenation of material and social circumstances causes the conflict to manifest itself in political actions, and, as a last resort, violence. By adopting the idea of an ideology as representing the position of a social interest group, Dahrendorf posits the existence of more than one 'consensus' or value system in a culture. According to his view, then, dissensus, conflict and change are as much a part of the essence of culture as are integration and consensus; either set of characteristics becomes dominant or more in evidence under certain historical conditions.

A minority position on the nature of culture, stressing human needs and intra-cultural conflict, has existed in anthropology from its beginning as an academic discipline. Malinowski (1960) related the concept of function directly to human biological and psychological needs, as well as to societal prerequisites. Sapir (1924) referred to culture as that which is 'potentially shareable' rather than that which is actually shared, opening the door for considerable diversity of interests and values within any cultural group. In the early years of American anthropology, a number of studies based on personal lives and experiences of American Indians reflected a sensitivity to the human dimension of culture and culture change, and others were also concerned with the often imperfect fit between culture and individuals, and consequent suffering (see e.g. Benedict, 1938; Henry, 1963; Radin, 1926; Thompson, 1950). The majority of anthropologists, however, assumed a view of culture as essentially in equilibrium, patterned, and, on balance, existing for the greater good of the whole despite maladjusted individuals.

CONFLICT THEORY AND GENDER ROLES

The view that conflict, coercion and dissensus are normal or intrinsic, rather than extrinsic conditions of society, opens the possibility of alternative value systems and world views within even a 'homogeneous' society. All societies consist of at least two groups with differing experiences: men and women. The common way of dealing with differences in pre-industrial societies has been through the idea of the division of labor by sex and age; feminist critique has charged that this functional approach glosses over differences in power, in access to wealth and resources, and in actual relative economic contributions of men and women, thus masking the latent conflict implied by differential economic positions of women and men (Rogers, 1978). Further, feminists have focused on the lack of investigation of women's views, values and beliefs by male or male-trained field workers. Ardener (1975) and others have discovered radical differences in attitudes, explanation of phenomena, and world views among women and men in societies they studied. Rogers (1978) believes that the lack of observation of these differences in past research results not so much from the fact that anthropology is male-dominated, as from the belief in our society that the ideologies and values of men and women are basically the same.

Applying Dahrendorf's model, according to which conflict, whether latent or manifest, derives from different social positions, it is probable that both women and men in a culture have a number of different ideologies, and that they may share some values while differing in others, or at least differing in the intensity with which they hold them. This coincides with casual observation and explains why women or other groups must experience 'consciousness raising' in order to appreciate their common interests. On this view, the interests and ideologies of men and women in US society, for example, are perceived as identical because of the emphasis on the nuclear family and the conjugal relationship, which places women and men in highly interdependent roles with identical interests. This contrasts with societies in which extended kinship groups bring adult women and men together with others of their gender in mutually dependent roles. Thus, in the United States, conflict between men and women is highly individualized; and only when women come to perceive that they share interests and needs with other women through 'consciousness raising' do they bring conflict to a public level.

Current research reveals that the status of women cross-culturally is a far more complex matter than formerly believed; thus, while men universally dominate the arena of formal political power, in some societies (notably peasant communities – Rogers, 1975) the areas of domestic life which women control are of critical economic and social importance. In some instances, traditional institutions provide economic and political powers and protections for women that are undermined by economic 'advancement' (namely, African women's trade networks) and the political forces of colonialism and nationalism; in other cases, practices which are restricting to women are exposed or removed through modernization. At times, both situations occur concommitantly (namely, education of Indian women and increase in dowry demands) or at different points in time; or traditional disadvantages of women may actually be reinforced or exacerbated by changing national politics (namely, 'dowry deaths').

In the Convention on the Elimination of all forms of Discrimination Against Women (1983), as part of the United Nations International Women's Decade, it is stated that appropriate measures shall be taken 'to modify the social and cultural patterns of conduct of men and women, with a view to achieving the elimination of prejudices' and practices based on stereotyped roles and inferiority of men or women (p. 141). This statement is a rejection of cultural relativism, and marks a significant departure from past actions, in which a 'hands off' policy in regard to 'cultural matters' has been practiced by UN agencies (see Hosken, 1979). If put into practice, the stated policy of the Convention could lead to social changes on a level with those of programs of economic development.

WOMEN'S RIGHTS AND HUMAN RIGHTS

Two cases of human rights violation are of particular interest in illustrating the application of a conflict model to society because (1) they show some of the special problems in applying basic human rights policies to women and (2) they show the complexity of the effects of socio-cultural change on women's status. The cultural practices of clitoridectomy and infibulation – genital mutilations of female children prevalent in North-eastern Africa and Muslim West Africa – are examples of customary practices which, despite modernization in other areas of life, have actually become more widespread. Clitoridectomy has also been practiced in the West, and in the United States until the late 1930s as a 'cure' for masturbation, and was at one time under consideration as a routine operation for female infants (Hosken, 1979). The other example – the 'dowry deaths' of Northwestern India – is partially a result of modernization processes. These two instances of violations of human rights have received much media attention in the past few years; because of sensitivities of Third World countries to outside interference, it is uncertain whether this attention will lead to active efforts to stop these practices by governments involved.

Genital Mutilations

It has been established that the practices ranging from cliteridectomy to more drastic mutilations including infibulation (nearly complete closure of the vaginal opening) have serious health effects on women, including fatalities from hemorrhage, infection, permanent damage to organs, obstructed labor, with possible brain damage and other ill effects to babies, as well as severe psychological trauma. Aside from these effects their avowed purpose is to restrict the sexuality of women, based on the idea that women cannot control their own sexuality because of innate inferiority (Abdalla, 1982; Hayes, 1975; Hosken, 1979).

The British attempted to outlaw the practices in Kenya in the 1920s and 1930s and in Sudan in the 1940s, with little effect (Hosken, 1979). During that time, promulgated by Islamic leaders, the practice actually increased. Although the custom was not originally Islamic nor required by Islamic law, religious leaders encouraged it as a kind of 'purification' rite, in a world view in which female sexuality was highly suspect. Christian missionaries did not oppose it, nor did they attempt to educate converts in the areas of health and sexuality; and the Catholic church authorities approved of the practice at one time (Hosken, 1979). In 1952, 1958, 1960 and 1961 the United Nations passed resolutions relating to these practices and in 1960 at the World Health Organization seminar in Addis Ababa a group of African women requested a study of the medical aspects of the operations (Hosken, 1979).

The health aspects of clitoridectomy and infibulation were finally given full hearing at the 1979 World Health Organization Seminar in Khartoum. At this meeting, while all of the negative aspects and hazards of the operations were acknowledged, there were disagreements on how to deal with the problem, largely along lines of sex. The male physicians and officials wanted to recommend an 'intermediate step', in which operations would be performed in hospitals under sanitary conditions to ameliorate serious effects. The women at the conference opposed this idea, pointing out that international funds would be used to carry out harmful mutilations; and that, moreover, the poor would have less access to hospitals and would continue the age-old methods. Finally, they pointed out that the practices would likely be continued as long as the physicians had a financial stake in their continuance (Hosken, 1979).

In rural areas, women carry out the operations and, in general, support the practices. In a functional analysis, Hayes (1975) holds that a 'latent' function of genital mutilations is the role they play in the financial and social status of women, especially midwives, and the power they give to the older women in the lineage. The 'manifest' function is to protect the honor of the patri-family through the restriction of female sexuality, and to protect women from social condemnation, since unmutilated women are considered prostitutes. Where infibulation is practiced, a man's family demands that a prospective bride be infibulated and that a woman be re-infibulated after each childbirth to ensure the legitimacy of heirs and the protection of lineage honor.

There is no consensus among either men or women on these practices. Some educated men oppose them for their daughters and their prospective brides. Many educated women oppose them and national women's organizations of Somalia, Sudan and Kenya are working to eliminate them (Abdalla, 1982). For older women in rural areas, much of their power and authority stems from their responsibility in controlling the behavior of young women in the interests of the patrilineage. They have little power to change the male-dominated system which victimizes them as children. The operations are kept secret from outsiders so women are involved in a conspiracy of silence; they are largely unaware of the health hazards of the operations, since there are strenuous efforts to keep complications and fatalities secret (Hosken, 1979). Many of the problems occur later, at menarche and childbirth, and therefore connections between the operations and traumas and fatalities are not readily made. Thus, a combination of special interests, social class differences, ignorance, and powerlessness keep women from uniting on this issue to bring about the abolition of female genital mutilations.

The functional analyses that have been made purport to show the functions of these practices with relation to the total society, rather than how they serve certain groups. Some of these explanations, including Hayes' (1975) 'manifest' functions appear to be rationalizations rather than explanations: thus, the idea that they prevent women from being wayward and protect their reputations merely begs the question of the need of such differential treatment of men and women in the first place. The argument that these practices are functionally related to the integrity of the patrilineage can be questioned by pointing to societies with strong patrilineages that do not practice female genital mutilations. Further, the practices are relatively recent in West African countries, having spread from the East with the introduction of Islam. While many other aspects of African societies have changed, and, in many instances, younger men have become less socially and economically dependent on lineages, these mutilations have persisted even among urban, middle-class professional families. In the latter cases, the ritual aspects of the operations are simplified or even absent; Hosken (1979) points out the absurdity of calling a practice traditional that is separated from ritual aspects, performed in Western hospitals with Western instruments. All of these considerations cast doubt on the view of culture as a 'complex homeostatic system' in which to change this one aspect is to change everything, leading to stress (see Barnes-Dean, 1985, p. 30). The latter caution seems misplaced, considering the amount of stress from trauma, ill health and death that is caused by the operations.

The above considerations lend support to the view that the aim of the customs is the coercion of a group, i.e. women, in the interests of other groups – men, older women and midwives, religious leaders. That such coercion involves the consent and cooperation of women is not surprising, given their vulnerability as children and their lack of options as they grow older. To argue that attempts to change or encourage changes in these practices is threatening to the functional integrity of culture is to ignore the different interests that are involved and the many cultural changes that have taken place. On this view, to assume a neutral stance is no less to support certain group interests than is support for abolition of these practices.

Dowry Deaths

The deaths by burning of brides, which have increased in frequency in recent years, primarily occur among urban middle-class families in North-western India. A death is usually reported as a suicide committed by a young woman in despair over the inability or unwillingness of her family to complete dowry payments. In many instances, however, it is suspected that the groom's relatives either drive her to kill herself or actually kill her. The victim's family and other protesters claim that this action is a cold-blooded attempt to pave the way for another marriage with a higher dowry (Sharma, 1984).

In rural settings, the dowry consists of household goods, apparel, jewelry, and small amounts of cash – items and amounts that are accumulated and produced over time by the bride's patri-family. The dowry is said to assure the status and well-being of the bride in her new home, and the responsibility of the bride's family continues after marriage, with yearly gifts at festivals, harvest time, and weddings of grandchildren (Aschenbrenner, 1967).

The institution of dowry has long been deplored by leaders and social thinkers as oppressive to poor people, and after Independence, laws were passed against it. However, it is difficult to enforce such laws, since for the bride's family, the possibility of marriage of a daughter is at stake, and for the groom's family, the financial gain is significant. Again, as in Africa, the custom persists in urban middle-class families; here demands are actually increased as the need for cash and the desire for expensive household goods intensifies (Sharma, 1984). Further, as caste restrictions are relaxed, hypergamy – the marriage of a woman into a higher caste – is more common; this leads to further material demands on her family to validate the bride's suitability.

The existence of the dowry has had a negative influence on women's status generally; girls are less valued than boys because they are a potential drain on family resources. As in Africa, older women, especially as mothers-in-law, exercise power in the patrilineage, here by receiving the household goods and distributing them, even using them for daughters' dowries. However, the payments of cash, which are expected to continue after a marriage, are appropriated by male heads. Undoubtedly, the difficulty in enforcing anti-dowry laws is increased by the benefit to men of higher caste, who receive the most payments of cash. Those with the most interest in doing away with the dowry are poor families, especially those with many daughters. However, the latter lack the power to ensure that the law is upheld, and they must try to make the best of the situation, often at the expense of daughters who must marry unsuitable men or are subjected to harsh treatment by in-laws.

As in Africa, social and economic changes have led to a weakening of the patrilineal kin group, here precisely in those families in which dowry deaths are most frequent. Again, this is an instance in which changes in family organization have not involved changes in oppressive practices relating to women, revealing a weakness in the functional argument. Here, also, the interests of women are divided; some educated women are leading the movement to enforce the law against dowry.

CONCLUSION

In the two instances of human rights violations – genital mutilations and dowry deaths – we have examined, situations similar to that in a totalitarian state exist, in which, according to Dahrendorf (1959), the submerged group lacks the means, organization, and power to emerge as a conflict group and initiate change. Given the history of these practices, however, dissensus, coercion, conflict, and at least the possibility of change are more applicable as models than functional stability and consensus. A conflict model offers a rationale to support human rights policies concerning these practices without violating an assumed cultural integrity or upsetting a cultural balance.

Hoskens (1979) has noted that none of the existing human rights organizations support movements against these cultural practices, nor do they deal with the economic issues of shelter, food and clothing, issues on which the International Women's Decade focused in the closing meeting in Nairobi in July 1985 (Perspective, 1985). During the Decade, there was a gradual shift from the emphasis on human rights at the beginning of the Decade to social and economic development with women benefiting equally and in decision-making roles (Steady, 1985). However, the main document of the meetings, signed by all countries represented, mentioned issues such as the disadvantages to women in some customary legal systems and the need to be aware of and fight any violence against women, including that within families, as victim or witness to human rights violations (Perspective, 1985, p. ix). Representatives from India noted success in gaining public attention to the abuses of dowry, but less success in convicting transgressors; they, like other women at the meetings stressed the need for economic advancement of Third World women, whose economic position has in many instances deteriorated in recent years (Butalia, 1985).

The conclusion to be drawn from these developments seems to be that the tasks concerning discrimination against women are too overwhelming to be handled by women's groups alone. Thus, human rights organizations should consider abuses such as genital mutilations, dowry deaths and others perpetrated on women, and those agencies concerned with economic development should deal with the pressing needs relating to general health and well-being of the women and children of the world.

References

ABDALLA, R. H. D. (1982) *Sisters in Affliction: Circumcision and Infibulation of Women in Africa* (London: Zed Press).

ASCHENBRENNER, Joyce (1967) *Endogamy and Social Status in a West Punjabi Village*. Unpublished manuscript, University of Minnesota.

ARDENER, Edwin (1975) 'Belief and the Problem of Women', in S. Ardener (ed.), *Perceiving Women*, pp. 1–17 (New York: John Wiley & Sons).

BARNES-DEAN, Virginia Lee (1985) 'Clitoridectomy and Infibulation', *Cultural Survival Quarterly*, 9: 26–30.

BENEDICT, Ruth (1938) 'Continuities and Discontinuities in Cultural Conditioning', *Psychiatry*, 1: 161–7.

BODLEY, John H. (1982) *Victims of Progress*, 2nd edn (Menlo Park, Calif.: Benjamin-Cummings).

BONFIL BATALLA, Guilermo (1966) 'Conservative Thought in Applied Anthropology: A Critique', *Human Organization*, 25: 126–30.

BROWN, J. S. (1952) 'A Comparative Study of Deviations from Sexual Mores', *American Sociological Review*, 17: 135–46.

BUTALIA, Urvashi (1985) 'Indian Women and the New Movement', *Women's Studies International Forum*, 8: 131–46.

CONVENTION ON THE ELIMINATION OF ALL FORMS OF DISCRIMINATION AGAINST WOMEN (1983), in House Committee on Foreign Affairs, *Human Rights Documents*. Washington, DC: Government Printing Office, pp. 139–49.

DAHRENDORF, Rolf (1959) *Class and Class Conflict in Industrial Society* (Stanford: Stanford University Press).

HARRIS, Marvin (1979) *Cultural Materialism: The Struggle for a Science of Culture* (New York: Random House).

HAYES, Rose Oldfield (1975) 'Female Genital Mutilation, Fertility Control, Women's Roles, and the Patrilineage in Modern Sudan: A Functional Analysis', *American Ethnologist*, 2: 617–33.

HENRY, Jules (1963) *Culture Against Man* (New York: Random House).

HOSKEN, Fran P. (1979) *The Hosken Report*, 2nd edn (Lexington, Mass.: Women's International Network News).

MAQUET, Jacques (1964) 'Objectivity in anthropology', *Current Anthropology*, 5: 47–55.

MALINOWSKI, Bronislaw (1960) *A Scientific Theory of Culture and Other Essays* (New York: Oxford Press).

MARIOTTI, A. and MAGUBANE, B. (1978) 'Urban Ethnology in Africa: Some Theoretical Issues', in J. Aschenbrenner and L. Collins (eds),

Processes of Urbanism: A Multidisciplinary Approach, pp. 45–68 (The Hague: Mouton).

PERSPECTIVE: UN DECADE FOR WOMEN, 1976–1986. *UN Chronicle*, 22: i–xii.

ROGERS, Susan (1975) 'Female Forms of Power and the Myth of Male Dominance: A Model of Female/Male Interaction in Peasant Society', *American Ethnologist*, 2: 727–54.

ROGERS, Susan C. (1978) 'Woman's Place: A Critical Review of Anthropological Theory', *Comparative Studies in Society and History*, 20: 123–62.

RADIN, Paul, (ed.) (1926) *Crashing Thunder: The Autobiography of an Indian* (New York: D. Appleton & Co.).

SAPIR, Edward (1924) 'Culture, genuine and spurious', *American Journal of Sociology*, 29: 401–29.

SHARMA, Ursula (1984) 'Dowry in North India', in Renée Hirschon (ed.), *Women and Property, Women as Property* (New York: St Martin's Press).

STEADY, Filmena Chioma (1985) 'African Women at the End of the Decade', *Africa Report*, 30: 4–8.

TOURÉ, Sékou (1973) 'A Dialectical Approach to Culture', in R. Chrisman and N. Hares (eds), *Contemporary Black Thought*, pp. 3–25 (New York: Bobbs-Merrill).

THOMPSON, Laura (1950) *Culture in Crisis: A Study of the Hopi Indians* (New York: Harper & Sons).

WEBSTER, Paula (1979) 'Politics of Rape in Primitive Societies', *Heresies*, 2: 16–21.

4 A Policy Approach to Human Rights Law: The Right to Development

Richard L. Siegel

The concept of human rights has expanded steadily since the close of the Second World War, and various, mostly Western, academic experts and national government representatives have opposed efforts to give priority to rights other than political and civil ones (Donnelly, 1981). Others defend, at least in part, efforts to incorporate and emphasize such claimed solidarity rights as self-determination, state control over natural resources, economic and social development, peace, and environmental protection into the body of fundamental human rights (Alston, 1981, p. 104; Falk, 1981, pp. 185–94). Intermediate between political–civil and solidarity rights stand largely welfare rights incorporated into the earliest United Nations human rights instruments, many of these reframed as 'basic human needs' to better relate them to the Third World context (Trubeck, 1984).

The issues in dispute are multiple, and may well have major implications for the future of international relations, developmental economics and many aspects of national public policy. The various academic commentators need to be aware that this debate is far from being merely academic – even as they uphold their personal principles and conceptions of their disciplines and the field of human rights. This debate may yet help influence actual progress or retrogression regarding development and established human rights throughout the Third World.

At issue is whether a substantial majority of Third World governments, with varying degrees of support from the Soviet bloc and several Western industrialized states, will consolidate efforts to link the restructuring of international economic relations with the substantial political and moral fervor of the international human rights movement. Supporters of this effort often seek to delegitimize various key aspects of the present international economic order (or orders) and to accelerate changes regarding power and outcomes in various international regimes (Krasner, 1985). Other major goals

72

advanced by some advocates of solidarity rights include the subordi-
nation of certain political–civil rights to social and economic ones
that are closely related to national development, the decoupling of
international aid from national choices of political–economic systems,
and the compulsory or automatic transfer of capital from North to
South.

Although such goals are rooted in one hundred years of writings
on imperialism, they have been pursued with notably increased
dedication from about the time of the 1968 Teheran Conference on
Human Rights. Major expressions concerning solidarity rights and
their relationship to earlier recognized rights are included in such
UN documents as the Declaration and Programme of Action on the
Establishment of a New International Economic Order (1 May 1974),
the Charter of Economic Rights and Duties of States (12 December
1974), and General Assembly Resolution 21/130 of 16 December
1977.

More recent steps towards their fulfillment include efforts in
virtually every available international forum to associate solidarity
rights and the proposed New International Economic Order with
new formulations of previously stated human rights, as was
evident in the contentious negotiation of the International Labor
Organization's 1984 supplementary recommendation concerning
employment policy. These efforts have also prominently included the
pursuit for nearly a decade of a major UN instrument recognizing
the right to development. Various General Assembly resolutions,
including 36/133 (1981), anticipated the declaration of such a right
by the General Assembly on 4 December 1986 (United Nations,
1987, pp. 365–9).

Any assessment of this drive to establish solidarity rights as a
claimed third generation of human rights and/or as a synthesis of
previously recognized rights must contend with strong evidence that
more than a few states seek to use such developments to gain a
degree of immunity from the application of human rights law
protecting various political–civil rights. It also needs to be recognized
that some UN member states apparently seek to blur any lines
separating international economic policies and human rights. Analysts
must also consider the often blatant character of efforts to use human
rights instruments to embarass certain Western states, these including
one-sided attacks on transnational companies, and the tendencies of
various states to denigrate the rights of the individual when they
stress the interdependence of all rights and focus on the rights of

collective bodies. (See comments by representatives of Cuba, Libya, Nicaragua and the Congo in Summary Record of the 20th Meeting of the UN Commission on Human Rights, 39th Session, 14 February 1983.)

These points must be balanced in part by the recognition that the records of the UN's Commission on Human Rights, Human Rights Committee, and Subcommission on the Prevention of Discrimination and Protection of Minorities have gradually improved regarding investigation and reporting on political–civil rights, this occurring during the very period of most active promotion of solidarity rights. These positive developments could not have occurred without significant support from various Third World states (Tolley, 1983; Forsythe, 1985).

Yet these contrasting developments serve as mere background to the issue of central concern here – the appropriateness of the right to development and other solidarity rights as human rights, and their proper relationship to the political–civil and socio-economic rights prescribed in earlier UN and regional instruments. The present writer believes that there is a strong claim to a human right to development, with such a right viewed as a necessary extension of the earlier acceptance of economic and social rights in the Universal Declaration and the covenants, among other foundational instruments of the global human rights regime. Further, the declaration of the right follows from a policy-oriented approach to human rights, one that recognizes the need to more firmly relate socio-economic and civil–political rights to the development process.

SOCIO-ECONOMIC RIGHTS AND DEVELOPMENT

The primary underlying argument for a right to develop is that the otherwise commendable drive to include economic, social and cultural (henceforth stated as ESC) rights in major UN and regional human rights instruments took place at a time when the primary reference point for such rights was the welfare state of advanced industrialized countries rather than the poverty and development needs of Third World states. Such an emphasis was rooted from 1919 in the priorities of the International Labor Organization and was carried forward by the Western-dominated UN Commission on Human Rights members that drafted the greater part of the UN Covenant on ESC Rights in the first decade of UN human rights activity (Trubek, 1984, pp. 214–15). This was even more the case regarding the Council of Europe's European Social Charter adopted in 1961.

The bulk of the socio-economic rights listed in the major global and regional human rights documents were actually drafted too early or too hesitantly to relate meaningfully to the problems of creating the socio-economic base needed for the enjoyment of those rights in most developing countries. The ESC Covenant does address state and international action 'to achieve progressively the full realization of the rights recognized in the present Covenant' (Article 2). Yet it generally avoids confronting the means of such realization, and in at least one major area – the rights of non-nationals – explicitly applies to developing states a lesser standard of state duties (Article 2). Further, the implementation procedures for ESC rights were clearly made less rigorous than those for civil–political rights from the start, and the quality and quantity of state reporting and international agency review of state performance in these areas under the ESC Covenant has been spotty or mixed at best (Mower, 1985, p. 63; Trubek, 1984, pp. 236–42).

The ESC Covenant does assure 'all peoples' the right of self-determination and derives from that right their entitlement to 'freely pursue their economic, social and cultural development' (Article 1). It also refers to international obligations regarding food distribution (Article 11). Yet UN and other globally-organized efforts at resource transfers, technical assistance and other programs that focus on development and the socio-economic needs of the Third World have occurred within a context of policy and administration that is mostly separate from international law generally and human rights law in particular. Human rights law has been applied to Third World states primarily in relation to 'grave' offenses against the rights of individuals to life and liberty, and to such liberal principles as non-discrimination, free association and the unacceptability of involuntary servitude.

Reviews of international experience with socio-economic rights point inexorably to a need to approach such issues in global structural terms and to broaden the approach of the ESC Covenant in relation to prescription and implementation (Mower, 1985, pp. 125–43). To a degree this effort can be accomplished by reading new conceptions of existing rights into earlier documents and by strengthening human right organs responsible for the review of information and the making of reports. Some small progress has been made on both of these points, as with the UN Economic and Social Council's 1985 decision to seek to fill its ESC rights monitoring body with experts serving in their personal rather than diplomatic capacities ('Human Rights', *UN Chronicle*, 1985, p. 44).

Yet such efforts seem of little consequence to the billions of people for whom the overall global approach to the promotion of socio-economic rights holds little promise. Real promise implies a recasting of the idea of economic and social rights in the light of state of the art knowledge concerning development and social justice in international economic relations. Such an effort by the UN was anticipated by the 1974 Manouchehr Ganji report on the realization of ESC rights in developing countries (Ganji, 1974), the Declaration of Principles and Programme of Action of the 1976 ILO World Employment conference (Follow-up of the World Employment Conference, 1979), and the above-noted confrontations over the 1984 ILO supplementary recommendation on employment policy. The idea that a right to development is a necessary extension of ESC rights has remained a major thrust of the UN Commission on Human Right's approach to this subject (Working Group, 1985), and is clearly reflected in the 1986 Declaration on the Right to Development.

It is not the purpose of this paper to defend the precise language of such documents, these often reflecting compromise and intentional vagueness. Rather, it seems most important to argue that it is both fitting and inevitable that the corpus of human rights instruments relate explicitly to identifiable policy issues of world socio-economic order and Third World development, and that this effort include a fundamental moral and political commitment by national governments and the international community to the meeting of basic human needs of all people.

A POLICY APPROACH TO INTERNATIONAL HUMAN RIGHTS LAW

The effective expansion of human rights law to incorporate the processes and needed outcomes of Third World development involves an implicit policy approach to the development of international human rights law. Some will object that this is a departure that bolsters their fears that human rights will be expanded *ad absurdum*. Yet it is clear that international human rights law has traditionally responded to new human needs considered fundamental in particular societies and eras.

This writer is uncomfortable with a positive law approach to international human rights law that merely rewards groups of states for successful advancement of certain international norms in a multiplicity of regional and global declarations, resolutions and other instruments. He is also less than fully comfortable with arguments based principally on conceptions of natural law, social or distributive justice, and other such normative foundations. Each of these approaches can partially justify the right to development. Yet the principal justification should perhaps be a policy-based one that places development in a policy and constitutive role as a critical right, or body of rights, required to achieve the goals established in the positive law of socio-economic human rights.

Impressive support for such a policy-oriented approach to the law of human rights is found in various works of Myres McDougal, Harold Lasswell, Lung-chu Chen, and W. Michael Reissman. Their foundational writings on human rights and world public order are, for the most part, highly abstract, and do not provide explicit advocacy of a human right to development or for other solidarity rights. Indeed, it is not clear that they would have approved such particular applications of their approach to human rights. Yet they provide critical intellectual support for an approach to international law that helps to justify a right to development.

McDougall and his colleagues advance such formulations as:

1. The goal of 'a constitutive process which both reflects, and is effective in securing, basic human dignity values' (McDougal, 1974, p. 415). This involves a broad structural and process-oriented approach to the fulfillment of human rights.
2. Development of a 'comprehensive set of goal values . . . commonly characterized as the basic values of human dignity or a free society' (McDougal, Lasswell and Chen, 1980, p. 90).
3. A perspective stressing global interdependence regarding human rights: 'The net aggregate in protection of human rights that a particular individual can achieve today is observably a function, not merely of the operation of social and decision processes within any single territorial community, but of the operation of such processes within a whole hierarchy of interpenetrating communities – from local, regional, and national to hemispheric

and global or earth-space' (McDougal, Lasswell and Chen, 1980, p. 88).
4. A combined individual- and collective-based perspective on human rights needs and demands: 'The ultimate actor in all social interaction is the individual human being, but individuals identifying with and making demands upon and on behalf of a whole range of groups and associations – including not merely nation states, but also the lesser territorial communities, international governmental organizations, political parties, pressure groups, tribes, families, and private associations of all kinds' (McDougal, Lasswell and Chen, 1980, p. 89).
5. The need for a continuous process of international legal prescription 'to respond effectively to the challenges of an ever-changing social and economic context' (McDougal and Reissman, 1981, p. 376).

These points go far to justify the prescription of solidarity rights generally and a right to development in particular. Other authoritative legitimizations of the foundations of such rights appear in works of Schachter (1976, 1977), MacDonald, Johnston and Morris (1978), Falk (1981), and Rich (1983). Schachter (1977) describes the existing role of law 'as a process for attaining [global] distributive justice and other social ends' (p. 143). He identifies the role of early solidarity-oriented international instruments in the delegitimizing of certain traditional legal and policy norms. MacDonald and his colleagues (1978) identify such issues as population growth, food and other resource shortages, and environmental pollution as 'key welfare issues central to human survival', while also taking the view that the international community had not yet accepted a legal obligation to meet its responsibilities regarding such issues (pp. 58–60). Rich, while ostensibly making a traditional argument for the right to development based on state practice, actually utilizes a policy-based approach when he seeks to describe as emerging international legal obligation such essentially policy-based areas of state practice as official development aid and trade preferences (pp. 302–11).

The major attraction of a policy-based approach is its combining of elements of structure, process, and goals with the affirmation of particular human rights. It seeks to extend the study and promotion of human rights by focusing on 'the inter-actions in social process by which values are shaped and shared' (McDougal, 1980, p. 84).

POLICY AND THE ANTECEDENTS OF SOCIO-ECONOMIC RIGHTS

Although contemporary conceptions of human rights owe much to natural rights approaches, they have also been shaped repeatedly by positive law approaches to the amelioration of misery and the promotion of economic security based on concepts other than rights. These non-rights policy antecedents reflect the welfare policy positions and innovations of such nineteenth-century Europeans as Bismarck and Pope Leo XIII as well as the more recent contributions of such figures as Beveridge, Myrdal and Brandt.

The decisions to incorporate ESC rights in the Universal Declaration, the UN's ESC Covenant, the European Social Charter, and other major human rights documents reflected processes of translating social policy advocacy into positive international law. The International Labor Organization has, for most of its history, avoided a human rights orientation in most areas of its work.[1] Yet the ILO has played a major role in the advancement of social and economic rights by affirming state duties regarding work, social security and other social and economic programs through its conventions and recommendations.

Although natural law and natural rights provide a core of human rights that is immune from the vicissitudes of positive law, natural law alone cannot provide an adequate frame of reference for human rights. Although natural law can be viewed as incorporating critical dimensions of distributive justice, as well as liberty and human dignity (Le Blanc, 1977, p. 63; Donnelly, 1982), distributive justice need also be a product of each era's conception of positive law and public policy.

The policy-based sources of a right to development include the various international development strategies adopted by the UN for each 'development decade' (Alston, 1981, pp. 72–3) and formulated by such widely respected bodies as the Brandt Commission on International Development Issues. While these and other sources vary considerably regarding ends and means, it is also true that the Western welfare state earlier responded to widely divergent approaches offered by socialists, Roman Catholics, conservatives, utilitarians and liberals, to name only some categories of contributors (Siegel, 1985).

A policy-oriented approach to international human rights should involve careful analyses of how human rights can be realized. Further, such an approach should fully consider global, national and sub-national mechanisms for advancing rights, and view these as complementary.

From policy studies, such an approach incorporates emphases on programs, structural adaptation, and processes of decision making and policy implementation. It should also emphasize methods that have been successful in one or more country and the negotiated basis of an international consensus concerning necessary steps toward human dignity. Sophisticated methods of analysis should be used to determine whether, for example, such particular methods as central planning or the assurance of basic human needs at all stages of development maximize subsistence and human dignity.

Such policy analysis need inform law and may justify broadening of international human rights law. Given the dominant approach of law in human rights regimes, there is clear advantage to the prescription as law of newly recognized critical requirements of human dignity and very carefully chosen structural or policy approaches to the meeting of such requirements. The welfare state was accepted into human rights law after scrutiny and acceptance as a requisite of human dignity. Some comparable range of state duties and individual rights relating to development, the indisputable key to the preparation of peoples for the enjoyment of welfare states, should also have recognition in law.

POLICY-BASED HUMAN RIGHTS LAW AND THE RIGHT TO DEVELOPMENT

In the space available it is possible only to highlight certain elements of a legitimate and useful policy-based right to development.[2]

First, the issue of obligation and duty needs to be faced squarely. Considerable value can be obtained from a formulation that invokes the name of human rights to augment, at least marginally, effective duties (legal and moral) of Third World governments and all states in a position to assist such countries. Further, the right of individuals and groups within Third World states to make effective claims against their own governments relevant to development would be augmented, and both these internal forces and Third World governments would have enhanced legitimacy when making claims on the resources of more developed states and intergovernmental organizations.

Forty years ago it would have been very difficult to imagine even the embryonic level of contemporary global and regional intergovernmental processes for investigating and criticizing states' behavior regarding rights issues ranging from torture and refugees to apartheid and denial of free association to trade unionists. A critical need exists to effectively extend duties of states to provide critical policies and resources vitally needed by their own citizens as well as to ensure the support and emergency aid required by peoples throughout the world.

The problems of setting out a policy-based human right to development are evident from a review of the two major reports of the Brandt Commission on International Development Issues (Independent Commission, 1980; Brandt Commission, 1983). These two reports stress economic policy analysis of development needs and largely ignore the potential of human rights law as a contributing element. Instead, they emphasize negotiation among the relevant state parties in search of breakthroughs concerning the identified economic problems and the structure of global regimes associated with them.

Yet the very frustration of the Brandt Commission, which labored on these issues between 1977 and 1983, supports the inclusion of a rights component in any possible solution. That commission was frustrated by the limits of existing or prospective state legal commitments to official development aid or to preferential treatment of developing countries in such spheres as debt and trade. Its analysis demonstrates that the norms supporting such obligations are still insufficiently recognized, and that progress toward their fuller acceptance has been halting at best.

It can certainly be argued that in the context of the continuing global dominance of *realpolitik* most developed states will never accept an internationally-established rights-based standard for levels of international economic assistance or for further concessions involving stabilized prices, access to markets, or debt restructuring. Yet bilateral economic assistance conforms less and less to the genuine needs of developing countries and has become – most dramatically in the cases of the two superpowers – primarily an element of strategic relationships with allies. One purpose of a strengthened international legal norm regarding the right to development would be to help delegitimize the unbridled sway of political–strategic considerations in the international dimensions of development.

Advancement of the Brandt Commission's (1980) proposal for a levy or surcharge on international trade generally or on arms trade in particular (pp. 244–6) would be a vital step towards a rights-based approach to development. Such a technique could be modeled on the European Community's sharing of VAT and other resources. This can be viewed as an alternative to the divisive demands of some radical states for compensation to developing states for colonial and neo-colonial exploitation.

Another major issue that deserves to be addressed in a rights context is that of Third World autonomy regarding basic political and economic policy orientations. This has been brought to the fore by harsh terms sometimes demanded by the IMF in its dealings with hard-pressed developing states. It also emerges from the practice of reserving certain multilateral grants and loans to countries which agree to take certain policy steps approved at a particular moment by agency staffs and/or dominant donor countries. The proposed Basic Needs approach to development advocated by World Bank President Robert McNamara and certain influential economists in the 1970s failed to establish itself as World Bank operational policy (Ascher, 1983; Ayres, 1983, pp. 83–91). Yet a major effort is being taken now to focus that agency's efforts on 'structural adjustment lending' designed to promote Third World countries' greater accommodation to free markets, both domestically and in international trade policies (Stokes, 1986, pp. 335–6).

Krasner (1985), among others, worries about international regime changes that point toward Third World preferences for 'the establishment of international regimes that legitimate authoritative, rather than market, allocation' (p. 15). Yet even more evident is the growing ability of certain Western states to utilize multinational financial agencies as well as their own programs to impose new political and economic directions and orientations towards development on Third World States (United States General Accounting Office, 1986). Such policies underlie the insistence in various draft UN declarations on the right to development that all peoples have a right to freely determine their political, economic and social direction (Working Group of Government Experts, 9 July 1982, p. 5; Draft Declaration, 22 May 1985, Annex II).

Implicit in the points made above is the acceptance of the right to develop as a collective as well as an individual right. This writer rejects any connotations of collective rights that can be used to subordinate fundamental civil – political or other human rights of individuals to the allegedly greater interests of the state. But the complete identification of socio-economic rights with the individual can be interpreted as limiting the potential of individuals. Effective claims in developed countries have long been advanced by such collective bodies as trade unions. In developing states demands also have to be made domestically by subnational organizations, these including trade unions, rural cooperatives, and tribal structures. Internationally, individuals generally depend on their government to voice their interests and rights. Such demands require a framework of rights for their fuller expression and implementation.

Finally, the right to development need be expressed as a comprehensive set of rights enlarging the dignity of each individual. It is in this central dimension that we return to the theme of the right to development as a necessary means to achieve progressively the full range of ESC rights without sacrificing civil–political ones. A human rights approach to development can strengthen civil–political as well as socio-economic claims of individuals in relation to the development process and its outcomes. It can strengthen claims, promote new vehicles for individuals and groups to participate in national decision making, and bolster recourse to law or revolution in the face of various forms of discrimination, corruption or repression.

CONCLUSION

Due to the central role of development processes and choices in efforts to 'progressively achieve' socio-economic human rights it is necessary to express and implement a policy-based human right to development. This right is defended here primarily as a necessary extension of socio-economic human rights. Its legitimacy is argued from the perspective of the policy-based approach to human rights law suggested by McDougal, Lasswell and Chen (1980) in *Human Rights and World Public Order* and the call for new intergovernmental measures advanced by MacDonald, Johnson and Morris (1978) in *The International Law and Policy of Human Welfare*.

The major argument offered here is that approaches to socio-economic rights adopted before 1967 failed to take adequate account of the centrality of the development process and its role as the engine that enables states to offer the material and non-material ingredients for healthful subsistence and any recognizable version of the welfare state envisioned in the ESC Covenant. An argument has been advanced for a tolerant and eclectic approach to development that strongly protects individual civil and political rights while allowing maximum choice regarding the character of political and economic systems and strategies for coping with international investment and trade.

The drawn-out debate in the United Nations and in many other forums during the past eight years concerning a right to development has forced a serious consideration of the elements and consequences of such a right. From the perspective of many Western (and some non-Western) governments and various scholars, the critical concerns include the potential use of a recognized right to development to subordinate individual civil–political rights and to further the polarization of North–South opinion regarding a New International Economic Order and related contentious issues. Yet a policy-based human right to development can augment the rights of individuals and collectivities at the global and regional levels. Such a right can be prescribed in ways that are consistent with democratic values, enlarging the obligations and duties of all states to individuals and groups who are presently not sufficiently protected by global and regional human rights regimes.

The moderate and gradualist approach taken by various Third World states in 1985 and 1986 made possible UN General Assembly adoption of a Declaration of the Right to Development on 4 December 1986 that enjoyed impressively broad support. Although the United States voted against the Declaration, America's principal industrialized allies split rather evenly between support and abstention. The US position was clearly aberrational insofar as the right to development had been prescribed in a manner generally consistent with the best traditions of global human rights. However, dangers as well as opportunities exist in the further prescription as well as implementation of the right to development.

Notes

1. Exceptions primarily involve the ILO's treatment of forced labor and free association.
2. The following discussion is based in part on a review of a wide range of materials available to the author from various international conferences beginning in 1978, and from the work of the UN Commission on Human Rights and its Working Group on the Right to Development between 1981 and 1985.

References

ALSTON, P. (1981) Prevention Versus Cure as a Human Rights Strategy. In Development, Human Rights and the Rule of Law, pp. 31–108 (Oxford: Pergamon Press).

ASCHER, W. (1983) 'New Development Approaches and the Adaptability of International Agencies: The Case of the World Bank', *International Organization*, 37: 415–39.

AYRES, R. L. (1983) 'Banking on the Poor: The World Bank and World Poverty' (Cambridge, Mass.: MIT Press).

THE BRANDT COMMISSION (1983) *Common Crisis North–South: Cooperation for World Recovery* (Cambridge: MIT Press).

DONNELLY, J. (1981) 'Recent Trends in UN Human Rights Activity: Description and Polemic', *International Organization*, 35: 633–55.

DONNELLY, J. (1982) 'Human Rights as Natural Rights', *Human Rights Quarterly*, 4: 391–405.

DRAFT DECLARATION ON THE RIGHT TO DEVELOPMENT: NOTE BY THE SECRETARY-GENERAL (1985) UN Economic and Social Council, 22 May, E/1985/70.

FALK, R. (1981) Human Rights and State Sovereignty (New York: Holmes & Meier).

FOLLOW-UP OF THE WORLD EMPLOYMENT CONFERENCE: BASIC NEEDS (1979) Report VII. International Labour Conference, 65th Session (Geneva: ILO).

FORSYTHE, D. P. (1985) 'The United Nations and Human Rights, 1945–85', *Political Science Quarterly*, 100: 249–69.

GANJI, M. (1974) 'The Widening Gap: A Study of the Realization of Economic, Social and Cultural Rights'. UN Commission on Human Rights, Thirtieth Session, 18 January E/CN.4/1131.

'HUMAN RIGHTS', (1985) *U.N. Chronicle*, 22, No. 5, 44.

INDEPENDENT COMMISSION ON INTERNATIONAL DEVELOPMENT ISSUES (Brandt Commission) (1980) North–South: A Program for Survival (Cambridge: MIT Press)

INDEPENDENT COMMISSION ON INTERNATIONAL DEVELOPMENT ISSUES (Brandt Commission) (1983) Common Crisis: North–South Cooperation for World Living.

KRASNER, S. D. (1985) *Structural Conflict: The Third World Against Global Liberalism* (Berkeley: University of California Press).

Le BLANC, L. J. (1977) 'Economic, Social and Cultural Rights and the Interamerican System', *Journal of Interamerican Studies and World Affairs*, 19: 61–82.

MacDONALD, R., JOHNSTON, D. M. and MORRIS, G. L. (eds) (1978) *The International Law and Policy of Human Welfare* (Alphen aan den Rijn: Sijthoff & Noordhoff).

McDOUGAL, M. S. (1974) 'Human Rights and World Public Order: Principles of Content and Procedure for Clarifying General Community Policies', *Virginia Journal of International Law*, 4: 387–421.

McDOUGAL, M. S., LASSWELL, H. and CHEN, L. (1980) Human Rights and World Public Order (New Haven: Yale University Press).

McDOUGAL, M. S. and REISSMAN, W. M. (1981) 'The Prescribing Function in the World Constitutive Process: How International Law is Made', in M. S. McDougal and W. M. Reissman (eds), *International Law Essays*, pp. 355–80 (Mineola, N.Y.: The Foundation Press).

MOWER, A. G., Jr. (1985) *International Cooperation for Social Justice* (Westport, Conn.: Greenwood Press).

RICH, R. Y. (1983) 'The Right to Development as an Emerging Human Right', *Virginia Journal of International Law*, 23: 287–328.

SCHACHTER, O. (1977) Sharing the World's Resources (New York: Columbia University Press).

SCHACTER, O. (1976) 'The Evolving International Law of Development', *Columbia Journal of Transnational Law*, 15: 1, 379.

SIEGEL, R. L. (1985) 'Socioeconomic Rights: Past and Future', *Human Rights Quarterly*, 7: 255–67.

STOKES, B. (1986) 'Liberals and Conservatives Struggling Over the World Bank's Proper Role', *National Journal*, 8 February, 334–7.

TOLLEY, H. (1983) 'Decision-Making at the United Nations Commission on Human Rights, 1979–82', *Human Rights Quarterly*, 5: 27–57.

TRUBEK, D. M. (1984) 'Economic, Social and Cultural Rights in The Third World: Human Rights Law and Human Needs Programs', in T. Meron (ed.), *Human Rights in International Law: Legal and Policy Issues*, Vol. I, pp. 205–71 (Oxford: Clarendon Press).

UNITED NATIONS (1983) Commission on Human Rights, 39th Session. Summary Record of the 20th Meeting. Geneva, 14 February, E/CN.4/1983/SR.20.

UNITED NATIONS (1987) Department of Public Information Press Section. Resolutions and Decisions Adopted by the General Assembly During the First Part of its Forty-First Session. Press Release FA/7463, 12 January.

UNITED STATES GENERAL ACCOUNTING OFFICE (1986) 'Foreign Assistance: US Use of Conditions to Achieve Economic Reforms', August.

WORKING GROUP OF GOVERNMENT EXPERTS ON THE RIGHT TO DEVELOPMENT (1985) Question of the Realization in All Countries of the Economic, Social and Cultural Rights. United Nations, 24 January, E/CN.4/1985/11.

WORKING GROUP OF GOVERNMENT EXPERTS ON THE RIGHT TO DEVELOPMENT (1982) Report on the Work of the Fourth Session. UN Commission on Human Rights, 9 July, E/CN.4/AC.39/1982/11.

WORK OF THE FOURTH SESSION (1982) UN Commission on Human Rights, 9 July, E/CN.4/AC.39/1982/11.

Part II

Measurement of Human Rights Practices

5 Some Thoughts on the Systematic Measurement of the Abuse of Human Rights

Andrew D. McNitt

During the late 1960s those social scientists who studied comparative politics were primarily concerned with the problem of political stability (Huntington, 1968; Gurr, 1970). Concern for human rights was largely confined to the somewhat tangential examination by pluralist scholars of the social preconditions for representative democracy (Kornhauser, 1959; Lipset, 1960). Only in the 1970s and 1980s did human rights emerge as a topic of serious study. New and expanded attempts were made to monitor the status of international human rights. Amnesty International vastly increased the scope of its reporting, Freedom House began to publish a yearly accounting of human rights abuses and the United States State Department was required by Congress to prepare a yearly report on the status of international human rights.

This sudden availability of annual reporting on the status of human rights for most of the nation states in the world today is an extremely valuable innovation. It opens up new avenues for empirically based research on human rights abuses and eventually will enable us to perform time series as well as cross-sectional analyses of human rights abuses. Yet the measurement of human rights abuses is a difficult task. There are strategic, conceptual and empirical problems which must be considered by anyone who wishes to work with these data.

STRATEGIC DIFFICULTIES

All researchers make a number of strategic decisions when analyzing the abuse of human rights. The choice of strategy, i.e. whether to treat violations of human rights as independent or dependent variables, and whether to conduct an intensive or extensive study profoundly influences the choice of measures.

To date, the abuse of human rights has been used as an independent variable by authors to explain political protest (Gurr, 1970) and as a factor influencing American foreign aid expenditures (Schloutz, 1981; Stohl, Carleton and Johnson, 1984; Cingranelli and Pasquarello, 1985; Pasquerello, 1986). When used as an independent variable there is a strong tendency to reduce measurement of the abuse of human rights to a single indicator variable. Although methodologically defensible this practice runs the risk of oversimplifying a complex variable. When treated as a dependent variable, the abuse of human rights has been analyzed as a consequence of the economic system (Strouse and Claude, 1976), socio-economic factors (Nixon, 1960, 1965), military government (Henderson, 1982) and dependency (Chomsky and Herman, 1979). Although a greater opportunity for detailed analysis of human rights abuses exists when they are treated as dependent variables, to date relatively few attempts have been made to study the abuse of human rights as a multifaceted phenomenon. The current tendency is to either use a simplified general measure of abuse (Strouse and Claude, 1976) or to look only at one aspect of abuse (Nixon, 1960, 1965).

The decision to conduct an intensive or extensive analysis also affects our efforts to measure human rights abuses. It is easier to find information about human rights abuses in single societies. Consequently there has been an abundance of case studies of human rights abuses. Unfortunately it is impossible to adequately test theories about either the causes or consequences of human rights abuses in general when working with data from a single society. Cross-sectional data sets are harder to develop because of the difficulty of finding comparable measures from the same period of time for a large number of societies. We would, however, substantially improve our understanding of human rights abuses if we did more cross-sectional studies. Still even cross-sectional data has its limitations. The cyclic nature of human rights abuses and the desire to discourage government human rights abuses means that we need to develop data sets which are both cross-sectional and time series in nature. Yet the desire to have cross-sectional time series data makes it even harder to obtain data and requires more consistent measurement than is characteristic of either the case study or cross-sectional models alone.

One way to reduce some of the data collection problems and at the same time maintain a comparative and time series perspective would be to restrict the analysis to regional subsets. It is much easier to obtain information about respect for human rights over time for the West European and Latin American nation states. The existence of such regionally based human rights reporting groups as Americas Watch, the better press coverage, and prior scholarly attention to related issues in these regions (Fitzgibbon, 1956; Fitzgibbon and Johnson, 1961) makes it much easier to develop an extensive times series data sets for these areas. The only difficulty is that this regional strategy substantially reduces the degree of political, cultural and economic variation which can be studied.

CONCEPTUAL DIFFICULTIES

One of the most serious problems with existing studies of human rights is the lack of conceptual clarity. The quantitative analysis of human rights requires us to make normative as well as empirical judgements. We make normative judgements when we decide what constitutes abuses of human rights. We make empirical judgements when we decide how to measure respect for those rights.

While it is possible to measure the extent to which government practices conform with explicitly stated sets of values, confusion is caused by the refusal to explicitly state those values, the lack of consensus on those values and the premature use of summated measures of those values. The failure to explicitly define respect for human rights is most evident in studies (Strouse and Claude, 1976; Henderson, 1982) which borrow existing scales from earlier works (Gastil, 1973). Since these scales grow out of a specific ideological position care should be taken to alert the reader to the normative and empirical implications involved when using a particular measure.

The lack of a consensus on the meaning of respect for human rights further complicates measurement. Respect for human rights, although part of the definition of democracy, is not equivalent to democracy. Democratic states on occasion fail to respect human rights and non-democratic states do not uniformly abuse those rights. Some of the earlier efforts to measure democracy deal with that concept almost exclusively in terms of popular sovereignty and electoral choice (Cutright, 1963; Neubauer, 1967; Cutright and Wiley, 1969) while others mix in some aspects of respect for human rights (Fitzgibbon, 1956; Fitzgibbon and Johnson, 1961; Smith, 1969; Jackman, 1973;

Bollen, 1980). Unfortunately even when information on respect for human rights is included in the definition of democracy the subscales relating to respect for human rights are usually not presented in the literature. Hence, existing measures of democracy are inadequate measures of respect for human rights.

A second area of disagreement involves the conflict between economic and political rights. There is a tendency for those on the left to include economic rights, income, health and physical conditions in their definition of human rights, and to distinguish those rights from a narrower set of procedural rights. While I would not want to excuse national states from their social responsibilities by defining those responsibilities away, for tactical reasons I prefer the narrower definition. We in the West live in a conservative society which defines human rights in legal and political terms. If we hope to influence that society we must adopt a similar restrictive definition.

A third area of controversy involves the judgements about the context within which human rights abuses occur. While there is some general agreement as to the standards of respect for human rights required from stable governments there is less consensus on how nations at war should behave. The stresses of both external and internal conflict often lead to government violations of individual liberties. How should we evaluate these violations? If we try to take circumstances into account we have to develop a second set of standards for evaluating belligerents. A second set of standards for belligerents might prohibit torture and arbitrary killings while allowing for some degree censorship and control over movement. While this approach would work for international conflicts, it would be difficult to apply in cases of internal war. Internal war is problematic because it is hard to determine precisely when such conflicts begin. If we take the narrower view that any violation of liberty is a violation of human rights we simplify our measurement problems, but end up having to classify many acts of self-defense as violations. Still if the focus of inquiry is the abuse of human rights, then it is probably best to ignore questions of justification and concentrate on the phenomenon whenever and wherever it occurs.

A fourth area of controversy involves the distinction between individual and group rights. Should the definition of human rights include rights that properly belong to groups? Such rights as the right to organize, to withhold services and to act collectively although most commonly associated with labor unions are also important to other kinds of secondary groups. However we choose to classify these rights, a decision must be made for inclusion or exclusion. That decision is particularly important when developing a single aggregate measure of 'human rights' because we must be careful not to include statistically and conceptually disparate measures.

One way to avoid the problems caused by global measures of human rights is to concentrate on a small subset of core rights (Forsythe and Wiseberg, 1979) which are usually defined as freedom from torture, freedom from imprisonment for the mere expression of a belief and freedom from political execution. The concept of core human rights is more universally acceptable than some of the legal and procedural definitions which have their origins in Western legal practices. Yet, even when we use the concept of core rights it is still difficult to reach a consensus. For example Amnesty International treats imprisoned conscientious objectors as prisoners of conscience and classifies all uses of the death penalty as violations of human rights. Although Amnesty International's practices simplify measurement, they interject additional normative conflicts into the measurement process. finally, restricting our analysis of human rights to core rights also results in our ignoring less extreme abuses of human rights and violations of political rights.

The lack of a consensus as to the meaning of human rights makes any attempt to use a single summated measure of those rights a risky endeavor. Too often authors have used summated scales without analyzing the interrelationship between items (Gastil, 1978, Strouse and Claude, 1976; Henderson, 1982). A preferable approach would be to begin either by examining individual practices or if scaling is desirable to use such scaling techniques as factor analysis or Gutman scaling to establish unidimensionality before employing summated measures. Amnesty International's (1983a) report on killings, Seymour's (1979) accounting of prisoners of conscience and Nixon's studies (1960, 1965) of freedom of the press are examples of studies which follow this first strategy of restricted analysis. Cingranelli and Pasquerello's (1985) study which uses factor analysis to dimensionalize human rights abuses is an example of the second type of scalar analysis. Value conflicts need not destroy our ability to study human rights abuses so long as we resist the temptation to rely exclusively upon summated measures of those rights. Individual variables such as the number of executions, the use of torture and the number of prisoners of conscience can be analyzed in their own right, and subscales can be developed to measure a variety of different categories of human rights.

EMPIRICAL DIFFICULTIES

The biases of informants and reporting groups, lack of information about abuses, and problems in attributing responsibility for abuses also makes it difficult to develop reliable measures. The biases of informants and reporting groups affect the collection of information in two ways. First, individual informants usually are allied with one side or the other in a political dispute. Exaggerated reports of atrocities are not uncommon propaganda technique; consequently such reports should not be taken at face value. Fortunately major reporting groups such as Amnesty International and the State Department do make some effort to verify accounts of human rights violations. Unfortunately these organizations have their own rather distinct points of view and have been criticized for their biases (McCamet, 1981; Scoble and Wiesberg, 1981). Amnesty International writes from a liberal perspective, Freedom House from a conservative perspective and the State Department from a more complicated perspective. The State Department must be frank enough to satisfy Congress and at the same time responsive to the president's wishes.

Probably the best technique for dealing with the biases of the reporting groups is to use two or three of their reports in combination when coding in an attempt to neutralize some of the bias or as Stohl, Carlton and Johnson (1984) did to construct three separate scales, one for each source, to use in the analysis. In addition it is also advisable to base our measurements on the descriptive portions of these reports and to ignore the more subjective measures. Estimates of the extent to which human rights abuses are changing, global categorizations of societies as free or unfree and non-quantitative comparisons between societies should be avoided because of their greater vulnerability to reporter group bias.

It is often difficult to obtain reliable information about human rights abuses because of the problems of collecting information about closed societies, difficulties in determining the number of abuses and the provincial location of some of those abuses. Closed societies such as the Soviet Union have harassed and imprisoned individuals for attempting to monitor human rights abuses (Amnesty International, 1983b, p. 286), others such as Burma have made it difficult for international monitoring groups to obtain even simple information about human rights abuses (Amnesty International, 1983b, p. 190).

Information on the actual number of abuses committed is even more difficult to obtain when a government wishes to disguise the extent of those abuses. This problem varies by type of abuse. Information on official executions, especially as happened in the Peoples Republic of China during 1984 when the executions were publicized as an example (Amnesty International, 1985, p. 205) are relatively easy to obtain. It is much harder to get an accounting when government forces, either with or without official sanction, murder individuals and hide their bodies. Estimates on the number of individuals who disappeared in Argentina during the late 1970s range from a low of 3900 confirmed by Amnesty International to a high of 15 000 in the view of Argentine human rights groups (Amnesty International, 1983b, p. 109).

Estimates of the number of people tortured are even more difficult to obtain. Many police departments, especially in the process of making arrests, brutalize individuals. The problem is to determine if an act of brutality is part of a pattern of abuse or only an isolated incident. Victims of abuse are afraid to come forward and most of the time only a small percentage of the more notorious incidents come to light. One alternative to estimating the exact number of abuses is to use either a rough ordinal scale or to code any substantial pattern of abuses as a violation.

The location of human rights abuses also influences our ability to detect them. Amnesty International and Freedom House do not prepare reports on all countries. The State Department's human rights reports now have sections on all members of the United Nations, but the entries for some of the smaller states are extremely brief. The location of abuses within a country also has an impact. Reports of human rights abuses are less precise when they deal with abuses committed outside of the major urban areas or in special security zones. In such countries as Columbia and Peru there are persistent reports of greater human rights abuses by government forces operating in rural as opposed to urban areas (State Department, 1983, pp. 510, 675).

It is not always easy to attribute responsibility for abuses. Individual disappearances may be a result of government policy or the responsibility of decisions made by independent members of a security service or the result of potential victims fleeing a dangerous situation. Further as can be seen by the history of lynchings in the American South, either the deliberate or unintentional failure of governments to enforce the law can contribute to the outbreak of vigilante activities and communal violence. This extra-governmental violence is extremely destructive of human rights, but is less directly the responsibility of government officials than is violence which results from the actions of government agents.

Finally there is the problem of how to deal with successful intimidation (Duval and Stohl, 1983). The lack of actual human rights abuses can result from either the absence of those abuses or from the intimidation of potential opponents by a highly repressive state. How should such a situation be treated? Although this problem is a genuine concern we usually can not measure psychological inhibitions with documentary data. Once again we are forced by methodological limitations to restrict the scope of our inquiries to specific overt behavior.

SOURCES OF INFORMATION

Expert opinion, events data analysis and organizational reports have all been used to develop measurements of human rights abuses. Summated expert opinion with all its problems has been used by Fitzgibbon and his associates (Fitzgibbon, 1956; Fitzgibbon and Johnson, 1961) to periodically measure democracy in Latin America, and by Nixon (1960, 1965) and Lowenstein (1968) to measure freedom of the press. In all of these cases panelists were given a list of countries and asked to rate them either in general terms or along a number of dimensions which were later summed up to produce single scale score. This technique, although roughly accurate, leaves too much to chance. General impressions, even expert ones, are only a crude method of classifying nation states. The problems of reliability and validity are particularly severe when the number of experts is much smaller than the total number of states. Expert opinion tends to rely on overall impressions of a society and hence is probably relatively insensitive to cyclic changes in performance.

Events data analysis has also been used to measure human rights abuses. In most cases this analysis is based on an accounting of government actions as reported in the *New York Times Index*. Taylor and Hudson (1972) developed a measure of government sanctions from this index which counts all government actions designed to control domestic opponents as sanctions. The accounting is available for all nation states, but mixes violent and non-violent events together and has not been updated. Markus and Nesvold (1972) used the *New York Times Index* to create a Gutman scale of government coerceiveness for ten countries. The Markus and Nesvold scale is an interesting effort to measure the coercive aspects of government actions. It has not, however, been extended in time or in scope beyond a few societies and ignores legal and procedural violations.

Organizational reports are the most promising sources of information on human rights violations. Amnesty International, Freedom House and the United States State Department all prepare annual human rights reports. Each report contains a brief country report on most of the nation states in the world which summarizes the status of human rights in that society during the year.

Amnesty International is the most respected of the reporting groups. It is a world wide organization which endeavors to act as an advocate for political prisoners. It has established a reputation for fairness and consistency in its reporting techniques and reports on the prevalence of torture, political executions, lack of minimal due process, and imprisonment of prisoners of conscience. Unfortunately substantially less attention is paid to violations of political rights and less drastic limitations on freedom of expression. Although founded in 1961 Amnesty's reports are difficult to obtain prior to the mid-1970s and even today do not report on all countries.

Freedom House prepares a series of country reports based on a careful examination of Arthur Banks data archive (Banks, 1979), *Worldmark Encyclopedia*, the popular press and State Department publications (Bollen, 1986, p. 584). In addition it also rates national states as free or unfree in comparison with other states and rates states on several numerical indices. Freedom House has been severely criticized for its conservative, free market, pro-United States biases (Scobel and Wiesberg, 1981). Even so, the country reports are consistent and the organization has criticized both right and left wing regimes.

The State Department's Country Reports on Human Rights Practices are the most detailed and complete of the annual reports. The reports are prepared by career foreign service officers for Congress. The entries relate specific incidents, quote conclusions of non-governmental monitoring groups and are two or three times as extensive as those of the other monitoring groups. Of all the monitoring organizations the State Department has the best resources for collecting information about human rights violations.

The first two reports, 1975 and 1976, were criticized by Congress which then officially turned to the Library of Congress for alternate information. As a result of this official rejection substantial changes were made in the way the reports were prepared. These changes improved the scope, quality and independence of the reports after 1979 (Scobel and Wisberg, 1981). A review of the 1983 reports in twenty-two nations which was conducted by Americas Watch, Helsinki Watch and the Lawyers Committee for International Human Rights (1983) concluded that 'For the most part distortions that appear in the Country Reports for 1982 are not so great as to prevent policy makers from grasping the essentials of the human rights situation' (p. 7). However, 'information about abuse in some friendly countries, but by no means all is presented in such a way to diminish its impact or explain it away' (p. 5).

The greatest problem with these reports seems to be with a small subset of nations where United States security interests are particularly involved. The reports on El Salvador, South Korea and Nicaragua have been singled out for particular criticism (Innes de Neufville, 1986).

Cigranelli and Pasquarello (1985) compared the State Department country reports with Amnesty International's annual report for 1980 for 100 randomly selected countries on use of torture and arbitrary imprisonment. They found substantial agreement, 81 per cent and 77 per cent respectively, in these two categories. On the other hand, Stohl, Carlton and Johnson (1984) found what they considered to be a relatively low correlation between the State Department and Amnesty International when they compared their ratings of twenty-two Latin American States for 1976 and 1981. However, Stohl, Carlton and Johnson's analysis of the relationship between human rights abuses and US foreign aid produced statistical relationships which were essentially the same when respect for human rights was measured with State Department, Amnesty International and Freedom House data.

Changes in presidential administrations have also influenced these reports. Under the Reagan administration the reports have been expanded to include information about human rights abuses caused by insurgent groups as well as governments, and to limit the presentation of economic and social information (Americas Watch, 1983).

The State Department reports are a frustrating source of information, too good to be ignored and yet flawed enough to require caution when using them. As a source the human rights reports are probably good enough to be used to construct a data base if we ignore the subjective portions of the reports, use a large number of cases and look only at general patterns of behavior. For more specific tasks, such as monitoring human rights abuses in specific societies, the country reports should only be used in conjunction with other sources.

Finally, a number of students of judicial behavior and criminal procedures have begun to look at conviction rates, sentencing practices, executions, and the extent of procedural protections provided in trial courts in the United States. Unfortunately only a very small amount of truly comparative studies of legal procedures and judicial behaviour have ever been attempted (Baar, 1976). If we could obtain a reasonably complete international data set, this kind of information would offer us much greater ability to analyze precisely human rights abuses. Short of that more complete comparative information about the use of the death penalty,[2] imprisonment rates and conviction rates would be of interest even though these variables are only indirectly related to actual abuse of human rights.

RECOMMENDATIONS

Major improvements in our knowledge of human rights abuses could be obtained if those social scientists who are interested in empirically studying this phenomena would at least initially follow a more multidimensional approach in developing measures of human rights abuses and at the same time cooperate more closely together in developing comprehensive data sets.

Human rights should be treated as a multidimensional phenomena. By separately analyzing specific aspects of respect for human rights and basing our scales on the statistical interrelationships between these variables we can avoid the necessity of developing a single definition of the concept. The normative problem of disagreement over the meaning of human rights can be solved by analyzing the different subcomponents of the concept.

Greater cooperation in collecting data sets would eliminate much of the current duplication of effort. The coding process for human rights data, even when we work from existing human rights reports is time consuming. A cooperative effort would allow us to experiment with alternative measurements, reduce the time required to develop a comprehensive time series data set and improve the comparability of the resulting research.

In addition, a cooperative effort might even allow us to shift our unit of analysis from the level of the national state to the level of the specific incident. For example rather than estimate the extent to which South Korea has imprisoned prisoners of conscience we could prepare a more detailed report on the circumstances surrounding the imprisonment of each individual prisoner of conscience. Although this strategy would tremendously improve our knowledge of human rights violations, it is much too time consuming for most individual scholars. The data coding requires either an extensive cooperation effort and/or the substantial long-term commitment of resources by a major research institution which has access to external sources of funding. Alternatively, one or more of the human rights monitoring organizations might be persuaded to both record and provide access to its initial reports in a machine-readable format.

We need to work toward the development of longer time series data sets so we can analyze human rights cycles. There is considerable historical evidence that several nation states have gone through cycles of repression and liberalization. Latin America, the United States, the Soviet Union and China have all exhibited cyclic changes in the degree to which they respect individual rights. In addition there is probably a long-term underlying secular trend towards greater respect for human rights. Any comparison of national states on the degree of abuse of human rights must take account of these changes. Multivariate techniques have been developed to allow us to perform quantitative analyses of these trends (Banks, 1986). We are just now at the point where we can develop data sets of a dozen years or so which although limited will allow us to begin to examine these trends.

CONCLUSION

Just as the natural science do not refuse to study important phenomena simply because they are difficult to measure so to the social sciences should not abandon the study of human rights simply because they to are difficult to measure. If we are careful, we can deal with most of the normative and empirical problems well enough to produce substantial improvements in our knowledge of how governments treat their citizens. The empirical problems are real, but thanks to the development of systematic annual human rights reports are less severe today than in the recent past. So long as we are willing to accept more modest levels of precision we have the data to identify major causal relationships and trends.

Notes

The preliminary work for this project was completed during a National Endowment for the Humanities summer seminar on theories of collective action. I would like to thank Sidney Tarrow and the National Endowment for the Humanities for their encouragement and support. I would also like to thank Andrea Bonnicksen for her comments.

1. Also see James Lemoyne's (1981, p. 1) report of CIA and embassy knowledge of the political killings of approximately 200 people in Honduras between 1981 and 1984. Lemoyne notes that 'Although the embassy human rights reports at the time mentioned abuses, they minimized the extent and seeming systematic nature.'
2. Amnesty International published a 1979 report on the death penalty. This report provides a comparative description of the application of the death penalty, but does not give an account of execution rates.

References

AMERICAS WATCH, HELSINKI WATCH, AND THE LAWYERS COMMITTEE FOR INTERNATIONAL RIGHTS (1983) *Review of Human Rights Practices for 1982* (New York: Americas Watch).

AMNESTY INTERNATIONAL (1983a) *Political Killings by Governments* (London: Amnesty International Publications).

AMNESTY INTERNATIONAL (1979) *The Death Penalty* (London: Amnesty International Publications).

AMNESTY INTERNATIONAL (1983b) *Amnesty International Report*. (London: Amnesty International Publications).

AMNESTY INTERNATIONAL (1985) *Amnesty International Report* (London: Amnesty International Publications).

BAAR, Carl (1976) 'Judicial Behavior and Comparative Human Rights Policy', in Richard Claude (ed.), *Comparative Human Rights*, pp. 353–81 (Baltimore: Johns Hopkins University Press).

BANKS, Arthur (1979) *Cross National Time Series Data Archive* (Cambridge, Mass.: MIT Press).

BANKS, David (1986) 'The Analysis of Human Rights Data over Time', *Human Rights Quarterly*, 8(4): 370–90.

BOLLEN, Kenneth (1980) 'Issues in Comparative Measurement of Democracy', *American Sociological Review*, 45(3): 370–90.

BOLLEN, Kenneth (1986) 'Political Rights and Political Liberties in Nations: An Evaluation of Human Rights Measures, 1950–1984', *Human Rights Quarterly*, 8(4): 567–91.

CHOMSKY, Noam and HERMAN, Edward (1979) *The Washington Connection and Third World Fascism* (Boston: South End Press).

CINGRANELLI, David and PASQUARELLO, Thomas (1985) 'Human Rights Practices and the Distribution of US Foreign Aid to Latin

American Countries', *American Journal of Political Science*, 27(3): 539–63.

CUTRIGHT, Phillip (1963) 'National Political Development: Measurement and Analysis', *American Sociological Review*, 28(2): 253–64.

CUTRIGHT, Phillip and WILEY, J. (1969) 'Modernization and Political Representation: 1927–1966', *Studies in Comparative International Development*, 5(1): 23–44.

DUVAL, Raymond and STOHL, Michael (1983) 'Governance by Terror', in Michael Stohl (ed.), *The Politics of Terror*, pp. 179–219 (New York: Marcel Dekker).

FITZGIBBON, Russell (1956) 'A Statistical Evaluation of Latin American Democracy', *Western Political Quarterly*, 9(3): 607–19.

FITZGIBBON Russell and JOHNSON, Kenneth (1961) 'Measurement of Latin American Political Change', *American Political Science Review*, 55(3): 515–26.

FORSYTHE, David and WISEBERG, Laurie (1979) 'Human Rights protection: A Research Agenda', *Human Rights Quarterly*, 1(4): 1–25.

GASTIL, Raymond (1973) 'The New Criteria of Freedom', *Freedom at Issue*, 17: 2–5, 20–24.

GASTIL, Raymond (1978) *Freedom in the World: Political Rights and Civil Liberties* (New York: Freedom House).

GURR, Ted (1970) *Why Men Rebel* (Princeton, NJ: Princeton University Press).

HUNTINGTON, Samuel (1968) *Political Order in Changing Societies* (New Haven: Yale University Press).

HENDERSON, Conway (1982) 'Military Regimes and Rights in Developing Countries', *Human Rights Quarterly*, 4(1): 110–23.

INNES de NEUFVILLE, Judith (1986) 'Human Rights Reporter as Policy tool: An Examination of State Department Country Reports', *Human Rights Quarterly*, 8(4): 681–99.

JACKMAN, Robert (1973) 'On the Relation of Economic Development to Democratic Performance', *American Journal of Political Science*, 17(3): 611–21.

KORNHAUSER, William (1959) *The Politics of Mass Society* (Glencoe, Il.: The Free Press).

LIPSET, Seymore Martin (1960) *Political Man: The Social Basis of Politics* (New York: Doubleday and Company).

LOWENSTEIN, Ralph (1968) 'World Press Freedoms', Freedom of Information Center. Report No. 201 (Columbia, Mo.: School of Journalism, University of Missouri).

LEYMONE, James (1986) 'CIA Accused of Tolerating Killings in Honduras', *New York Times*, 14 February, p. 1.

MARKUS, Gregory and NESVOLD, Betty (1972) 'Governmental Coerciveness and Political Instability', *Comparative Political Studies*, 5: 231–44.

McCAMET, John (1981) 'A Critique of Present Measures of Human Rights and an Alternative', in Ved Nanda, James Scarritt and George Shepherd (eds), *Global Human Rights* (Boulder, Col.: Westview Press).

NEUBAUER, Deane (1967) 'Some Conditions of Democracy', *American Political Science Review*, 61(4): 1002–9.

NIXON, Raymond (1960) 'Factors Related to Freedom in National Press Systems', *Journalism Quarterly*, 37(1): 13–28.

NIXON, Raymond (1965) 'Freedom of the World's Press: A Fresh Approach with New Data', *Journalism Quarterly*, 42–1): 13–4.

PASSQUARELLO, Thomas (1986) 'Human Rights and Other Determinants of US Aid to African Nations'. Unpublished paper presented at the annual meeting of the American Political Science Association.

SALZBERG, John (1979) 'Monitoring Human Rights Violations: How Good is the Information?' in Peter Brown and Douglas MacLean (eds), *Human Rights and US Foreign Policy* (Lexington, Mass.: Lexington Books).

SCHLOUTZ, Lars (1981) 'US Foreign Policy and Human Rights', *Comparative Politics*, 13(1): 149–70.

SCOBLE, Harry and WISEBERG, Laurie (1981) 'Problems of Comparative Research on Human Rights', in Ved Nanda, James Scarritt and George Shepherd (eds), *Global Human Rights* (Boulder, Co.: Westview Press).

SEYMOUR, John (1979) 'Indicies of Political Imprisonment', *Universal Human Rights*, 1(1): 99–100.

SMITH, Arthur (1969) 'Socioeconomic Development and Democracy: A Causal Analysis', *Midwest Journal of Political Science*, 13(1): 95–125.

STATE DEPARTMENT (1983) *Country Reports on Human Rights Practices* (Washington, DC: US Government Printing Office).

STOHL, Michael, CARLTON, David and JOHNSON, Steven (1984) 'Human Rights and US Foreign Assistance from Nixon to Carter', *Journal of Peace Research*, 21(3): 215–16.

STROUSE, James and CLAUDE, Richard (1976) 'Empirical Comparative Rights Research: Some Preliminary Tests of Developmental Hypotheses', in Richard Claude (ed.), *Comparative Human Rights* (Baltimore: Johns Hopkins University Press).

TAYLOR, Charles and HUDSON, Michael (1972) *World Handbook of Political and Social Indicators* (New Haven: Yale University Press).

6 Measuring Social and Economic Rights Performance in the People's Republic of China: A Comparative Perspective Among Developing Asian Countries

Stephen C. Thomas

What has been the People's Republic of China's social and economic rights performance since 1949 and how does it compare to other developing Asian countries as measured by the Physical Quality of Life Index (PQLI)?[1] To answer I will first present data on China's performance from 1949 to 1978 and from 1978 to the present for each major rights area identified in the 1966 Covenant on Social and Economic Rights. Second, the data on China will be evaluated using PQLI criteria. Finally, China's PQLI performance will be compared with other developing Asian countries.

CHINA'S SOCIAL AND ECONOMIC RIGHTS PERFORMANCE

The first right, listed in *Article 6* of the Social and Economic Rights Covenant, is the right to work. The Chinese Constitution, like that of the Soviet Union and virtually every other socialist country, guarantees to everyone the right to work, but it also requires it. From 1949 to 1978, underemployment and unemployment were greatly reduced through jobs created by high levels of investment in industrialization and controlled urban migration, and through collective work

104

arrangements in the countryside that included virtually all rural dwellers. These programs and reforms reduced unemployment to a low of 4.7 per cent by 1982 (Taylor, 1985).

Economic reforms that began in 1978 have addressed remaining unemployment through the creation of new jobs, particularly in construction, and through allowing the establishment of small individually-owned businesses, especially in needed services. In the countryside, where 80 per cent of Chinese still live and work, new jobs in manufacturing, as well as in mining, in construction, and in transportation industries, allowed nine million of the total rural labor force of 380 million to leave agricultural labor in 1986. In the cities, new employment has been expanding more slowly than the 1953 to 1983 average of 5.2 per cent increase per year, but still has increased a respectable 3.8 per cent per year since 1983 (*Beijing Review*, 1986).

Despite China's impressive progress, millions remain unemployed or underemployed. Underemployment has resulted in part from the Chinese government policy of trying to provide work for everyone, even if this means labor redundancy. Despite post-1978 reforms and resulting increased employment opportunities, labor redundancy is still as high as 30–40 per cent in the countryside. Without successful economic reforms, redundancy could increase to 60 per cent by the year 2000 (Taylor, 1985).

Article 7 contains the rights to enjoyment of just and favorable conditions of work, to equal remuneration for work of equal value, to a decent standard of living, and to rest and leisure, including reasonable limitation of working hours and periodic holidays with pay. These rights seem to have been well protected from 1949 to 1978, with wages of urban workers supported through subsidization of basic needs (housing, grain, clothing, medical care) and the consumption levels of the much poorer rural peasants supported through collective structures that assured access to at least a minimum level of food (the 'basic consumption grain' allotment) and to other basic needs (the 'five guarantees' of food, housing, clothing, medical care, and burial) (Lardy, 1984). There has also been a policy of decreasing interprovincial and urban–rural inequalities through investing in poor provinces and rural areas. Though equal pay for women is guaranteed, in practice women are often unable to get the more skilled and higher paying jobs. They therefore have lower wages as a group.

Chinese work a six-day week, at least in urban enterprises and government jobs, not counting time spent going to political meetings.

They are guaranteed a daily rest period of about one hour and they have seven days vacation per year, three days at Chinese New Year, two days on National Day, 1 October, one day for 1 May, and one day for 1 January. The major post-1978 reform has been to shift the responsibility for rural support services from the communes to the townships. Otherwise, reforms have so far not done much to undermine these rights.

Article 8 sets out trade union rights. Trade unions, or 'worker's unions' as they are called in China, have been available to Chinese workers except during the 1966–76 Cultural Revolution, when unions were virtually abolished. Although workers are permitted to discuss and vote on factory production plans, Chinese trade unions, as well as labor unions in all socialist countries except Yugoslavia, serve more to mobilize labor and manage of employment benefits than to advocate improved labor conditions. While former Chinese Communist Party Chairman Mao Zedong explicitly allowed for the right to strike in the 1975 Cultural Revolution Constitution, China's 1982 Constitution rescinded that right. Current Chinese leaders are encouraging unions to play a more active role in increasing productivity and efficiency, but are trying to prevent the 'Polish Disease', i.e. union independence from Communist Party control.

Article 9 provides the right to social security. In theory, all Chinese have a form of social security based on membership in their *danwei*, or work unit. In practice, urban dwellers working for state-run industries or institutions do receive social security through a universal and adequate retirement system. Peasants, however, have depended mostly on their families because children are obligated by law to support their parents and because peasants are still expected to depend for their support only minimally on the commune or government. The lack of a comprehensive social security in the countryside, despite the promise of access to basic social needs through the 'five guarantees' of food, clothing, housing, medical care, and burial, is one of the forces inhibiting implementation of a successful voluntary population limitation program.

With the post-1978 reforms allowing for bankruptcy of a state enterprise, provisions have been made to provide unemployment benefits for a year to laid-off workers. Another reform is that cities, rather than individual businesses, will begin to administer pensions because of the disparity in the ratio between pensioned and employed workers in different enterprises. Steps have also been taken to strengthen social security benefits for peasants in order to facilitate the one-child family policies (Platte, 1984–5).

Article 10 provides for protection of the family. Chinese performance has been both impressive, and extremely controversial. The general availability of services such as paid maternity leave, child care, infant food allocations, and affordable medical care, has lead to impressively low infant mortality rates and would seem to meet the requirements of Article 10 (Table 6.1).

At the same time, official Chinese policies, such as setting quotas for the number of children in a family, have caused great controversy, both in China and abroad. While the in-quota family receives all the above-mentioned services, families who have unplanned children can lose various social benefits: e.g. apartments, food allowance, clothing rations, child subsidies.

Population-control measures to limit a family to one child, first established in 1979, were particularly stringent from 1982 to 1984. During that period, a second pregnancy, if beyond the state quota, was to be terminated. If a second pregnancy was permitted for some reason, one of the two parents was supposed to be sterlized after the birth of the child (Bannister, 1985).

Such harsh measures would not be popular in any country and have caused much controversy in China, and in the United States (Mosher, 1983). Prompted in part by domestic reports of female infanticide (see Table 6.1 for total infant mortality rates), and in part by embarrassing foreign reports of forced abortions, some late in pregnancies, Chinese authorities reviewed their population policy in early 1984. On 13 April 1984, they issued Central Document 7, that prohibits coercion and 'starts from reality', i.e. that some rural couples, particularly those with a female child, can be allowed a second child. To permit the increases that may result from a more flexible population policy, the population target for the year 2000 was changed from 1.2 billion to 'about' 1.2 billion. Chinese leaders have also begun to recognize the possible negative conequences of a too-rapid fertility decline (Greenhalgh, 1986).

Article 11 recognizes the right of everyone to an adequate standard of living for himself and his family, including adequate food, clothing and housing, and to the continuous improvement of living conditions. The rights in Article 11 are both the broadest so far, and perhaps the hardest to measure. Nevertheless, some judgements can be made about Chinese performance for this category of rights. Even though

Table 6.1 Reconstruction of social data on China, 1953–82

Year	Mid-year population (millions)	Crude birth rate (per thousand)	Crude death rate (per thousand)	Natural population increase rate (per thousand)	Total fertility rate	Expectation of life at birth (years)	Infant mortality rate (per 1000 births)
1953	584.2	42.2	25.8	16.5	6.06	40.3	175
1954	594.7	43.4	24.2	19.2	6.28	42.4	164
1955	606.7	43.0	22.3	20.7	6.26	44.6	154
1956	619.1	39.9	20.1	19.8	5.86	47.0	143
1957	633.2	43.3	18.1	25.1	6.40	49.5	132
1958	646.7	37.8	20.7	17.1	5.68	45.8	146
1959	654.3	28.5	22.1	6.5	4.31	42.5	160
1960	650.7	26.8	44.6	−17.8	4.02	24.6	284
1961	644.7	22.4	23.0	−0.6	3.29	38.4	183
1962	653.3	41.0	14.0	27.0	6.03	53.0	89
1963	674.2	49.8	13.8	36.0	7.51	54.9	87
1964	696.1	40.3	12.5	27.8	6.18	57.1	86
1965	715.5	39.0	11.6	27.4	6.07	57.8	84
1966	735.9	39.8	11.1	28.7	6.26	58.6	83
1967	755.3	33.9	10.5	23.4	5.32	59.4	82
1968	776.2	41.0	10.1	30.9	6.45	60.3	81
1969	798.6	36.2	9.9	26.3	5.73	60.8	76
1970	820.4	37.0	9.5	27.4	5.82	61.4	70
1971	842.5	34.9	9.2	25.6	5.45	62.0	65
1972	863.4	32.5	8.9	23.6	4.99	62.6	60
1973	883.0	29.9	8.6	21.3	4.54	63.0	56

Year							
1974	28.1	8.3	19.8	4.17	63.4	52	901.3
1975	24.8	8.1	16.7	3.58	63.8	49	917.9
1976	23.1	7.8	15.2	3.23	64.2	45	932.7
1977	21.0	7.7	13.4	2.85	64.6	41	946.1
1978	20.7	7.5	13.2	2.72	65.1	37	958.8
1979	21.4	7.6	13.8	2.75	65.0	39	971.8
1980	17.6	7.7	10.0	2.24	64.9	42	983.4
1981	21.0	7.7	13.3	2.69	64.8	44	994.9
1982	21.1	7.9	13.2	2.71	64.7	46	1008.2

Source: The table was prepared by Judith Banister, Representative of the Bureau of Census, for her testimony before the Subcommittee on Human Rights and International Organizations and the Subcommittee on Asian and Pacific Affairs, US House of Representatives, 31 October 1985. For further detail see Judith Banister, 'Analysis of Recent Data on the Population of China', *Population and Development Review*, Vol. 10, No. 2 (June 1984): pp. 241–71; 'Perspectives on China's 1982 Census', in *Proceedings of the International Seminar on China's 1982 Population Census*, State Statistical Bureau, People's Republic of China, forthcoming; and *China's Changing Population* (Stanford, Cal.: Stanford University Press, 1988).

farm production barely kept up with population until 1977, almost all Chinese were able to have enough to eat through a combination of price setting, rationing, and government subsidies where necessary. Simple but adequate clothing has been available through rationing since 1949. Housing has been scarce, particularly in the cities, but it has been reasonably equally distributed. As mentioned above, welfare programs for the unemployed, the widowed, the sick, and those in other severe circumstances beyond their control, are available only at very modest levels, particularly in the poorer parts of the countryside. Nevertheless, for most of the period after 1949, China's guarantees, though minimal, have been sufficient to overcome past patterns of massive famines and severe maldistribution of food. The exception, and it is a major one, was the 1959–61 Great Leap period when a massive famine caused an estimated 20–30 million above-normal deaths (Aird, 1985).

Since 1978, agricultural production has increased 8.98 per cent per year while population has increased only about 2 per cent yearly. Chinese consumption levels have therefore greatly improved, particularly in the countryside where higher grain prices and free-market sale opportunities have lead to a 17.2 per cent increase in income per year from 1978 to 1984, as compared with 5.5 per cent per year from 1953 to 1978 (*Beijing Review*, 1986). On the negative side, China's rural Gini coefficient is rising (a sign of increasing inequality), and the gap between rich and poor regions is widening. For the moment, the government seems to think that increasing inequalities are not only a natural part of continued growth, but that they may be necessary for 'mobilizing enthusiasm for production' (*Beijing Review*, 1986).

Article 12 calls for the highest attainable standard of physical and mental health. In terms of health and well-being, government policy has been to provide basic medical care to all so that past public health threats such as venereal disease, yellow fever, diphtheria, polio, and smallpox cannot continue to ravage the population. The Chinese government has also tried to provide a sufficiently healthy living environment for mothers and children to reduce infant mortality to the minimum possible. These two policies have resulted in tremendous improvements in life expectancy and infant mortality since 1949 (Table 6.1). It is again worth noting, however, that past progress was radically reversed for several years during and immediately after the Great Leap when both life expectancy and infant mortality rates surpassed even pre-1949 levels. Post-1978 reforms also seem to have begun a slight negative trend in life expectancy (Table 6.1).

Articles 13 and 14 guarantee educational rights. China has made a special point of trying to increase literacy among its people and to ensure that everyone has the right to at least primary school education. Of workers over fifteen years of age, 28 per cent are illiterate or semi-literate, with 48.9 per cent of female workers (who are a smaller percentage of the workforce than men) being semi-literate or illiterate, and 20.8 per cent of male workers being semi-literate or illiterate (Taylor, 1985). China has not, however, made primary education free, and the tuition plus fees that even a poor peasant family has to pay can be a major disincentive to enrolling a child for even primary education.

Article 15 guarantees the right to take part in cultural life. Chinese are encouraged to take part in culture but at times the government has very narrowly circumscribed what art and literature is acceptable, particularly during periods of high political mobilization. During the 1966–76 Cultural Revolution, for example, the government virtually prohibited everything except proletarian or people's art.

Two interesting questions arise in relation to China's social and economic rights performance. First, to what extent are social and economic benefits not universally available? Access to social and economic programs, at least until very recently, has been totally in the hands of local authorities – the leaders of one's work unit or danwei. Any conflict with these leaders, whether personal or political, could lead to losses in rights of all kinds. During both the anti-rightist campaigns of the 1950s and the 1966–76 Cultural Revolution period, persons condemned as rightists or counter-revolutionaries often suffered major degradation of their social and economic rights. A politically condemned individual might be moved into the smallest possible living dwelling available, lose housing altogether by being sent to the countryside for re-education, find his salary reduced to bare minimum, and even be denied basic medical care. Although it does not appear to have been official policy to deprive those politically criticized of their social and economic rights, and many have, since 1978, been given back pay and compensation for their losses, the practice of depriving political victims of their basic social and economic rights was common and lead to untold suffering for millions of Chinese.[2] China's behavior in this regard offers support to Donnelly (1982) who contends that the political conditionality of social and economic rights makes them less than absolute rights in many settings.

The second question is whether social and economic rights are inhibited by rapid economic growth or whether they can have a neutral or even positive effect. Until at least 1978, it seemed to be possible for China to meet basic social needs and to achieve relatively successful economic growth. According to a World Bank Report (1981) on China: 'Per capita GNP appears to have grown at an annual rate of 2.0–2.5 per cent in 1957–77 and 2.5–3.0 per cent in 1957–79. Even the former rate is significantly above the average for other low-income developing countries (1.6 per cent in 1960–78).'

However, China's average annual food production and GNP growth rates, while reasonably impressive compared to most other poor countries, depended on extremely high and rising investment rates, and therefore left little for increased consumption (Subramaniam, 1986). Chinese per capita food consumption increased little from 1957 to 1976, and may actually have slightly decreased. The post-Mao leadership addressed the problem of levels of consumption in 1978 reforms by establishing a 'responsibility system' to stimulate agricultural production. Results have been impressive, with both agricultural and industrial production expanding at over 7 per cent per year from 1979 to 1984, a much accelerated rate for agriculture (*Beijing Review*, 1986).

The effects of the reforms on future social and economic rights performance are still to be determined. Nevertheless, some observations are already possible. First, reforms in the countryside, particularly the dismantling or privatization of the commune clinics, may be having a negative effect on the ability of poorer peasants to have their basic social needs met (Hsiao, 1982). It is possible to discern a disturbing trend that supports this contention. Namely, since 1978, crude death rates, infant mortality rates, and (therefore) life expectancy rates have all been moving against past progressive trends, the first such negative movement since the disasters of the 1959–61 Great Leap (Table 6.1). Although the regressive changes are still modest and the time period short so far, the direction is disturbing and the trend should be watched during the coming years.

Second, the factor that has most adversely affected Chinese access to basic social needs since 1949 has been economic crises, such as during the Great Leap. Although few would characterize 1978 as a time of economic crisis, some analysts (e.g. Harding, 1986) feel that it was a crucial decision period when political and economic problems, including an increasingly inefficient industrial structure and stagnating levels of consumption, demanded major reform. Thus, if the current reforms are able to increase agricultural productivity (as they have), to raise levels of consumption for the vast majority of Chinese peasants (which they seem to have), and to increase efficiency in both agriculture and industry, then current negative movements in crude death rates, infant mortality, and life expectancy may be more the consequences of economic adjustment leading to major economic improvement than portenders of a downward spiral. Jack Donnelly's argument that meeting basic needs reinforces successful industrialization would also support a more positive interpretation of China's post-1978 trends, particularly Donnelly's point that Korea suffered a slight decrease in its equality of distribution of income during some stages of its recent impressive economic growth (Donnelly, 1984).

APPLICATION OF THE PQLI TO CHINA

China's record of meeting the basic social and economic needs of its people based on its performance in the rights categories enumerated in the Covenant of Social, Economic, and Cultural Rights, seems, on the surface, to be quite respectable. But it would be helpful to measure China's performance and to be able to compare it with that of other developing countries.

Several approaches to measuring basic human needs have been suggested by scholars and practitioners. According to the authors of the 1981 World Bank Report on China, the best single indictor of the level of basic social needs is life expectancy: 'whose dependence on many other economic and social variables makes it probably the best single indicator of the extent of real poverty in a country.' A more complex approach is the Physical Quality of Life Index (PQLI), developed by Morris (1979), which combines life expectancy, infant mortality, and literacy into one indicator on a scale of 1 to 100. Various authors have offered criticisms of the PQLI. The most telling criticisms are that the three measures (life expectancy at age one, infant mortality, and literacy) correlate so highly as to be redundant and that the index itself correlates so highly with GNP as to be unnecessary (Hicks and Streeten, 1969; Larson and Walton, 1978; and Ram, 1982).

The case of China also raises several problems for the PQLI that are probably typical of developing countries. First, the index depends on statistics provided by the country, statistics that can be unreliable.

China in particular has been plagued with questionable statistics since at least the Great Leap of 1957–59. At present, however, Chinese and foreign analysts believe that they have reasonably good figures, and it is these statistics that have been used so far in this paper.

A second problem is that the PQLI may maks both particular problems in a country as well as country-specific variations in the three areas of scaling that could be of importance when comparing one country with another. As mentioned earlier, the PQLI does not hint at the very serious implications of China's current population control program, a program that may be resulting, for example, in increased infant mortality rates for female babies, and perhaps also in decreased life expectancy for women. The PQLI also does not permit examination of whether certain groups are being severely restricted in their access to basic social needs. Such exclusion of rights could be masked if the affected group (such as the hundreds of thousands of Chinese branded as rightists and counter-revolutionaries) is a small enough percentage of the whole population.

COMPARISON WITH OTHER DEVELOPING COUNTRIES

Despite its limitations, the PQLI does permit quantification of basic social needs with sufficient representational accuracy to be able to roughly evaluate a country's performance over time. The PQLI also seems to be very useful for making crude comparisons of social needs performance between countries with different social, economic, or political systems but similarly low levels of economic development. The Overseas Development Council, for example, has used Morris' index for several years in their publication series, *US Foreign Policy and the Third World* (Sewell, Feinberg and Kallab, 1985).

According to the Overseas Development Council, in 1981 China had a per capita income of $US 310, a life expectancy of 67, an infant mortality rate of 71 per thousand, and a literacy rate of 69 per cent. Based on an equal weighting of China's life expectancy at age one, infant mortality, and literacy rate, China's PQLI in 1981 was 75 on a scale of 1 to 100 (Sewell, Feinberg and Kallab, 1985).

From the data in Table 6.2, China can be shown to have a proportionally far better PQLI than almost all countries at a comparable economic level and even many countries with two to three times the per capita GNP. Pakistan, with a GNP of $US 380, $70 more than China in 1981, is the most comparable to China according to

Table 6.2 PQLI index for selected lower and lower-middle income Asian countries

	Population mid-1984 (millions)	Physical Quality of Life Index (PQLI) 1981	Physical Quality of Life Index (PQLI) 1970–75 Average	Per Capita GNP 1982 ($US)	Per capita GNP (Real) growth rate 1960–82 (%)	Population growth rate (%)	Life expectancy at birth (years)	Infant mortality per 1000 live births	Literacy (%)	Per capita public education spending 1980 ($US)
Low-Income (12)	2133.3	60	n.a.	280	3.2	1.8	59	97	53	11
Afghanistan	14.4	17	18	220	n.a.	2.5	37	205	20	5
Bangladesh	99.6	37	35	140	0.3	3.1	48	135	26	2
Bhutan	1.4	25	n.a.	120	n.a.	2.3	44	149	5	n.a.
Burma	38.9	59	51	190	1.3	2.4	54	98	66	3
China, People's Republic	1034.5	75	69	310	5.0	1.3	67	71	69	17
India	746.4	46	43	260	1.3	2.0	52	121	36	7
Kampuchea	6.1	33	40	120	n.a.	1.9	43	201	48	n.a.
Laos	3.7	39	31	80	n.a.	2.4	43	126	44	n.a.
Nepal	16.6	30	25	170	-0.1	2.5	45	148	19	2
Pakistan	97.3	39	38	380	2.8	2.8	50	123	24	5
Sri Lanka	16.1	85	82	320	2.6	1.4	69	43	86	8
Vietnam	58.3	54	54	190	n.a.	2.4	66	99	78	6
Lower Middle-Income (7)	277.9	65	n.a.	665	4.0	2.2	57	79	68	13
Indonesia	161.6	58	48	580	4.2	2.1	53	92	62	10
Maldives	0.2	57	n.a.	440	n.a.	3.0	48	120	82	n.a.
Mongolia	1.9	77	n.a.	780	n.a.	2.8	64	54	80	60
Philippines	54.5	75	71	820	2.8	2.5	63	53	75	11
Thailand	51.7	79	68	790	4.5	2.0	63	53	86	23
Yemen, Arab Republic	5.9	28	27	500	5.1	2.7	43	160	21	19
Yemen, People's Dem. Republic	2.1	38	33	470	6.4	2.9	45	143	40	18

Sources: John W. Sewell, Richard E. Feinberg and Valeriana Kallab (eds), US Foreign Policy and the Third World: Agenda 1985–86, Overseas Development Council, pp. 218–19 (New Brunswick: Transaction Books, 1985).
Morris D. Morris, Measuring the Condition of the World's Poor: The Physical Quality of Life Index, Overseas Development Council, pp. 128–31 (New York: Pergamon Press, 1979).

the figures. However, Pakistan had a life expectancy of only 50, an infant mortality rate of 123 per 1000 live births, and a literacy rate of only 24 per cent, for a PQLI of only 39, almost half of China's. No country in the world with an equal or lower GNP than China's had a higher PQLI. Instead, China scored better on meeting these three areas of basic social needs than many countries with double or more the GNP per capita.

Indonesia, for example, with a per-capita income of $US 580, almost twice that of China ($US 310), had an infant mortality rate of 92 deaths per 1000, a life expectancy of 53, and a literacy rate of 62 per cent, giving it a PQLI of 58, some seventeen points below China (75). The Philippines had a per capita GNP of $US 820, about two and a half times that of China, but a life expectancy of 63, an infant mortality rate of 53, and a literacy rate of 75 per cent, for a PQLI of 75, exactly that of China. Even Malaysia, with a per capita GNP of $1860, or some five times that of China, had a lower PQLI.

In fact, China had a PQLI that was fifteen points higher than the average for the low-income countries ($280 average per capita), and ten points higher than the lower middle-income countries ($665 average per capita). Even if the questionable cases of the two Yemens are excluded, China would be roughly comparable in PQLI with countries twice her GNP per capita. China's comparative PQLI performance is similar to China's rating on a World Bank scale of 126 countries with a population of one million or more. Although China was near the bottom in per-capita income, 102nd, it ranked 62nd in per-capita calorie intake, 60th in infant mortality, 47th in adult literacy, 46th in life expectancy, and 32nd in birth rate, making it similar to many medium income countries (*Beijing Review*, 1986).

China's record is all the more impressive because it is still a primarily agricultural country that has nearly the worst arable land per capita ratio in the world (.12 hectares of cultivated land per person), a ratio that is half of Japan's (.25), less than one-third of India's (.42), and less even than those of Egypt (.15), Indonesia (.16), or Bangladesh (.15) (World Bank, 1981). Only Sri Lanka, a country with a comparable GNP level that is known for its commitment to meeting basic social needs, surpasses China in terms of PQLI. Even in the 1970–75 period, before the post-Mao reforms, China's PQLI performance was a respectable 69, also higher than any other comparably poor Asian country except Sri Lanka.

Of historical interest also is the case of India. In 1952, both China and India were reasonably comparable in terms of GNP, and probably also in terms of meeting basic social needs, and therefore in terms of PQLI. From 1952 to 1981, however, India achieved slower GNP growth rates and even slower increases in PQLI such that by 1981 it was a full twenty-nine points behind China. That difference, translated back into social needs, meant that in 1981 the average Indian lived fifteen fewer years, had an 80 per cent higher chance of losing a newborn child, and was only a little more than half as likely to be literate as his Chinese counterpart.

SUMMARY

In this paper, China's social, economic, and cultural rights performance has been evaluated, her efforts at meeting basic social needs have been measured using the Physical Quality of Life Index, and China's PQLI has been compared with the PQLIs of other developing countries in Asia. China's social and economic rights performance seems respectable, even impressive, from 1949 to 1982, except for the massive loss of life during the Great Leap of 1959–61 and for the exclusion of those branded rightists and counter-revolutionaries from minimum acceptable levels of social needs. A brief comparison of China's PQLI with other countries' PQLIs seems to support the conclusion that China also performed very well in comparison to equally poor and even economically more developed poor Asian countries. China's performance compared to other poor Asian countries also does not seem to have significantly deteriorated between 1970–75 and 1981 despite possible decreases in social and economic rights performance in the wake of post-Mao economic reforms. The results of both comparisons are consistent with a World Bank estimate of China made in 1981.

China's most remarkable achievement during the last three decades has been to make low-income groups far better off in terms of basic needs than their counterparts in most other poor countries. They all have work, their food supply is guaranteed through a mixture of state rationing and collective self-insurance; most of their children are not only at school, but being comparatively well taught; and the great majority have access to basic health care and family planning services. Life expectancy – whose dependency on many other economic and social variables makes it probably the best single indicator of the extent of real poverty in a country – is, at 64 years, outstandingly high for a country at China's per capita level (World Bank, 1981).

Notes

1. The PQLI is composed of the averages of figures for life expectancy, infant mortality, and literacy.
2. Estimates of the number of Chinese persecuted during the Cultural Revolution range from three to 100 million.

References

AIRD, J. S. (1985) Responses to Ten Questions on Family Planning Policies in China by the US House of Representatives Subcommittee on Human Rights and International Organizations, Subcommittee on Asian and Pacific Affairs, 19 October. Unpublished paper, Washington DC.

BANNISTER, J. (1985) Statement of the Representative of the Burea of Census Before the Subcommittee on Human Rights and International Organizations and the Subcommittee on Asian and Pacific Affairs, US House of Representatives, 31 October. Unpublished paper, Washington DC: US Bureau of Census.

BEIJING REVIEW (1986) 'Economic Growth and Rural Development, 10, 15 March, 14–21.

DONNELLY, J. (1982) 'Human Rights and Human Dignity: An Analytical Critique of Non-Western Conceptions of Human Rights', *American Political Science Review* 76(2): 303–16.

DONNELLY, J. (1984) 'Human Rights and Development: Complementary or Competing Concerns?', *World Politics* 36(2): 255–83.

GREENHALGH, S. (1986) 'Shifts in China's Population Policy, 1984–1986: Views from the Central, provincial, and Local Levels', 18 May. Unpublished paper (New York: Center for Policy Studies, The Population Council).

HARDING, H. (1986) 'Political Development in Post-Mao China', in A. Doak Barnett and Ralph N. Clough (eds), *Modernizing China: Post-Mao Reform and Development* (Boulder, Co.: Westview Press).

HICKS, N. and STREETEN, P. (1979) 'Indicators of Development: The Search for a Basic Needs Yardstick', *World Development*, 7: 567–80.

HSIAO, W. (1982) Transformation of Health Care in China. *New England Journal of Medicine* (5 April).

LARDY, N. R. (1984) 'Consumption and Living Standards in China, 1978–1983', *China Quarterly* (100): 849–65.

LARSON, D. and WALTON, W. T. (1979) 'The Physical Quality of Life Index: A Useful Social Indicator?' *World Development*, 7: 581–4.

MORRIS, M. D. (1979) *Measuring the Condition of the World's Poor: The Physical Quality of Life Index* (New York: Permagon Press).

MOSHER, S. (1983) *Broken Earth: The Rural Chinese*. New York: Macmillan.

PLATTE, E., (1984–85). 'China's Fertility Transition: The One-Child Campaign', *Pacific Affairs*, 57(4): 646–71.

RAM, R. (1982) 'Composite Indices of Physical Quality of Life, Basic Needs Fulfillment, and Income: A "Principal component" representation', *Journal of Development Economics*, 11: 227–47.

SEWELL, J. W., FEINBERG, R. E. and KALLAB, V. (1985) US Foreign Policy and the Third World. Overseas Development Council US Third World Policy Perspectives, No. 3 (New Brunswick, N.J.: Transaction Books).

SUBRAMANIAM, S. (1986) 'A Comparative Perspective of the Economic Growth of China and India: 1870–1985', ch. 3, *Efficiency in the Use of Resources and Equity in the Distribution of Incomes*. Unpublished book manuscript (Cambridge, Mass.: Harvard University).

TAYLOR, J. R. (1985) *Employment and Unemployment in China: Results from 10-Per cent Sample Tabulation of 1982 Population Census*. Foreign Economic Report No. 23 (Washington DC: US Department of Commerce).

WORLD BANK (1981) *China: Socialist Economic Development (In Nine Volumes), The Main Report*. World Bank Report No. 3391-CHA (Washington DC: The World Bank).

7 Gender/Generic Language in the United States Constitution: Gender Bias Versus Democratic Ideals

Eileen L. McDonagh and Edward C. McDonagh

The Constitution of the United States, as the law of the land, offers an objective measure over time of the development and change in meaning of the ascriptive characteristics of Americans who may be considered to be participants in the body polity under the rubric 'We, the People'. A determined effort is made to identify classes of 'people' who were intentionally or unintentionally omitted from viable citizenship in the first great social experiment in representative democracy. Particular attention is directed to the two largest categories of the population: men and women. Certainly the thrust of the proposed Equal Rights Amendment to the Constitution was to clarify and neutralize the Constitution's numerous masculine gender references. However, since the ERA was not ratified on 30 June 1982, it becomes important to understand precisely how the Constitution specifies significant gender and generic relationships in a document basic to the principles underlying human rights.[1]

I

The United States' 'founding fathers' completely rejected 'hereditary-determined', that is to say, 'genetically determined' leadership exemplified by the monarchy of King George III. However, at the same time, all American women were excluded from any direct participation in the new 'Democracy'. Centuries prior to the American Revolution, women in England, and in other monarchies, might become the acknowledged sovereign of the nation with the title

120

queen. Indeed, classic historical examples include rivalry *between* competing queens, such as Elizabeth and her cousin, Mary Queen of Scots, where support from respective Protestant and Catholic adherents added religion as a still more important criterion than gender for determining leadership of a monarchical body politic.[2]

Thus, the early history of the establishment of 'democracy' in the United States is more the chronicle of substituting one ruling group for another, rather than the shedding of barriers preventing full participation in politics by all citizens.[3] Charles Beard contends that fundamental private property rights were anterior to government and 'morally beyond the reach of majorities' (Beard, 1941, p. 65). On this basis not even a majority of adult males participated in the ratification of the Constitution. A candid appraisal of the participation of the 'people' in the framing of the Constitution discloses the following categories of Americans excluded or unfairly represented: property poor whites, Roman Catholics, black slaves, Indians, and an entire gender, women. Ferdinand Lundberg makes the point that 'the fact that a few people framed and ratified the Constitution is no decisive point against it, and one must concede, doesn't impugn it. However, it is a decisive point against the myth that they did' (Lundberg, 1980, p. 19).

The Preamble to the Constitution proudly proclaims that 'We, the People' initiated the machinery for a more perfect union; however, constitutional historians and others have frequently observed that Colonel George Mason of Virginia refused to sign the Constitution on the grounds that it lacked a Bill of Rights. Patrick Henry, a spectacular Revolutionary leader, complained during the period when the Constitution was undergoing the ratification process in the Virginia Legislature that 'I have the highest regard for those gentlemen; but, Sir, give me leave to demand, what right had they to say, "We, the People?" – Who authorized them to speak the language of "We, the People", instead of "the States"? The people gave them no power to use their name' (Leedham, 1964, p. 2–30). While the word 'people' has an extraordinarily 'generic ring' to it, the founding fathers apparently had in mind a population of *white male protestant patricians* who came to constitute the collectivity known by the ubiquitous phrase, 'We, the People'. Of course, some of the strident opposition to the word 'people' came from anti-federalists who feared that the federalists were simply using the sloganized platitude of 'We, the people' as a distraction from their determined effort to have a powerful national government. Leonard Levy suggests that 'the framers of the Constitution had a genius for studied imprecision or calculated ambiguity' (Levy, 1972, p. 17).

Some of the underlying forces accounting for the exclusion of American women from participating in the rights of citizenship in the New Republic are not too difficult to identify. The Judaic-Christian culture accepted as a centerpiece of faith that the Deity was masculine and thus was naturally referred to as our 'Father'. Organized religion in the colonies failed to permit women to hold important offices as religious leaders; however, male theologians in Europe did 'Saint' selected women after their demise for reported miraculous and extraordinary works. A good many of the colonists accepted literally that man's downfall in the Garden of Eden should be attributed to Eve's weakness and willingness to be tempted by Satan. The notorious hangings in Salem of 'witches' attest to the prevailing consensus that skill in sorcery was primarily restricted to women. Thus, it is perhaps not surprising that all women were excluded from participating as citizens in the New Republic; the Constitution reflected simply the anti-feminist attitudes of men of power and the religious mores of the period.[4] The fact that the First Amendment tackled the issue of neutrality of the government supporting or rejecting organized religion intensifies the conclusion that religious considerations were of utmost importance in the minds of the framers of the Constitution – a moral tide of indifference which ignored the possibility that women could serve in any capacity as legitimate decision makers.[5]

II

Prior to an examination of specific gender/generic references cited in the Constitution, attention is directed to the words 'sex' and 'gender' to identify the property of a noun or pronoun by which the 'sex' of the object may be categorized. Most behavioral scientists consider 'gender' behavior a product of socialization and learning, especially with reference to 'sex roles'. Hence, in their explication, the word 'gender' signifies an achieved status or characteristic rather than an ascribed one. Yet, in analyzing the gender/generic language of the Constitution, we also must realize the fact that written language tends to lag behind contemporary connotations and usages. No doubt, on this point C. K. Ogden and I. A. Richards are correct in observing that 'the power of words is the most conservative force in our lives'

(Ogden and Richards, 1936, p. 25). Certainly this is true of the United States Constitution – a document difficult to change and largely representative of the prevailing beliefs and values of Americans two centuries past.

Of neglected attention but of paramount importance is the fact that the Constitution is a document embodying a traditional use of the English language in which it is ambiguous whether masculine specific terms – such as he, his, him, and himself – are meant to be interpreted generically to refer to 'all human beings' or whether, indeed, such terms are meant to signify only 'males'. Further, and of equal importance, there are *no* parallel feminine gender terms cited in the Constitution, thereby adding to the ambiguities inherent in interpretations of constitutional meanings.

The use of masculine/gender terminology creating such ambiguities is today defined as 'sexist'.[6] Wendy Martyna refers to this practice as the 'He/Man' language and develops a convincing argument for the conscious reduction of this form of sexist linguistics in order to correct the inequalities created by such practices (Martyna, 1980, p. 483). Others refer to the 'category confusion' that necessarily involves women because of such linguistic usages and to the fact that 'language can constrain concept formation' and lead to the conceptualization of women as 'second class citizens' (Kramarse, 1980, p. 58–66).

Let us explore the nature and frequency of the use of masculine generic referents in the United States Constitution as a basis for analyzing sexist language and some of its political consequences inherent in the very establishment of the American political system.

III

A comparative analysis of masculine/generic referents in the United States Constitution is presented in Table 7.1 under eighteen categories. There are some fifty-four masculine citations and 170 references to terminology that may be defined as generic. Equally notable is the complete omission of any specific reference to the female gender.[7]

The most frequently used word to describe an American constituent is a generic one, namely *person*, which appears forty-eight times. Though it would seem incontrovertible that the word 'person' would linguistically signify equality for all so designated, the Constitution itself as well as historical test cases contain remarkable limitations

Table 7.1 Gender/generic terminology usage in the constitution of the United States

Constitution	Masculine gender — He, his, him, himself, male	Generic terminology — Person, their, citizen, they, elector, member, people, them, inhabitant, our, ourselves, sex, we						Adopted
Preamble						1		1787
Article I								
Section 2	1	3	2	1	1	1		"
Section 3	2	2	1	4				"
Section 5	1	1	1					"
Section 6	4 1	1	3	5				"
Section 7	1 3	1	2					"
Section 8			1					"
Section 9		3	1					"
Article II								
Section 1	5 4	8	2	6	2	3*	1	1791
Section 2	4		1					"
Section 3	7							"
Article III								
Section 1			3					"
Section 2		1	1	5				"
Section 3	1		1					"
Article IV								
Section 2	1	2						"
Amendments								
I		2	1	1				1791
II	2	2						"
IV		2	1					"
V								"
VI								"
IX								"
X			2	2				"
XI								1797
XII	3	10	3	1	2	3	2	1804
XIV	3	5	1	2	1	2	3	1868

	1870	1913	1920	1933	1951	1961	1964	1967	1971	
XV								1	1	1
XVII									1	1
XIX									5	5
XX									6	6
XXII			2						9	9
XXIII									15	15
XXIV			2				2 1		18	18
XXV	1 1		2						22	22
XXVI		1	2			2			25	25
	3 5		2						48	48
Totals	28 18	4 1	3			3 9			48	

* Included under this rubric is one (1) 'themselves'.

on the meaning of this term in relation to political rights. Perhaps most notorious is Article I, Section 3 of the Constitution which defines apportionment (in order to determine the number of Representatives and direct taxes for each state) in the following language: 'by adding to the whole number of *free persons*, including those bound to service for a term of years, and excluding Indians not taxed, *three fifths* of all other *persons*' (emphasis added). Here we have the linguistic presentation of slaves as 'fractional persons' who were not citizens. (The interposition of the terms person and citizen is a topic that will be discussed in more detail under the provisions of the Fourteenth Amendment.)

In addition to a constitutional provision counting black people as 'three-fifths of a person' is the astonishing historical fact that women also were not always recognized as fully a 'person'. The state of Virginia's bar admission act specified that 'any "person" who had been licensed to practice in any other state or in the District of Columbia could practice in Virginia'. However, Belva A. Lockwood was denied a license to practice law in Virginia, despite the fact that she had been admitted to the bar of the District of Columbia. 'In this instance, the Supreme Court of Appeals of Virginia decided that "person" meant "male" even though the Court had stated that women were both "persons" and citizens in *Minor*' (Sachs and Wilson, 1978, p. 106). Thus, we see that even the explicitly generic term, 'person', has been used to discriminate against groups in the denial of their political rights. On the other extreme, it is astonishing to realize that the high court has been able to define corporations as *persons* and give birth to the concept of 'artificial persons as distinct from natural persons' (Beth, 1971, p. 173).

The second most frequently used gender/generic term in the Constitution is *he* which occurs twenty-eight times. All but three citations are restricted to the first four Articles of the Constitution. In general, the use of the pronoun 'he' is restricted to members of the Congress and presidential responsibilities, thereby promoting a tendency to perceive the pronoun 'he' as highly associated with executive authority and to a lesser extent with legislative personnel. Here we can see a more explicit problem with the use of language to convey a sense of political equality to women as well as men, particularly in relationship to access to leadership roles. If 'person' was interpreted to mean 'male', how much more inevitable that 'he' should be interpreted to mean 'male', thereby excluding women from even a conceptualization of participation as heads of state.

Citizen is cited twenty-two times and is used five times in Article III, an article dealing largely with controversies between states and citizens. However, it is in the Fourteenth Amendment that the term 'citizen' begins to take on some very important qualitative distinctions of planned discrimination against all women. We find two references to 'male citizens' and one to 'male inhabitant'. In this Amendment there are explicitly identified two types of citizens for the very first time: *full* citizens, as represented by *males* in the population and *non-male citizens*. Under paragraph 1 of this amendment we learn that:

All persons born or naturalized in the United States are *citizens* of the United States and of the State wherein they reside. No State shall make or enforce any law which shall abridge the privileges or immunities of citizens of the United States; nor any State deprive any person of life, liberty, or property, without due process of law; nor deny to any person within its jurisdiction the equal protection of the laws (italics added).

However, under paragraph 2 of the Fourteenth Amendment it is indicated that in participating in the political process of the federal and state governments, the franchise is neither a privilege nor a right for non-male citizens. On the other hand, *male inhabitants* of a state may not be denied the franchise if they meet certain rudimentary qualifications and are not in rebellion or guilty of other crimes. The consequence is that all non-male (i.e. women) citizens are denied the franchise along with male citizens who are known criminals – an extraordinarily disjunctive categorization of half the population that constitutes 'We, the people'.

By injecting the phrase 'male citizens', the writers of the Fourteenth Amendment enfranchised black males and deftly denied suffrage to all American women regardless of race, religion, education, and social class. Many women leaders in the abolition movement were shocked to learn how the Fourteenth Amendment supported black males yet excluded all women from suffrage. These women, many of whom had collected many petitions to enact the Thirteenth Amendment to terminate slavery, became appalled by the turn of events and gathered some 10 000 signatures to a petition to remove the key word *male* from the Fourteenth Amendment (Grimes, 1978, p. 61). The opportunism of northern congressmen is sardonically observed: 'It was one thing for northern male abolitionists to free southern slaves – little would change in their personal lives as a result. It was entirely another matter for them to free their own women' (Sachs and Wilson, 1978, p. 107).[8]

The pronouns *their* and *they* appear twenty-five and eighteen times respectively. All but six citations to the word *their* appear in the first ten Amendments and a majority of the references to the term *they* also appear in these early amendments. A cursory reading of these amendments will disclose that the referents to *their* and *they* (as well as the objective case, *them*) are clearly to masculine intended gender terms, again illustrating implicit sex bias even when technically gender-neutral terms are used.

The term *elector* is cited eighteen times in the Constitution. Article II refers to elector six times concerning the qualifications for voting in a presidential election (which was later superseded by the Twelfth Amendment dealing with the same issue). However, in this Amendment *persons* is cited ten times and *electors* only three times. In both these instances generic language or neutral sexist language prevails.

Member, another generic term, is quoted fifteen times in the Constitution with eight citations found in Article I (which describes the way the two houses of congress may judge the qualifications of their members). The Fourteenth Amendment employs the term *member* three times, and it occurs twice in Article II and the Twelfth Amendment.

Other masculine terms cited in the Constitution have the following frequencies: *his* eighteen times, *him* four times, *male* three times, and *himself* once. The remaining generic terminology is used as follows: *people* nine times (notably in the first ten Amendments), *them* six times, *inhabitant* five times, and a singular use of *we*, *our*, *ourselves*, and *sex*. (We have omitted from categorization all titles of office.)

IV

How does the United States Constitution compare with the constitutions of a number of other countries on matters of generic/gender referents and expressed human rights? It should be appreciated that most of these constitutions are of recent origin and that some of them have been influenced to some extent by idealistic discourse on the American Constitution. There emerges a somewhat mixed achievement in the elimination of gender specific references and in some intances while the intention is clear to avoid gender limitations, there remains the cultural habit of using masculine gender terminology and expecting readers to 'translate' such language to mean generic referents.

The popular slogan 'the rights of man' with its implied generic symbolism is an excellent example of the diffusion of a political ideal from the United States to France and the major role of an enlightened aristocrat, Lafayette, in this process. Peter Buchman observes that during the Summer of 1789 the Constituent assembly 'referred his proposals to its committees, and the Declaration of the Rights of Man and the Citizen that finally passed the assembly on August 27th owed much to Lafayette's initiative' (Buchman, 1977, p. 144).

The latest Constitution of France adopted 28 September 1958 proclaims, 'Its principle is government of the people, by the people and for the people' (Blaustein and Flanz, 1985, p. 4). Another reference to the generic 'People' may be found in the description of sovereignty where it is stated, 'National sovereignty belongs to the people, which shall exercise this sovereignty through its representatives and by the means of referendums' (Blaustein and Flanz, 1985, p. 4). Nevertheless, when we turn to the description of the duties of the President under Title III, Articles V–XVIII, an alarming number of these Articles concerning the President and 'his' subordinates begin with the words 'He shall' (Blaustein and Flanz, 1985, p. 5–10). In retrospect, the French might have avoided 'gender backsliding' by simply using the word 'President'. The fact that such terminology was not used can be seen as related to principles and practices of sex discrimination in French society. For example, as late as the mid-1960s a French husband had the legal right to oppose his wife's independent gainful employment and a French husband had the sole right to be considered head of the household (Davidson, Ginsburg and Kay, 1974, p. 935).

The 'Basic Law' of the Federal Republic of Germany (West Germany) issued December 1974 under Article III states:

1. All persons shall be equal before the law;
2. Men and women shall have equal rights;
3. No one may be prejudiced or favored because of his race, his language, his homeland and origin, his faith, or his religious or political opinions (Blaustein and Flanz, 1974, p. 6).

No doubt, the foregoing statement assures that men and women, among other considerations, have equal rights. Yet, writers of Article III defined all the other aspects of prejudice under the rubric 'his'. Taken out of context, a literalist might be unsure that 'his', is used as a generic pronoun. Certainly the intent of the statement is gender equality. Nevertheless, it does inject, by the use of 'his', an insensitivity to problems inherent in what can be viewed as sexist terminology. Furthermore, as late as the 1970s West German courts developed a 'separate but equal' doctrine in relation to family issues based 'on the assumption that in marriage, the wife's province is the home and the husband's the outside world', thereby reflecting sex discrimination principles endemic to West German culture and to its Constitution as well (Davidson, Ginsberg and Kay, 1974, p. 934).

Sweden adopted in the 1976–77 Ordinary Session of the Riksdag the Basic Principles of the Constitution in Article II: 'Public power shall be exercised with respect for the equality of all human beings and for the freedom and dignity of the individual' (Blaustein and Flanz, 1985, p. 1). However, the Swedish Constitution does use the masculine pronoun 'his' in somewhat the same manner as observed in the West German Constitution, but with an important affirmative action clause in Article XVI: 'No law or other decree may imply the discrimination of any citizen on account of *his* sex, unless the relevant provision forms part of efforts to bring about between men and women or concerns compulsory military service or any corresponding compulsory national service' (Blaustein and Flanz, 1985, p. 14, emphasis added).

Sweden has, among modern nations, one of the highest percentages of women as elected members of its parliament – 29.2 (Blaustein and Flanz, 1985, p. 8). For the most part, the Swedes tend to use the word 'citizen' most often to describe the rights and duties of their inhabitants rather than resorting to personal pronouns.

The Soviet Union promulgated a new constitution on 4 October 1977 during the L. I. Brezhnev period which defines in Chapter 6, Article XXXIV the rights of citizenship in this manner: 'Citizens of the USSR are equal before the law, without distinction of origin, social or property status, race or nationality, sex, education, language, attitude to religion, type or nature of occupation, domicile or other status' (Blaustein and Flanz, 1985, p. 26).

It is indeed difficult to reconcile the expressed constitutional rights of various populations in the USSR with the current antagonism towards several religious minorities. However, a highly centralized one-party government simply does not permit a citizen the right to demand the 'equality' proclaimed in its Constitution. Membership, in fact, in the Communist Party is not open to all citizens of the Soviet Union. Gary Thatcher's recent analysis of the demographic and occupational characteristics of representatives to the 27th Communist Party Congress meeting in Moscow during the last week of February 1986 suggests some of the desparateness inherent in a one-party government:

> First of all, only about 9.5 per cent of the adult population – or 19 million people – are card carrying members of the Communist Party. And it is a rather elite group. Twenty-two per cent of its membership is from the intelligentsia: one out of every two PhDs, two out of every three master's degree holders, and schoolteachers, half the country's writers, and a quarter of its engineers are members.
>
> It's a male-dominated organization. Only one-third of its members are women (Thatcher, 1986, p. 1).

On 3 November 1946 a new Constitution of Japan was completed which incorporated some of the spirit of the United States Constitution, and while abolishing hereditary rule, permitted the Emperor to remain as a symbol of Japanese unity. In Chapter III, Rights and Duties of the People, Article XIV, a very bold statement of equality is incorporated in these words: 'All of the people are equal under the law and there shall be no discrimination in political, economic or social relations because of race, sex, social status or family' (Blaustein and Flanz, 1946, p. 2). The two groups that benefited significantly by these reforms were women and the Eta caste (formerly almost an outcaste segment of the Japanese people).

The Italians in their current Constitution follow the general guidelines concerning 'equality' expressed in the constitutions discussed above. Article III addresses the subject of equality in this manner: 'All citizens are invested with equal social status and are equal before the law, without distinction as to sex, race, language, religion, political opinions and personal or social conditions' (Blaustein and Franz, 1973, p. 1). In addition, Article 51(1) of Italy's 1948 Constitution 'guarantees all citizens of either sex equal right to enter public office' (Davidson, Ginsburg and Kay, 1974, p. 935). However, as late as 1958 the 'Constitutional Court held that it was not unconstitutional to exclude women from the judiciary', though the legislature established by ordinary statute five years later the provision that 'women are eligible for judicial and other public offices' (Davidson, Ginsberg and Kay, 1974, p. 935).

V CONCLUSION

The social movement of several women's groups in the United States has focused considerable attention on women in politics, and, no doubt, some readers may consider this a brand new development. However, women have been 'movers and shakers' in the Greco-Roman myths, the monarchies of France, Great Britain, Spain, Russia, China, and Egypt. Obviously, these women, as leaders, tended to represent a caste of society so selective that gender could not be considered a political handicap. Yet, when the shift in America was made away from monarchism, the emphasis was placed firmly on elected leaders rather than hereditary criteria. In pragmatic terms elections were translated narrowly to mean the election of 'free white men' by other 'free white men'.

Blacks have tried to delete the word 'white' from the Constitution and women have struggled also to remove the word 'man'. The latter case posed special difficulties due to the linguistic ambiguity implied by the word 'man' which can signify 'human beings', thereby including women, or can signify 'males', thereby excluding women. Nevertheless, women have sought to ignore the literalness of the word 'man' and have empowered themselves as candidates for every major office except the presidency.

It is true that some of the more recent national constitutions do acknowledge equal rights for both sexes, yet there remains a significant lag in observing the expressed gender equality in the top rungs of political power. There are, however, a few examples of women holding, or having held key elected positions, of their respective governments: Margaret Thatcher (Great Britain), Indira Ghandi (India), Golda Meier (Israel), and Corazon Aquino (Philippines). Two of the foregoing countries do not have formal written constitutions (Great Britain and Israel). The so-called egalitarian government of the USSR has made only token progress in offering high political positions to its women citizens.[9] While nations have overthrown monarchies and their hereditary rulers (albeit preference always assigned to the first male heir rather than the first born, if female), a tradition of male dominance largely prevails irrespective of emerging gender equality and scientific evidence of symmetry in the distribution of abilities between the sexes.

Bolinger describes the role of language in preserving gender inequalities in political documents and laws, such as constitutions:

> The inertial mass of language is like the inertial mass of society. Women inherit their place as speakers inherit their word. We drag a vast obsolescence behind us even as we have rejected much of it intellectually . . . Roles are made over but stereotypes [expressed in language] remain . . . The gun of sex-biased language may be rusty, but it is there and the greatest danger is unawareness that it is a gun, and is loaded (Bolinger, 1980, pp. 103–104)

The use of language in the United States Constitution offers clear evidence of sex bias at the initiation of this country's political community and throughout most of its political history. Though many are familiar with the racist principle introduced in the Constitution for counting 'persons' (Article I, Section 3), the manifest sexism embodied in the prevailing language of the Constitution has remained relatively unexplored. This study offers a critical assessment of the use of gender/generic terminology in the United States Constitution in order to understand more completely the scope of language-based sex discrimination of women so antithetical to the egalitarian ideals of democratic society.

Notes

1. It is important to remember that the first Equal Rights Amendment was proposed as early as 1923 by Alice Paul (Pole, 1978, p. 319). Thus, efforts beginning in 1972 to pass the ERA are a continuation of a very long struggle – as yet unsuccessful – to obtain gender parity in the language of the United States Constitution.
2. Nevertheless, some confusion developed when rival Queens – for example, Elizabeth and her cousin, Mary Queen of Scots – contested each other for support from their Protestant and Catholic adherents. When Mary went to the block on the charge of treason (though Mary purported correctly that the charge was unfair in as much as she was not a *citizen* of England), there appeared to be a contrived 'sufferance' by her son, James VI of Scotland and I of England that he might now become the 'sole King' (Frazier, 1970, pp. 545–6).
3. See the work by William J. Crotty for an insightful appraisal of the belief

that property was a person's true measure of worth (Crotty, 1977, p. 4–9).

4. Classical democratic theory was predicated upon a conception of an autonomous individual and his property rights. However, with the exception of chattel slaves, married women had the least proprietary rights over themselves compared to any other group. Some argue that this denial to women of the 'right' to their 'own persons' or 'their own property', resulted in women's social and economic dependency upon men and their exclusion from politics (Du Bois, 1978, pp. 44–45). However, not all women suffered from social and economic deprivation, yet political rights were universally denied on the basis of gender.

5. In fact, in the post-Colonial period, public opinion and politicians usually were more sympathetic to the economic demands and rights of women than to the political rights of women. As early as 1839 in tradition bound Mississippi, married women were allowed to have equal property rights compared to men (Pole, 1978, p. 312), and by 1860 as many as fourteen states had passed legislation protecting women's property. The most comprehensive of these was the 1857 legislation in New York granting all the economic demands of feminists while stonewalling on women's right to vote (Du Bois, 1978, pp. 41–2).

6. William F. Buckley, Jr. takes to task the National Council of English Teachers for its attempt to eliminate sexism by quoting the following example: 'Anyone who wants to go to the game should bring *his* money tomorrow' to 'Anyone who wants to go to the game should bring *their* money tomorrow' (Buckley, 1978, p. 582, emphasis added). However, a better construction – certainly emanating from English teachers – might be to substitute a plural word for 'anyone' and simply announce: 'Students who want to go to the game tomorrow should bring their money.'

7. The proposed ERA Amendment should have made explicit *individual* rights rather than 'equal rights' between the two genders. Eventually, language similar to the following example will stand a better chance of being ratified by a sufficient number of states: *Men and Women in the United States are to enjoy equality under the law according to their individual mental abilities and physical capacities.* Hence, with language that places emphasis upon individual differences rather than assumed stereotyped gender differences, the policy of the Secretary of Defense, Caspar W. Weinberger, could not exclude *all* Army women from sixty-one military positions (about one-sixth). He explained his policy in quasi-chauvinistic whispers to President Ronald Reagan: 'There will be no women in combat, and all the criticism was that we are closing off too many jobs that were associated with combat units. And so what we've done is that until there is an actual imminence of war, there will be *women grease monkeys* if they want to and things like that' (*Washington Post*, 5 July 1983, A, 3, emphasis added).

8. Susan B. Anthony felt keenly the betrayal of the writers of the Fourteenth Amendment and stated with mounting vehemence, 'I will cut off this right arm of mine before I will ever work for or demand the ballot for the Negro and not the woman' (Cary and Peratis, 1977, p. 20). The conventional explanation for the exclusion of full citizenship for women

was that northern Republicans felt that to enfranchise a large white population of women would be too risky for them. Additionally, republicans felt that ex-male slaves could be depended upon to remember who their 'friends' had been.

9. In the last 25 years only two women have been appointed to high positions in the Communist Party. The late Yekaterina A. Furtseva, who served in the Politburo from 1956 to 1961 and the recent appointment (6 March 1986) of Aleksandra P. Biryukova, a textile engineer, who will be concerned with consumer goods (*The New York Times*, 7 March 1986, p. 3).

References

BETH, L. (1971) *The Development of the Constitution, 1877–1917* (New York: Harper & Row).

BEARD, C. (1941) *An Economic Interpretation of the Constitution of the United States* (New York: Macmillan).

BLAUSTEIN, Albert P. and FLANZ, Gisbert H. *The Constitutions of the World*, Vols 5, 6, 8, 15 (New York: Oceana Publications).

BOLINGER, D. (1980) *Language: The Loaded Weapon: The Use and Abuse of Language Today* (New York: Longman Group).

BUCKLEY, W. (1978) 'Unsex me now', *National Review*, Vol. XVIII: 582–3.

BUCKMAN, P. (1977) *Lafayette: A Biography* (New York: Paddington Press).

CARY, E. and PERATES, K. W. (1977) *Women and the Law* (Skokie, Ill.: National Textbook).

CROTTY, W. J. (1977) *Political Reform and the American Experiment* (New York: Thomas Y. Crowell).

DAVIDSON, K. M., GINSBURG, R. B. and KAY, H. H. (1974) *Text, Cases and Materials on Sex-Based Discrimination* (St Paul, Minn.: West Publishing).

DU BOIS, E. C. (1978) *Feminism and Suffrage: The Emergence of an Independent Women's Movement in America, 1848–1869* (Ithaca, NY: Cornell University Press).

FRAZIER, A. (1970) *Mary Queen of Scots* (New York: Delacorte Press).

GRIMES, A. (1978) *Democracy and the Amendments to the Constitution* (Lexington, Ma.: Lexington Books).

KRAMARAE, Cheris (1981) *Women and Men Speaking: Framework for Analysis* (Rowley, Mass.: Newburg House).

LEEDHAM, C. (1965) *Our Changing Constitution* (New York: Dodd Mead).

LEVY, L. W. (1972) *Judgments: Essays in American History* (Chicago: Quadrangle Books).

LUNDBERG, F. (1980) *Cracks in the Constitution* (New Jersey: Lyle Stuart).

MARTYNA, W. (1980) 'Beyond the "He/Man" Approach for Nonsexist Language', *Signs: Journal of Women and Society*, 482–93.

OGDEN, D. K. and RICHARDS, I. A. (1936) *The Meaning of Meaning* (New York: Harcourt & Brace).

POLE, J. R. (1978) *The Pursuit of Equality in American History* (Berkeley, Calif.: University of California Press).

SACHS, A. and WILSON, J. H. (1978) *Sexism and the Law* (New York: The Free Press).

THATCHER, G. (1986) 'Gorbachev Should Have Congress Under Control', *Christian Science Monitor*. Syndicated 23 February.

Part III

Explanations of Cross-National Variations

8 Comparative Human Rights: Promise and Practice

Kathleen Pritchard

INTRODUCTION

The comparative study of human rights is a relatively recent academic undertaking. Scholarly efforts in this area have focused on three major research questions. These central themes include: 1) the theoretical question of defining human rights; 2) the methodological issue of measuring human rights; and 3) the explanatory problem of accounting for the variation found in human rights conditions in different nations. While the focus of this chapter is on explanatory conditions, any attempt to wrestle with the third of these themes requires at least a peripheral discussion of the first and second questions.

Defining and Measuring Human Rights

Much of the literature on human rights is characterized by conceptual arguments regarding the 'true' meaning of the term. There does, however, seem to be agreement on the points that the meaning of human rights has changed over time (Donnelly, 1981) and that human rights have emerged prominently on the contemporary scene through the attention accorded them by the United Nations (Forsythe, 1983). The *contemporary* meaning of human rights then, stems from the universalization of rights, defined, through a political process, by international agreements. Specifically, contemporary human rights are defined here as those embodied in the United Nations' Universal Declaration of Human Rights and its subsequent covenants, and include civil, political, and socio-economic rights.

Admittedly, there is something offensive about discussing human rights in terms of statistics and models. Reducing the rights of human beings to numerical rankings, correlations and probabilities undoubtedly masks the meaning both of the enjoyment and violation

139

of human rights. Nevertheless, the field of human rights is characterized by random observations and subjective opinions, and perhaps because the very words 'human rights' provoke such an emotional response, quantification is necessary. Having stipulated a definition of human rights and attempting to move to the explanatory question, it is necessary to select the measures generally accepted as the best available comparative indicators of civil, political and socio-economic rights conditions.

Assessments of political and civil rights are those of Gastil (1978). Data are for 1974 and represent an assessment of the rights of the population as a whole. Although the Gastil data are not without criticism, even the critics view the data as providing adequate quantitative information regarding civil and political rights conditions over a relatively large sample (Dominguez, 1979; McCamant, 1984).

The measure of socio-economic rights comes from Morris' (1979) Physical Quality of Life Index which is based on indicators of literacy, infant mortality and life expectancy. It was developed for the Overseas Development Council and is considered to be a relatively straightforward way to quantify the extent to which the most basic human needs are being fulfilled (Shue, 1980).

For this research, each indicator has been converted to a seven-point scale, with one being the lowest and seven the highest. The population of the study consists of 133 independent nation states. The time period under consideration is generalized to the early 1970s. Interestingly, the correlations among the three types of human rights are positive and statistically significant,[1] indicating substantial relationships among the different types of rights. Nations that score high on civil rights enjoyment are likely to score high on political rights and, to a lesser degree, on socio-economic rights as well.

Having identified the indicators of human rights enjoyment, a seven-point composite index[2] was then calculated by averaging the three summary indicators, giving equal weight to each of them. Equal weighting is conceptually consistent with the stipulated definition of human rights given the United Nations resolution (32/130) which declares that all rights are indivisible and interdependent and that none of them ranks in priority over any others. Beyond conceptual consistency, equal weighting has the advantage of limiting the influence of any one indicator and assuring that no indicator can affect the human rights index by more than seven points.

The median ranking on the human rights index is 3.40. Fifty nations (37.6 per cent) are classified on the lowest end of the human rights scale (1 and 2), while only thirty nations (22.5 per cent) are rated at the highest end of the scale (6 and 7). The overall conclusion that may be drawn from this assessment is that, at the national level, the enjoyment of human rights is quite low, and thus a deserving issue for the international and scholarly concern recently afforded the topic. That there is variation among nations in human rights conditions is certainly not surprising. What is surprising is the lack of empirically verified explanations for this variation. The index of human rights conditions is intended to address this problem by permitting the cross-national exploration of three common explanations.

Common explanatory themes

The following propositions represent three general themes purporting to explain the variation exhibited in human rights conditions in different countries.

1. Human rights must have some *lawful basis* if governments are expected to uphold and respect these rights.
2. Some *mechanism of redress* must be made available by the government if the interference with the enjoyment of rights is experienced.
3. The availability of *economic resources* enhances the government's ability to protect and provide for human rights.

The first proposition is a traditional explanation of human rights offered by many legal scholars and suggests that a necessary condition for the enjoyment of human rights is the government's recognition of, and commitment to, these rights. Accordingly, adherents to this explanation rely heavily on constitutional rights, contending that the basic human rights provisions found in a nation's constitution serve as the starting point from which to assess the official national commitment to their protection (Claude, 1976; Duchacek, 1973). Greater national commitment to human rights, then, is thought to be associated with more extensive enjoyment.

The second proposition, offered by scholars of comparative government, is a structural explanation. The core idea of this tradition is that the form of government decision making affects the enjoyment of human rights. The explanation rests heavily on the tradition of limited government and the assumption that a judicial branch, differentiated from other governmental structures, produces a greater likelihood of justice. Thus the existence and proper functioning of an independent judiciary are frequently cited as essential conditions for the respect and protection of human rights under the law (Blondel, 1969; Cappelletti, 1971; Shapiro, 1981).

The final proposition provides an economic explanation of human rights. Theoretically, this tradition suggests that the greater the government's level of economic resources, the more widespread the enjoyment of human rights (Shue, 1980; Moon and Dixon, 1985). It rests on the assumption that respect for human rights requires a positive obligation on the part of the government, and that a greater availability of resources results in greater respect for human rights.

These explanations of human rights conditions share several characteristics which limit their usefulness. First, the explanations themselves have seldom been tested empirically. The literature in each of the areas is characterized by frequent assertions that these factors – whether legal guarantees, judicial independence or economic resources – have some impact on human rights, and much lamenting that no one has undertaken a study which systematically attempts to test these assertions. Second, the individual explanations are discipline bound; too often they are seen as competing explanations with little consideration given to their possible interdependence.

To begin to address these problems, indicators of the legal, structural and economic explanations were developed[3] and correlated with the assessment of overall human rights conditions. In each case, a statistically significant relationship was found (See Table 8.1), but given the apparent theoretical inadequacy of each individual explanation, the need for an integrative model was suggested. The

Table 8.1 Correlation matrix of variables in the general model

	Constitutional Promise	Judicial Independence	Government Revenue	Human Rights Practice
Constitutional promise	1.000	.087	−.371	−.254
Judicial independence	.087	1.000	.138	.436
Government revenue	−.371	.138	1.000	.617
Human rights practice	−.254	.436	.617	1.000

following is an attempt to include, on one multivariate model, measures from these commonly offered explanations of human rights conditions.

A GENERAL MODEL OF HUMAN RIGHTS CONDITIONS

In a behavioralist's conception of human rights, *acknowledgement* of the right by the duty bearer is a necessary condition for its respect (Danelski, 1966). This implies the need to begin with something that establishes the existence of, or entitlement to, a right – in this case, governmental acknowledgement. From the legal perspective, rights are claims, grounded in titles, recognized as valid by established social rules and principles. The source of the right establishes its domain. Using national constitutions as the source of rights, with the domain being limited to the duty bearer's (government's) obligation toward the right-holders (citizens), the initial bivariate relationship confirmed an obvious suspicion that rights may be widely recognized by governments but ignored in practice. Existence of a right does not imply the enjoyment (the actual practice or attainment) of the right. Other factors intervene. One such intervening force is the government's respect for rights. Governmental *respect* for rights is therefore seen as an intervening force which may be either negative or positive.

From the structural explanation, comes one mechanism of respect often claimed to protect human rights; that is, assuring that courts have sufficient power to intervene when the opposition to the practice of rights is experienced. Exploration of this relationship suggested that providing courts with significant independence does help to secure the practice or attainment of human rights (Pritchard, 1986). But courts, of course, provide only a single method of respect.

Initial findings further suggested that respect depends not only on *mechanisms* of respect but also on the government's *capacity* to provide for human rights. National government financial resources were then considered as a measure of the government's capacity or ability to respect rights, and greater economic resources were found to be associated with greater enjoyment of human rights.

Theoretically then, the model predicts that human rights conditions are a function of acknowledgement, capacity, and mechanisms of redress. Operationally, these were explored in terms of constitutional provision for rights, per capita government revenue and independent courts. To further integrate the theory, however, it is necessary to look not only at the bivariate relationships between an identified explanatory variable and human rights conditions, but also at how these explanatory variables are related to each other.

Several interesting observations can be drawn from the correlation matrix. Regarding the direction of the relationship, with the exception of constitutional rights, the variables are positively related, indicating that an increase in one is associated with an increase in the others. As national government resources increase, we would expect an increase in overall human rights and, to a lesser extent, an increase on the judicial independence index. Constitutional rights are negatively associated with both per capita government revenue and human rights, but positively associated with judicial independence. Additionally, the strength of the relationships suggests that of the three independent variables, national government revenue correlates most highly with the dependent variable, so that economic resources may be thought of as the single most important explanatory variable, followed by judicial independence and finally constitutional commitment.

Still, correlation coefficients are only measures of association and do not imply any sort of causal process. Consequently, path analysis was employed to estimate the magnitude of the linkages between the variables, and then to provide information about the underlying causal process of human rights. Figure 8.1 depicts the hypothesized relationships among the concepts representing the individual explanations. Assumptions of the model are specified below.

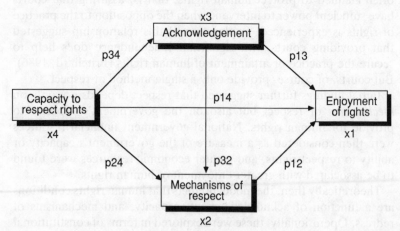

Figure 8.1 Explaining human rights conditions: general four-variable model

First, I assumed that economic resources are exogenous, that is they are not determined by any other variable in the model. In general, I assume that economic variables are causally prior to the legal or structural variables. Economic variables are thought to shape the environment in which nations operate and at a very general level, the ability to promise and protect human rights. Thus, for example, if economic resources have an impact on human rights, it may be a direct one or it may operate by shaping the promise or protection of human rights. The remaining three variables were assumed to be endogenous, or determined in part by at least one other variable model. Second, I assumed that constitutional commitment and judicial independence are influenced by economic resources, and that the degree to which nations afford power to courts depends both on economic resources and constitutional commitment. Finally, I assume that human rights conditions are directly influenced by all three independent variables.

Figure 8.2 shows the results of the initial path analysis for the overall measure of human rights conditions. Economic resources are

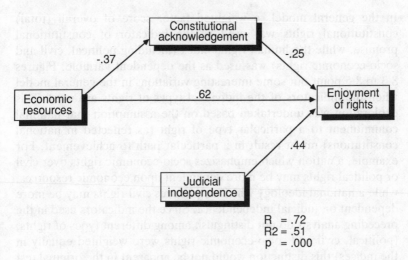

Figure 8.2   Overall human rights

seen to have the greatest direct effect on human rights conditions, followed by the direct effect of judicial independence and the negative impact of the constitutional promise of rights. Additionally, economic resources are found to have an indirect effect on human rights by affecting the constitutional promise of rights, meaning that nations with greater economic resources promise fewer rights, and the lesser the constitutional promise, the greater the actual practice. Two paths, from economic resources to judicial independence and from constitutional rights to judicial independence, are not statistically significant. Substantively, this means that judicial independence is not directly influenced either by economic resources or constitutional commitment, and therefore judicial independence should be considered an exogenous variable.

In the model explaining overall human rights conditions, approximately 51 per cent of the total variance has been accounted for by economic resources, judicial independence and constitutional promise ($R = .72$). These results are actually quite impressive, given the difficulty of substantially increasing the R^2 by including additional variables, and suggest a good causal model.

VARIATIONS ON A THEME

In the general model, a weighted factor score of overall (total) constitutional rights was used as the indicator of constitutional promise, while the human rights index (including political, civil and socio-economic rights) was used as the dependent variable. Figures 8.3 to 8.5 point out some interesting variations in the general model when the indicators of the individual types of rights are used. This exploration was undertaken based on the assumption that national commitment to a particular type of right (as reflected in national constitutions) might result in a particular path to achievement. For example, a nation which emphasizes socio-economic rights over civil or political rights may be more dependent upon economic resources, while a national ideology which emphasizes civil rights may be more dependent on judicial independence. Since the indicators used in the preceding analysis do not distinguish among different types of rights, (political, civil and socio-economic rights were weighted equally in the indices) this distinction would not be apparent in the original test of the model. Substituting indicators of the individual types of rights for the overall indices previously used in the model yields some interesting variations. In fact, as Figure 8.3 to 8.5 reveal, when the impact of the constitutional promise of a particular type of right on the actual practice of that right is examined, three distinct paths to human rights enjoyment emerge.

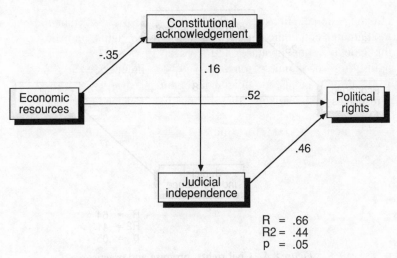

Figure 8.3   Political rights: promise and practice

Figure 8.3 presents an intriguing variation of the original model. Government economic resources have a direct effect on the constitutional promise of political rights, but the effect of constitutional promise on political rights is not statistically significant. In this case, the constitutional promise of political rights has only an indirect impact on the practice of rights by influencing judicial independence. That is, constitutional commitment to political rights leads to increased judicial independence. Thus in the case of political rights, the model more closely resembles that which was originally posited (Figure 8.1).

As Figure 8.4 suggests, the path analysis of civil rights presents less variation from the model used to explain overall human rights conditions. The direct and indirect paths to rights enjoyment remain unchanged. Interestingly, however, the direct impact of judicial independence on civil rights is virtually equal to the impact of economic resources.

Figure 8.5 presents a third variation of the model. Looking at socio-economic rights, the indirect effect of national government resources on the constitutional promise of socio-economic rights, a relationship that has held throughout, is greatly reduced (−.37 in the overall model to −.04 here) and loses statistical significance. Per capita national government revenue has no direct effect on whether constitutions promise or provide for the protection of socio-economic

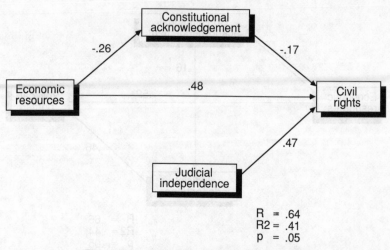

Figure 8.4   Civil rights: promise and practice

rights. In this case, the constitutional promise of socio-economic rights, judicial independence, and national government revenue have only direct effects on the practice of socio-economic rights. Note too that for the first time, the relationship between the constitutional promise of rights and the actual practice of rights is positive, suggesting that as the constitutional promise of socio-economic rights increases, so does the actual enjoyment of socio-economic rights.

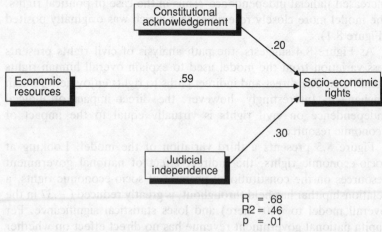

Figure 8.5   Socio-economic rights: promise and practice

CONCLUSION

The preceding analysis calls for two sets of concluding remarks, one which pertains to the need for further research, and a second which relates to the substantive implications of the findings.

Research Conclusions and Recommendations

Particularly in assessments of human rights conditions, statistical evaluations have a tendency to be accepted or rejected on the basis of ideological or political beliefs. The debate regarding the 'appropriate' rights to be included in any such assessment provides an example. Most criticisms of quantitative assessments of human rights conditions are based on the charge that they exclude what others see to be primary rights (e.g. evaluating human rights only in terms of civil or political rights to the exclusion of socio-economic rights, or vice versa). The measure of human rights conditions created for this research attempts to address this problem by building an index based on the recognition of the contemporary definition of human rights. Theoretically, it reflects the universalization of human rights. Its individual indicators were chosen on the basis both of face validity and statistical reliability. This is not to suggest that the measure cannot be improved, only that it represents an improvement over present measures.

Secondly, this research points to the need to cross disciplinary lines and recognize the difficulties inherent in trying to explain complicated phenomena from a single perspective. Integrating the explanations from the legal, structural and economic perspectives provides insights which explain human rights conditions better than any of the individual explanations. It also points to interesting interactive effects among the explanations which would quite possibly be ignored if the research were more strictly discipline bound.

Finally, as in any comparative research on a relatively large sample, deviant cases (nations which do not conform to the specified model) were found.[4] The approach chosen here has the advantage of identifying such cases and indicates that the research could be fruitfully supplemented with comparative case studies. The identified cases, then, suggest appropriate areas of research that could yield some illumination on the general model. Here, more indepth studies of constitutional promise, judicial independence, and government revenue, as well as specific human rights conditions, could be undertaken. Sources which are of little value in large-scale, macro-level research because they are neither quantitative nor comparative could be quite useful in such a comparison and could help to lend a sense of balance and perspective to the statistical analysis presented here.

Substantive Conclusions

One reason for undertaking a study on human rights conditions is to attempt to understand them because in and of themselves they are interesting phenomena. Another, or course, is the belief that efforts to understand human rights conditions can lead to their improvement. Most of the research on human rights implies that belief. What tentative (and cautious) substantive conclusions can be drawn from this effort?

First, is the finding that human rights conditions are skewed toward lower rather than higher enjoyment. Given the recognition of universal human rights it is not particularly comforting to recognize the lack of universal realization. While attention afforded human rights conditions varies with political philosophy, circumstances and administration, this finding suggests the need for continued interest and effort in this area.

Second, human rights conditions were found to vary together. While specific exceptions can be cited, nations which perform well on civil rights tend to score high on political rights, and socio-economic rights as well. Despite differing philosophies, there is no empirical evidence which justifies emphasizing a particular type of right over the others.

Third, performance on human rights conditions tends to be influenced most by national economic resources (per capita government revenue). This applies particularly to socio-economic rights, but is also true in the case of political, and to a lesser extent, civil rights. This finding has implications for government leaders, and policy makers of concerned countries as well as foreign governments and international organizations. Other things being equal, it suggests that increasing national government revenue may go a long way in improving human rights conditions. For nations with little potential for significantly increasing government revenue, this is depressing news. Alternatively, given an awareness of the potential impact of government revenue on human rights conditions, it could be used to inform internal budgeting, foreign assistance and international aid processes and priorities, potentially resulting in improved human rights conditions.

Additionally, it should be noted that the impact of judicial independence on civil rights conditions is almost identical to the influence of economic resources on civil rights. Thus, a particular concern for civil rights conditions might be addressed with efforts to improve the independence of the courts, which, theoretically at least, could be accomplished without increased economic resources. In fact, the findings indicate that judicial independence is not influenced by economic resources, and that it does have a respectable positive influence on all types of human rights conditions. Substantively, this suggests that efforts to influence the independence of the judiciary, such as those undertaken by the Center for the Independence for Judges and Lawyers, and other NGOs, may provide an appropriate mechanism for improving the enjoyment of human rights. While not dependent on economic resources, this strategy does have organizational costs and may require structural changes which may be as difficult to implement. While it is clearly most effective in improving the enjoyment of civil and political rights, increased judicial independence has a positive, if moderate, impact on socio-economic rights as well.

Finally, the constitutional acknowledgement of rights was a factor thought to be necessary for governmental respect and therefore for the enjoyment of human rights. It was found to be influenced by government resources however, substantially indicating that nations with higher government revenue promise fewer rights in their constitutions. And, greater acknowledgement of rights in constitutions was found to result in lower actual enjoyment of rights. Prescriptively, this might argue for a return to national constitutions which follow the traditional model of limited rights, rather than the more extensive lists included in many of today's newer constitutions. Of course, it also indicates that the gap between promise and practice is not to be ignored in attempting to improve human rights conditions. Finally, there is an important difference in the constitutional promise of socio-economic rights and its impact on actual socio-economic rights conditions. Here the relationship is positive and indicates that increased constitutional commitment to this type of rights, in fact, has an effect on their practice.

Notes

1. The correlations between different indicators of human rights are as follows:

	Socio-economic rights	*Civil rights*
Civil rights	.4878	
Political rights	.5473	.8744

2. Prior to constructing the multi-item scale, coefficient alpha were computed as a reliability check. Cronbach's Alpha, (.85) provides good reason to assume that the scale is reliable.

3. Data on *constitutional rights* is from Boli-Bennet (1976). Original data codes all rights found in national constitutions in 1970. These data were then factor analyzed, resulting in three factors: civil, socio-economic, and political rights. The Constitutional Factor Score, used in the general model, is an equally-weighted index of the three types of rights. The measure of *judicial independence* is a Guttman scale which includes the following variables: separation of powers (Banks and Textor, 1968 and Banks, 1970); presence of judicial review (Blondel, 1969); type of judicial review (Kommers, 1970); and effect on judicial review (Kommers, 1970). The measure of *economic resources* is National Government Revenue per capita, from Banks (1976) and Kurian (1976). It was initially compared to the standard economic measure (GNP per capita) and found to be theoretically and statistically superior in explaining human rights conditions. For further discussion of each of these measures, see Pritchard (1986).

4. Nations identified as outliers, at different points in the research (and of course to different degrees and for different reasons) include the following; Libya, Chile, Jamaica, Barbados, Bahamas, Panama, Gambia, Botswana, Burundi, Dominican Republic, Uganda, Switzerland, Spain, Paraguay and Argentina.

References

BANKS, A. (1971) *Cross Polity Time Series Data* (Cambridge, Mass.: MIT Press).

BANKS, A. and TEXTOR, R. (1963) *A Cross Polity Survey* (Cambridge, Mass.: MIT Press).

BLONDEL, J. (1969) *An Introduction to Comparative Government* (New York: Praeger).

BOLI-BENNET, J. (1976) The Expansion of Nation States, 1870–1970. PhD Dissertation, Stanford University.

CAPPELLETTI, M. (1971) *Judicial Review in the Contemporary World* (Indianapolis: Bobbs-Merril).

CLAUDE, R. (1976) *Comparative Human Rights* (Baltimore: Johns Hopkins University Press).

DANELSKI, D. (1966) 'A Behavioral Conception of Human Rights', *Law in Transition Quarterly*, 3: 63–73.

DOMINGUEZ, J. (1979) *Enhancing Global Human Rights* (New York: McGraw-Hill).

DONNELLY, J. (1981) What are Human Rights: An Historical and Conceptual Analysis. PhD Dissertation, Berkeley University.

DUCHACEK, I. (1973) *Power Maps: Comparative Politics of Constitutions* (Santa Barbara, Calif. ABC-Clio).

FORSYTHE, D. (1983) *Human Rights and World Politics* (Lincoln: University of Nebraska Press).

GASTIL, R. (1978) *Freedom in the World: Political Rights and Civil Liberties* (New York: Freedom House).

KOMMERS, D. (1970) Cross National Comparisons of Constitutional Courts: Toward a Theory of Judicial Review. Prepared for the annual meeting of the American Political Science Association.

KURIAN, G. (1979) *Book of World Rankings*. (New York, New York: Facts on File, Inc.).

McCAMANT J. (1984) 'A Critique of Present Measures of Human Rights Development and an Alternative', in V. Nanda and G. Shepherd (eds), *Global Human Rights, Public Policies, Comparative Measures and NGO Strategies* (Boulder, Co.: Westview Press).

MOON, B. and DIXON W. (1985) 'Politics, The State, and Basic Human Needs: A Cross-National Study', *American Journal of Political Science*, 29, 4: 661–694.

MORRIS, M. (1979) *Measuring the Condition of the World's Poor: The Physical Quality of Life Index* (New York: Pergamon Press).

PRITCHARD, K. (1986) Comparative Human Rights: An Integrative Explanation. PhD Dissertation, University of Wisconsin–Milwaukee.

SHAPIRO, M. (1981) *Courts: A Comparative and Political Analysis*. (Chicago: Chicago University Press).

SHUE, H. (1980) *Basic Rights* (Princeton: Princeton University Press).

9 Correlates of Due Process

David Louis Cingranelli and Kevin N. Wright

One widely recognized method of constraining the abuse of coercion by the state is due process, which requires that the government does not deny or remove an individual's property or freedom without showing cause and following proper legal procedures. The strategy of due process is to 'present formidable impediments' to the state's use of force against its citizens (Packer, 1968, p. 163). Due process is the most fundamental right of free people because it is the primary mechanism through which all other individual rights and liberties are protected from encroachment by the government. In a seminal work, Packer (1968) presented two models of the judicial system representing competing value systems. The central value of his 'crime control' model was the repression of criminal conduct. A judicial system incorporating crime control values would operate in a way that would be analogous to an assembly line. The movement from arrest to incarceration would be efficient; though some innocent persons might be punished, few guilty persons would go free. The central value of the 'due process' model was protection of individual rights and liberties from violation by the state. If the crime control model resembled an assembly line, the due process model resembled an obstacle course. Each stage of the process was designed to present formidable impediments against state abuses. A guilty person might be released by a system of justice operating with due process values, but few innocent persons would be punished.

Packer applied the two models to criminal justice practices in the US to identify movement towards one model of values or the other. However, the application of his conceptual framework to cross-national variations is straightforward. Societies fearing that the social order would be disrupted by individuals who abused their rights and liberties would tend to enact laws establishing crime control systems of justice. Societies having greater fear of abuses of state power would tend to establish due process systems.

This study is a comparative analysis of variations in the provision of due process rights across 152 nations in 1980. Though several disagreements remain, a number of international tribunals have agreed upon minimum due process rights which should be respected by every nation. Internationally recognized rights include freedom from violations such as: invasion of the home in order to search for and seize evidence, arbitrary arrest or imprisonment, arbitrary abduction, the use of torture to extract confessions, and denial of a fair trial. Nations adhering to the letter and spirit of such international agreements would have criminal justice systems which, in effect, conformed with Packer's due process model. This report describes variations in due process practices among nations and develops a typology of national systems of justice based upon the extensiveness and consistency of due process practices by governments. This system of justice typology then is utilized to investigate the factors in a nation's historical experience, political system, social system, and economy that affect the type of justice system it has.

ECONOMIC AND CRIMINAL JUSTICE SYSTEMS

Weber (1947) and Durkheim (1958) suggest that legal systems developed to serve the purpose of conflict resolution in society, thus promoting social and political stability. One of the key characteristics of a system of justice conforming to the theoretical conceptions of Weber and Durkheim is that legal safeguards for contract and property rights and for non-economic personal rights such as due process are essential (Schmidhauser, 1982, pp. 38–9). For Roscoe Pound (1942), another principal figure advocating this perspective, the law adjusted and reconciled conflicting interests in society in order to produce consensus and to maintain and ultimately improve the social order. In formulating his theory of the role of the law in society, he looked upon the law as reflecting the needs of a well-ordered society. It not only represented the product of adjusted and reconciled interests; it was a social engineering force towards a better society (Pound, 1942, pp. 98–9).

Critics of this 'conflict resolution' conception have posited an alternative conceptual framework and historical evidence to argue that law often serves as a partisan instrument of the powerful rather than as a neutral instrument for the resolution of conflict (Tigar and Levy, 1977; Galtung, 1971; Quinney, 1969). Proponents of this perspective view society as characterized by diversity, conflict, coercion, and change, rather than by consensus and stability. They view law only as a product of conflicting interests, not as a beneficial force operating outside of particular interests. Perhaps most importantly, the law is not viewed as the product of the interests of all members of society. Rather, it is characterized as 'made by men, particular men representing special interests, who have the power to translate their interests into public policy' (Quinney, 1969, p. 25).

Dependency and world-systems theorists not only accept the above tenets, but posit a relationship between economic systems and the role of law. They emphasize that legal safeguards for property and contract are essential in all systems of justice, but non-economic rights such as due process are expendable when the bourgeoisie has achieved effective control of a nation in order to participate in the world economy. If this conception of the purposes of the law in society is correct, we would expect that due process would be less extensive and less consistently administered in less developed, more dependent, capitalist nations, a thesis which will be examined in this chapter.

LITERATURE REVIEW

The only research which has developed typologies of criminal justice systems based upon empirical research has utilized the case history approach. Substantive changes in the legal system of a nation tend to be explained by the introduction and diffusion of legal concepts and values from Germanic, Roman, and Canon law during historical periods when each was dominant. David and Brierly (1978) argue that, as a result of this process, nations can be categorized as belonging to one of several families of laws (e.g. socialist laws, the Romano-Germanic family of laws, and common law). Critics have argued that the plethora of variables and combinations of variables used to construct the families of law taxonomies results in confusing and contradictory classifications (Krislov and Kvavik, 1984) which may be useless theoretically and descriptively (Friedman, 1969). Furthermore, the proponents of this families of law approach tend to focus on one nation at a time, making cross-national comparisons difficult.

Not only have few empirically based typologies been developed, there has been very little comparative research of any kind regarding due process or other criminal justice practices. Several case studies have described the judicial systems of particular nations. Most of these case studies have been focused upon economically developed countries. Comparisons of criminal justice practices are relatively scarce, and rarely have included more than a handful of countries (e.g. Cappelletti and Garth, 1978; Doleschal, 1977; Stephens, 1976). A very few studies have broadly described cross-national variations in particular criminal justice practices (Cingranelli and Wright, 1985; Wright and Cingranelli, 1985), but even these works did not attempt to identify major dimensions of system differences. In general, previous research has been rich in detail, providing invaluable insights into the administration of justice in other national contexts, but it has not provided a general framework within which individual cases could be located.

A somewhat broader perspective has been provided by Duchacek (1973), who analyzed formal provisions contained within the bills of rights of over 100 national written constitutions. But formal provisions within constitutions and actual practices by governments often diverge. While Duchacek reported that 'All constitutions ban torture, which may or may not result in death' (p. 149), there is no doubt that some governments torture their citizens. Formal constitutional provisions rarely condone due process practices that are condemned in international law. Boli-Bennett (1981) also examined the constitutions of a large number of countries. Among other findings, he reported that, over the period from 1870 to 1970, explicit mentions of due process protections such as trial by jury, reasonable bail, and habeous corpus had increased (p. 179).

One aspect of criminal justice which has been the subject of considerable comparative research by political scientists is judicial decision making. Although most of this research has used the case study approach and has been focused mainly on economically developed countries, there have been similarities in the kinds of research questions which have been raised, making some comparisons of findings possible. Several studies, for example, have examined the relationships between social background characteristics of judges and various attributes of judicial decisions. The principal methods of data collection used in research about courts and judges in other nations has been content analysis of judicial reports (c.f. Schubert and Danelski, 1969) and surveys of judges (c.f. Schubert, 1968). Becker (1970), in an especially ambitious effort, even proposed a rudimentary theory of the interrelations among courts, the judicial structure, judicial processes, and politics that was intended to have cross-national and cross-cultural utility. Though the adjudicative stage might be viewed as the focal point of the judicial system, the analysis which follows will demonstrate that there is as much, if not more, variation among systems of justice at other stages of the judicial process.

There have also been a few comparative studies of human rights practices. All have considered due process to be a fundamental human right and a few have ranked actual national practices (c.f. Cingranelli and Pasquarello, 1985; Schoultz, 1980; Strause and Clause, 1976). But none allow the disaggregation and separate treatment of due process practices from other human rights practices such as freedom of speech, assembly, religion, unionization, and participation in government decision making. And none have measured the practices of more than a small subset of nations.

THE DATA

Information about the criminal justice systems of countries was gathered through a content analysis of the 1981 volume of the Department of State's report on human rights practices (the *Country Reports*). This annual volume contains information about criminal justice and other government practices relevant to human rights in all foreign countries which are members of the United Nations, all countries which are recipients of United States foreign assistance, North Korea, and Taiwan. The US State Department collects information about the human rights practices of other nations through an annual questionnaire sent to US ambassadors, review of reports issued by American intelligence agencies, and review of newspapers and reports issued by other human rights organizations including Amnesty International. Initial drafts of each country's human rights report are prepared by American embassies. The reports are edited by appropriate area and country experts within the State Department in consultation with the embassy and the Bureau of Human Rights. While the State Department reports are not an ideal source of information about due process practices abroad, they are comprehensive both in the number of countries reported upon and in the variety of human rights practices described. They are consistent in format and are widely respected.

Content analysis of the *Country Reports* as a method for measuring US State Department perceptions of human rights and criminal justice practices in other nations has advantages over data collection methods which have been employed in previous studies. Though most previous works have not attempted to rank or otherwise quantify human rights or criminal justice practices, quantification is necessary in order to compare and evaluate the practices of nations. Some scholars have simply located one, two, or a few nations on a criminal justice system continuum on the basis of their own expertise (Ali, 1969), or have relied on self-reporting (Skoler, 1975). The results are often interesting, even compelling, but rarely replicable or generalizable. The *Country Reports* are the only centralized source of detailed information about due process practices throughout the world. The findings reported here in effect summarize the results of the State Department study of such practices in 1980 and should be interpreted accordingly.

A system was classified as dependent if economic processes within the system were contingent upon processes external to it. Of course, all nations are dependent upon others to some degree, especially with respect to raw materials. In general, dependency theorists refer to a country as dependent only if it is less developed and more economically dependent than others. In order to test the hypothesis that greater dependency was related to less extensive due process protections of citizens and less consistent application of due process rules and principles, economically developed nations were excluded from the analysis. Then, each less developed nation's degree of dependence and type of economic system were measured.

In this analysis, we used a simple and intuitively appealing indicator of economic dependence developed by Rosh (1987). His index of dependency is produced by multiplying the percentage of a country's exports concentrated in its primary commodity by the percentage of its exports that is accounted for by trade with its most important trading partner. Theoretically, the index suggests that the degree of dependence increases geometrically as both concentration in the production of a particular commodity and reliance upon a particular trading partner increase. Rosh computed his index using information describing each nation's export commodity concentration and trading partner concentration in 1975. Therefore, in the analysis which follows, degree of economic dependency in 1975 will be related to criminal justice practices in 1980.

Data concerning economic policies and the structure of each nation's industrial sector were gathered by Gastil (1980) and used to categorize nations along an economic spectrum ranging from socialist to capitalist. Gastil's measure was very strongly correlated ($r = .82$)

with a similar indicator of economic orientation as formulated by Kurian (1982). As such, it serves as a solid foundation for relating the extensiveness of due process rules and the consistency of their administration to the types of economic systems found in Third World nations. Gastil's eight categories were collapsed into four classifications in order to display the underlying patterns in the data better. Third World nations were designated as 'capitalist' if they had a market based industrial sector in which the private sector predominated. 'Socialist' nations were those which had nationalized or were striving to nationalize the entire industrial sector. Moreover, the central government in such nations tended to claim jurisdiction over the productive capacity of land. Third World nations, falling between socialist and capitalist classifications often had nationalized major industries but had retained free market activity. These were broken into two groups. 'Capitalist–socialist' nations included those that provided social services on a large scale through government institutions such that private control of property was largely sacrificed. 'Capitalist–statist' nations were characterized by a very large public sector spearheaded by government enterprise.

THE TYPOLOGY

Extensiveness

Since there is some disagreement over what due process requires and over what constitutes a denial of a fundamental due process right, some preliminary definitions are useful. The system of justice (or judicial system) consists of a series of interactions between accusers and the accused beginning at the point at which an individual is suspected of illegal behavior and ending with release or incarceration. Due process protections are necessary at each stage. In general, protections during the early stages are necessary if the protections during later stages are to be considered meaningful. If a government allows evidence to be fabricated or confessions to be extracted through torture, for example, it would be difficult for that same government to conduct a 'fair trial'. In this analysis we examined five justice system attributes related to the extensiveness of due process: pre-trial guarantees against unreasonable searches, arbitrary arrest or imprisonment, arbitrary abduction, and torture. We also evaluated the fairness of trials themselves.

A government was classified as safeguarding citizens and their homes from unreasonable searches and seizures of evidence if it required that warrants be issued before searches took place. Since every government has recognized that, under some circumstances, the purpose of the search would be defeated by the delay in obtaining the warrant, governments were classified as respecting this right if searches with warrants were the rule followed rather than the exception. Arrest and imprisonment were classified as arbitrary if: the individual was not informed of charges against him; release on bail was not allowed; or if there was a usual practice of pretrial detention (arresting and detaining individuals without making formal charges and without the intention of holding a trial). Arbitrary abductions or disappearances occured when a government had a policy of kidnapping its citizens, depriving them of all rights and liberties from the point of abduction onward, and failing to notify the public that arrests and imprisonments had occurred. Abduction is, in one sense, the most extreme form of arbitrary arrest and imprisonment. Torture refers to the practice by some governments of inflicting pain on individuals accused or convicted of criminal behavior in order to gain information, force confessions, punish, intimidate, or terrorize. Though it is treated as a pre-trial practice here, it may occur before or after trial.

Governments were classified as violating the right to a fair trial if they did not allow the accused to hire his own lawyer or if the judges were not impartial and independent of the regime in power. There are, of course, many other due process rights that might be viewed as necessary conditions for a fair trial such as adequate preparation time before trial, the right to a public defender, and the presumption of innocence until proven guilty. These rights were rarely mentioned in the *Country Reports*, so they could not be considered in this analysis.

The most common violation was unreasonable searches of homes and property. Nearly one-half of the nations in our sample violated this right. The next most commonly violated right was the protection against arbitrary arrest and imprisonment, violated by approximately one-third of the nations. As noted above, violations of pre-trial rights are especially detrimental to due process, since unjust acts by the state at the pretrial stage are difficult to correct later. Only about one-fourth of the nations in our sample were classified as having unfair trials. Nations which provided any one of the due process protections examined were also likely to provide the others. The correlations among the due process protections were positive and significant at the .05 level. Though there were positive relationships among the five due process rights examined, few of the relationships were strong, indicating that few of the nations in our sample provided all of the due process rights to their citizens.

Nations were categorized as offering 'very extensive' due process protections to citizens if respect for at least four of the five due process procedures were affirmed in written constitutions (if these existed), were reaffirmed in statutory laws, and in customary judicial and police practices. Nations in the second category, providing 'extensive' protections to citizens, offered due process protections to citizens in theory, but because of various obstacles, struggled to offer those protections in practice. Some common obstacles mentioned in the *Country Reports* were lack of a legal tradition supporting due process, poor training of criminal justice personnel, and too few lawyers. Thirty nations, categorized as offering 'moderate' due process protections, established extensive rights for citizens in theory and respected those rights in practice except for those accused of anti-activities. Finally, due process rights were classified as 'not provided' if the government was classified as offering three or fewer of the due process rights examined in this analysis, thus apparently subordinating individual rights and liberties in the criminal justice system completely or nearly completely to the interest of the state. Fifty-four, or more than one-third of the nations, were classified in the 'not provided' category.

Consistency

Building an extensive set of due process rules and principles to guide decisions in individual cases usually leads to improvement in the quality of justice provided to individuals by their governments. But, in many nations, for a wide variety of reasons, the rules and principles are not followed consistently. In the US, this problem of inconsistency is usually attributed to discretion on the part of those who administer the system of justice (Davis, 1971). Though the extensiveness of due process protections offered by nations and the consistency of the application of those protections were positively correlated among the nations in our sample, it was possible for a nation to rank high on one of these but low on the other.

In classifying nations as consistent or inconsistent in the implementation of due protections, we evaluated the consistency of rule application and principle adherence among groups of citizens, and classes of offenders over time. For many nations, the *Country Reports* contained some mention of allegations that one or more due process rights had been violated in specific cases. It is virtually impossible for an observer unfamiliar with all the facts in such cases to judge the accuracy of the allegations. Therefore, a nation was not classified as inconsistent in the application of due process protections if only a few allegations had been reported or if the *Country Reports* indicated that the government was conducting a good faith investigation, with the intention of remedying any wrongdoings, if any were found. Similarly, suspensions of due process occurred in several nations in 1980 because of declarations of national emergencies. Only in those cases where suspensions of due process protections lasted longer than one month out of the year, were nations classified as inconsistent in the administration of due process.

In general, a nation which was classified as 'consistent' in the implementation of its criminal justice constitutional protections and statutory laws followed closely established legal traditions and where departures from those established traditions by those who administer the laws of the land were punished whenever possible by government leaders (based upon reported incidences during calendar year 1980). Only sixty-four, or about 42 per cent of the nations in our sample were classified as 'consistent' in the administration of their criminal justice laws. The remaining nations were classified as 'inconsistent' because constitutional provisions and statutory laws were routinely violated. This category includes those nations where government leaders pay lip service to formal rules and principles, but make little effort to control arbitrary implementation.

On the basis of the distinctions we have proposed among nations which offer their citizens relatively extensive or few due process protections and the distinction between consistent and inconsistent administration explained above, we propose at least eight classifications of national systems of justice. There was a positive relationship between the extensiveness of due process protections and the consistency of their application ($r = .42$). Table 9.1 displays the names of the countries placed into each category of the typology. This classification is based upon national practices during calendar year 1980, and undoubtedly some changes in classifications would be made if we were to re-classify on the basis of practices during the current calendar year. However, we would be surprised if that re-classification were to result in major changes in the classifications of more than 10

Table 9.1 A typology of criminal justice systems

The implementation of the law is:	Due process protections are:			
	Very extensive	**Extensive**	**Moderate**	**Not provided**
Consistent	Australia, Austria, Barbados, Belgium, Canada, Costa Rica, Cyprus, Denmark, Dominica, Finland, France, Gambia, German Federal Republic, Greece, Iceland, Israel, Italy, Japan, Luxembourg, Malta, Mauritius, Mongolia, Netherlands, New Zealand, Papua New Guinea, Saint Lucia, Senegal, Solomon Islands, Norway, Sweden, Switzerland, Egypt, Ireland, Fiji, Western Samoa	Bhutan, Botswana, Central African Empire, Sri Lanka, Equatorial Guinea, Maldive Islands, Saudi Arabia, Tunisia	Bahrain, Cape Verde Islands, Guinea-Bissau, Ivory Coast, Jordan, Kuwait, Malaysia, Bangladesh, Qator, Sao Tome and Principe, Seychelles, Sierra Leone, Singapore, Swaziland, Zimbabwe Rhodesia, USSR	Kenya, Lesotho, Malawi, Niger, Sudan
Inconsistent	Hungary, Bahamas, Dominican Republic, Jamaica, Portugal, Spain, Trinidad/Tobago, United Kingdom	Brazil, Zaire, Ecuador, Gabon, Ghana, Honduras, Lebanon, Mexico, Morocco, Nigeria, Oman, Panama, Peru, Rwanda, United Arab Emirates, Venezuela, Zambia	Algeria, Taiwan, Colombia, India, Republic of Korea, Nepal, Nicaragua, Yemen PDR, Surinam, Tanzania, Thailand, Turkey, Yemen Arab Republic, Yugoslavia	Afghanistan, Albania, Angola, Argentina, Bolivia, Burma, Burundi, Kampuchea, Cameroun, Chad, Chile, China, Comoro Islands, Congo Republic, Cuba, Czechoslovakia, Benin, Djibouti, El Salvador, Ethiopia, German Democratic Republic, Grenada, Guatemala, Guinea, Guyana, Haiti, Indonesia, Iraq, Korean People's Republic, Laos, Liberia, Libya, Madagascar, Mali, Mozambique, Pakistan, Paraguay, Philippines, Poland, Romania, Somali Republic, South Africa, Syria, Togo, Uganda, Upper Volta, Uruguay, Vietnam

per cent of the nations in our sample. A 'major change', in our view would be a movement from 'consistent' to 'inconsistent' in the implementation of laws (or a movement in the opposite direction) or a movement of more than one category on the extensiveness dimension.

Kenya and four other African nations were classified as not providing due process protections yet consistently implementing their laws. All of the nations in this category have adopted some constitutional provisions and some statutory safeguards against violations of due process in their criminal justice systems. However, each has also adopted formal provisions which supercede most or all of the apparent safeguards. For example, Kenya revised its omnibus Public Security Act in 1978. The *Country Reports* suggest that 'in practice the Act supercedes constitutional safeguards, since it empowers the state to undertake actions in a wide range of circumstances to control the activities of individuals and groups normally regarded as lawful, without recourse to the judiciary or any other authority' (1981, p. 129).

Classification of the criminal justice practices of some nations presented special problems; Israel was one of these. Criminal justice practices in Israel are described by the report as differing depending upon whether the practices occur in Israel or in the Arab territories Israel has occupied since the 1967 war. Within Israel, due process protections are very extensive and consistently implemented. Within the occupied territories, Israelis receive the same protections as other citizens, but Arabs sometimes receive worse treatment. Furthermore, it is not clear whether Arabs in the occupied territories are considered or even wish to be citizens of Israel. The United Nations holds that the Fourth Geneva Convention concerning the protection of civilian populations under military occupation applies to Israel's governance of the occupied territories. Israel declares that it voluntarily observes most of the Fourth Convention's provisions, but that it does not accept that these territories are within the purview of the convention (*Country Reports*, 1981, p. 1001). Our classification of the criminal justice system of Israel and of other nations which might be viewed as governing occupied territories (e.g. the USSR in Afghanistan) ignores the practices of a government beyond its internationally recognized national borders.

On the basis of this decision, the United Kingdom, which played a leading role in the development of due process principles and in the application of those principles, was classified as inconsistent in the application of its laws because of the practices of its security forces in Northern Ireland. Northern Ireland is recognized in international law as an integral part of the United Kingdom, not as an occupied territory.

The Union of Soviet Socialist Republics, according to the *Country Reports*, is an example of a nation which formally provides extensive due process safeguards to all citizens except those accused of anti-state activities. The Soviet Union is described as having formal provisions which made it difficult for some classes of offenders to oppose the overwhelming coercive power of the state. For example, defendants in political cases in the Soviet Union had the right to a 'fair trial', but the impartiality and independence of judges in 'political' cases was questionable. In addition, though defendants in such cases were allowed to choose their own legal counsel, they were forced to choose among those given a special government clearance for 'secret' matters (*Country Reports*, 1981, pp. 894–908).

Although it is true that many of the United States' adversaries do not fare well in the *Country Reports*, nations which are friendly with the US and/or important to US foreign policy do not receive 'whitewashed' descriptions either. Criminal justice practices in China, El Salvador, the Korean People's Republic, the Phillipines (under Marcos), and South Africa are described as inconsistent and lacking in due process. The accounts of abysmal practices in these nations are evidence that the *Country Reports* are relatively objective in their descriptions of human rights practices abroad.

DEPENDENCY, CAPITALISM AND CRIMINAL JUSTICE PRACTICES

Table 9.2 displays the relationship between the degree of economic dependency of less developed countries and the extensiveness of due process protections provided citizens and the consistency of the implementation of those protections. Although 119 of the nations in our sample were classified as 'less developed', Table 9.2 summarizes the relationship among those seventy-three nations for which a dependency index had been constructed by Rosh (1987). Less developed nations were found to provide less extensive protections and to provide protections less consistently than others. Among less developed nations, there was no statistically significant relationship between the degree of economic dependency of a country and either the extensiveness of due process protections or the consistency of implementation of those protections.

The relationship between the type of economic orientation and criminal justice practices among third world nations is presented in Table 9.3. While dependency theory led us to hypothesize that more capitalist nations would offer less extensive due process protections to their citizens than socialist nations, the opposite pattern was found. None of the eighteen nations classified by Gastil as socialist were found to have extensive or very extensive due process protections. Forty-six per cent of the fifty nations classified as capitalist provided extensive or very extensive due process protections. Within each economic system category, however, a majority of nations did not provide extensive protections of their citizens. A similar relationship between type of economic system and the consistency of criminal justice rule implementation was found and also is displayed in Table 9.3. Again, a majority of nations within each economic category inconsistently applied criminal justice rules and principles, with capitalist nations performing slightly better than the other.

CONCLUSIONS

The purpose of this research was not to rank national systems of justice from best to worst, but rather to identify meaningful differences among them. The first step in scientific inquiry into cross-national variations in justice systems is to describe and measure important variations. Relying upon information contained in the *Country Reports* for calendar year 1980, we have done that. Comparative policy analysis requires that the units of analysis – in this case nations – be measured by some common standard. Such efforts are often fraught with the dangers of ethnocentrism. We chose to measure the 'extensiveness of due process protections' and the 'consistency of the implementation of criminal justice laws' partly because Packer (1968) and Davis (1971, 1976) have presented compelling arguments suggesting that these two attributes of criminal justice systems are intimately related to the quality of criminal justice and partly because these two standards appear to be acceptable cross-culturally. Most nations have signed international agreements proclaiming that all defendants in criminal cases have fundamental due process rights such as the right to a fair trial. Since several nations have philosophically endorsed and instituted *sharia*, or Islamic law, which punishes theft

Table 9.2 Relationship between degree of economic dependency and the extensiveness and consistency of due process among less developed nations (N = 73)

Degree of dependency	Due process protections are:					
	Not provided/moderate	Extensive/very extensive	Row % row (N)	Inconsistently administered	Consistently administered	Row % row (N)
Very low	83.3 (15)	16.7 (3)	24.7 (18)	83.3 (15)	16.7 (3)	24.7 (18)
Low	63.1 (12)	36.9 (7)	26.0 (19)	63.2 (12)	36.8 (7)	26.0 (19)
High	66.6 (12)	33.4 (6)	24.7 (18)	83.3 (15)	16.7 (3)	24.7 (18)
Very high	50.0 (9)	50.0 (9)	24.7 (18)	77.8 (14)	22.2 (4)	24.7 (18)
Col 90 Col (N)	65.0 (48)	35.0 (25)	100.0 (73)	76.7 (56)	23.3 (17)	100.0 (73)

Somer's D = .12
p = .24

Somer's D = −.02
p = .42

Table 9.3 Relationship between type of economic system and extensiveness and consistency of due process among less developed nations (N = 119)

Economic system	Due process protections are:					
	Not provided/ moderate	Extensive/ very extensive	Row % row (N)	Inconsistently administered	Consistently administered	Row % row (N)
Socialist	100.0 (18)	0.0 (0)	15.1 (18)	83.3 (15)	16.7 (3)	15.1 (18)
Capitalist– socialist	66.7 (16)	23.3 (8)	20.2 (24)	75.0 (18)	25.0 (6)	20.2 (24)
Capitalist– statist	55.6 (15)	44.4 (12)	22.7 (27)	66.7 (18)	33.3 (9)	22.7 (27)
Capitalist	54.0 (27)	46.0 (23)	42.0 (50)	52.0 (26)	48.0 (24)	42.0 (50)
Col 90 Col (N)	63.9 (76)	36.1 (43)	100.0 (119)	64.7 (77)	35.3 (42)	100.0 (119)
			Somer's D = .27 p = .01			Somer's D = .28 p = .05

with amputation, a classification of nations on the basis of the harshness of punishments, for example, would be more ethnocentric.

When thinking about national systems of justice or, in fact, the availability of any human right within a nation state, it is useful to distinguish between symbolic statements, the intents of regimes in power, and the ability of governments to translate policy intent into action. At the symbolic level, due process rights are guaranteed in the vast majority of national constitutions. However, our analysis indicated that fewer than one-half of the national governments in the world have made commitments to provide extensive due process protections to citizens, and only about one-half of those which have made the commitment have been able to deliver those protections on a consistent basis.

While dependency theory led us to expect that dependent and capitalist nations in the Third World would place less emphasis on the rights of the individual, the evidence did not support those expectations. Our findings did show that poorer nations tended to have governments which provided fewer due process rights to their citizens and administered the protections which did exist more inconsistently than richer nations. This evidence alone does not provide support for the dependency or world-systems conception of the organization and purposes of criminal justice systems unless one views all less developed nations as economically dependent. More likely, richer nations have more lawyers, better educated police, judges, prosecutors, and correctional personal, and are, therefore, better able to translate policy intent into action.

References

ALI, B. (1969) 'Treatment of Prisoners in Nine Nations: A Pilot Study on Standard Minimum Rules', *Criminologica*, 7: 2–18.

BECKER, T. L. (1970) *Comparative Judicial Politics* (Chicago, Ill.: Rand McNally).

BOLI-BENNETT, J. (1981) 'Human Rights or State Expansion: Cross-National Definitions of Constitutional Rights, 1870–1970', in Ved P. Nanda, James R. Scarrett and George W. Shepherd, Jr. (eds), *Global Human Rights: Public Policies, Comparative Measures, and NGO Strategies*, pp. 289–304 (Boulder, Co.: Westview Press).

CAPPELLETTI, M. and GARTH, B. (1978) *Access to Justice: A World Survey* (Milan, Italy: Sijthoff and Noordhoff Publishing Company).

CINGRANELLI, D. L. and WRIGHT, K. N. (1985) 'A Comparison of

National Criminal Justice Practices', *Journal of Crime and Justice*, 8: 93–114.

CINGRANELLI, D. L. and PASQUARELLO, T. N. (1985) 'Human Rights Practices and the Distribution of US Foreign Aid Among Latin American Countries', *The American Journal of Political Science*, 29: 539–63.

DAVID, R. and BRIERLY, J. E. C. (1978) *Major Legal Systems in the World Today: An Introduction to the Comparative Study of Law* (London: Stevens and Sons).

DAVIS, K. C. (1971) *Discretionary Justice: A Preliminary Inquiry* (Urbana, Ill.: University of Illinois Press).

DAVIS, K. C. (1976) *Discretionary Justice in Europe and America* (Urbana, Ill.: University of Illinois Press).

DOLESCHAL, E. (1977) 'Race and Length of Imprisonment: How Does the US Compare with the Netherlands, Denmark and Sweden', *Crime and Delinquency*, 23: 51–6.

DUCHACEK, I. D. (1973) *Rights and Liberties in the World Today* (Santa Barbara, Calif.: ABC-Clio).

DURKHEIM, E. (1958) *Professional Ethics and Civic Morals* (Glencoe: The Free Press).

FRIEDMAN, L. M. (1969) 'Legal Cultures and Social Development', *Law and Society Review*, 4, 1: 29–44.

GALTUNG, J. (1971) 'A Structural Theory of Imperialism', *Journal of Peace Research*, 8: 81–113.

GASTIL, R. (1980) 'The Comparative Survey of Freedom', *Freedom at Issue*, 54: 3–14.

KRISLOV, S. and KVAVIK, R. B. (1984) 'Political Development and Emergent Theories of Legal Evolution'. Paper presented at the 1984 Annual Meeting of the American Political Science Association.

KURIAN, G. (1982) *Book of World Rankings* (New York, NY: Facts on File).

PACKER, H. (1968) *Limits of the Criminal Sanction* (Stanford, Calif.: Stanford University Press).

POUND, R. (1942) *Social Control Through Law* (New Haven, Conn.: Yale University Press).

QUINNEY, R. (1969) *Crime and Justice in Society* (Boston, Mass.: Little, Brown).

ROSH, B. (1987) 'Ethnic Cleavage as a Component of Global Militarization', *Journal of Peace Research*, 24, 1: 21–30.

SCHMIDHAUSER, J. R. (1982) 'The Circulation of Judicial Elites: A Comparative and Longitudinal Perspective', in Moshe M. Czudnowski (ed.), *Does Who Governs Matter?* (De Kalb, Ill.: Northern Illinois University Press).

SCHOULTZ, L. (1980) 'U.S. Foreign Policy and Human Rights', *Comparative Politics*, 13: 149–70.

SCHUBERT, G. (1968) 'Ideological Distance: A Smallest Space Analysis Across Three Cultures', *Comparative Political Studies*, 1: 319–50.

SCHUBERT, G. and DANELSKI, D. J. (1969) *Comparative Judicial Behavior* (New York: Oxford University Press).

SKOLER, D. L. (1975) *World Implementation of the United Nations Standard*

Minimum Rules for Treatment of Prisoners (Washington, DC: American Bar Association Commission on Correctional Facilities and Services).

STEPHENS, O. H. (1976) 'Equal Justice and Counsel Rights in the United States and Canada', in Richard P. Claude (ed.) *Comparative Human Rights*, pp. 161–83 (Baltimore, Md.: Johns Hopkins University Press).

STRAUSE, J. C. and CLAUDE, R. P. (1976) 'Empirical Comparative Rights Research: Some Preliminary Tests of Development Hypotheses', in Richard P. Claude (ed.), *Comparative Human Rights* (Baltimore, Md.: Johns Hopkins University Press).

TIGAR, M. E. and LEVY, M. R. (1977) *Law and the Rise of Capitalism* (New York: Monthly Review Press).

US DEPARTMENT OF STATE (1981) *Country Reports on Human Rights Practices* (Washington, DC: US Government Printing Office).

WEBER, M. (1947) *The Theory of Social and Economic Organization* (Glencoe: The Free Press).

WRIGHT, K. N. and CINGRANELLI, D. L. (1985) 'Inhumane, Cruel, and Degrading Treatment of Criminal Prisoners Throughout the World', *Justice Quarterly*, 2, 3: 345–62.

10 Democracy and Economic Human Rights in the Third World

Nancy Spalding

INTRODUCTION

The question, 'does politics matter?' has been the focus of comparative policy analysis since Dawson and Robinson wrote their iconoclastic piece in 1964. To address the question, more complex measures of political and economic variables have been developed; the subject area has also expanded, from the north American states, to western Europe, and most recently throughout the world, touching on the problems of newly independent states. Within the context of these developing societies, the question is particularly important. To what extent does the political system of a country, aside from the economic structures and resources, have an impact on the provision and protection of economic human rights, or alternatively, 'basic needs'? This question, significant to students of basic needs and human rights, as well as comparative politics and policy analysis, will be addressed below.

HUMAN RIGHTS

Historically, human rights as we think of them have only been a social concern for a few hundred years.[1] As both Polanyi and Scott have demonstrated, in entirely different contexts, societies have until recently survived by taking care of their members, in reciprocal sharing arrangements.[2] More recently however as the market has replaced older forms of organization, older motivations, and as the world has become more interdependent, communities are no longer able to exist independent of the larger world, and the basic reciprocity and redistributive systems have been replaced or superseded or undermined (Gilpin, 1977).

In a world which refuses to care for its members, and which is built around individual rather than communal principles or organizations, the question of 'rights' arises. A right is a power or a privilege, belonging to a person by law or by nature. As was argued in the *Declaration of Independence* of the United States of America, 'all men . . . are endowed by their creator with certain inalienable rights; that among these rights are life, liberty, and the pursuit of happiness'. This implies that these rights are inherent, or perhaps intuitive (Renteln, 1987, p. 4). These general civil rights, and the more specific formulations that stem from them, can be seen as rights to 'benign neglect' on the part of the government, and are central to the Western Liberal political tradition. That is, they provide freedom for the individual, and do not prevent him or her from acting in self-interest. These freedoms and rights are vital. Confessions extracted by torture, arbitrary arrest and imprisonment, and restrictions on speech and worship are fundamentally derogations of the ability to pursue life, liberty and happiness, however they may be defined.

To the basis of civil rights were added rights to participate in one's society, the rights of self-determination or self-government. These 'political' rights included representation, expanded suffrage, and the right to participate in a wide range of political activities, especially political parties. They were instituted following the period of rapid industrialization, and the expansion of the economic power (and therefore effective demands) of the middle and working classes.

Political rights expanded the 'relevant' population of societies while severe economic hardships prevailed, especially those which resulted from rapid industrialization. The effective demands on systems then began to include what can be called economic or social rights, which include subsistence, health care and education.[3] The domestic process of increasing the level of effective demand in the Western industrialized market economies, which followed logical steps, was not followed around the world. This 'logical process' included increasing economic productivity, in addition to the increasing economic (and later political) power of the newer economic actors, accompanied by social and political stability. The political structures were able to handle the increasing demands upon them, in part because the demands were increasing slowly enough that political capacity could keep up. After the Second World War, there was an explosion in the number of independent states. The national liberation movements which had won independence for many of the states, and the new governments which were created, were often unable to deal with issues of civil and political rights immediately, in part due to problems of unrest and social instability (see especially Huntington and Nelson, 1976). However, an immediate and unavoidable problem for these states was poverty, along with the critical need for rapid economic growth.

With this shift has come an international concern, as expressed in the United Nations' 'Universal Declaration of Human Rights' (1948), for the well-being of the poorest people in the world (see especially Articles 23, 35). The concern can be attributed to humanitarian motives, but also to the number and growing political influence of the poor states in the world system. Increasingly, economic human rights are becoming a concern and a source of problems and dissent, both as a domestic political issue in many countries, and as an international political and financial issue.

The concept of economic human rights itself is subsumed in a far-ranging body of human rights, the basic premise of which is that there are some rights inherent in human beings *qua* human beings, and that these rights should be protected (Spalding, 1987, p. 18). Economic human rights include the right to at least some minimal level of subsistence (Shue, 1980; Donnelly, 1985; Drost, 1951). These rights are justified on the ground that they are *basic*, or necessary for the enjoyment of other rights. Clearly, if one is starving, or ill with no medical attention possible, one is not actively enjoying freedom of speech or the secret ballot. Of course, if human beings have a right to something, an obligation on the part of others (usually represented by the state) either to safeguard actively the rights at issue, or alternatively, to refrain from interfering with their exercise, is generally assumed. Once economic and social rights are included in the accepted pantheon of human rights which are the appropriate subject of social policy, the implications for policy makers of their inclusion are problematic. As Drost (1951) stated, 'Human rights form an intrinsic part of the province of law but they require a favorable political, economic and social climate if they are to be consummated.'

To give a 'human right' the status of law is to require social and governmental action, which may not be quickly forthcoming. A variety of political problems accompanies the protection of economic and social rights. The issues raised include the definition and measurement of economic and social rights (or alternatively, level of well-being or standard of living), and the conception, passage, implementation, funding, and evaluation of philosophically supportable and economically feasible programs aimed at improving conditions. Even prior to these very real obstacles to formulating and implementing policies which will raise standards of living, are the problems of political will and access to resources. Therefore, however high the professed priority given to economic human rights, little can be done in their support without the financial and institutional prerequisites of social action. To state simply that economic human rights are important, whether you are a head of state, an IGO, or an aid agency, is not to bring improvements about. It must also be noted that, even in the industrialized West, the full range of rights suggested by the UN's 'Declaration' is not protected.

The issue of safeguarding of rights, which is an obligation that the state holds with regard to its members, brings me to the question which motivated this study. To what extent does the political system of a country, aside from the economic structures and resources, have an impact on the provision and protection of economic human rights, or alternatively, basic needs? I will address this question by first discussing the operational meaning of economic and social rights, and their measurement, as well as the relation of democracy to economic human rights. I will then present the research design of the study. The findings and analysis will follow.

Economic Human Rights as the Provision of Basic Needs

Marshall (1964) has suggested that social and economic rights include the rights to education, employment, subsistence and medical care. Economic human rights can be defined as a minimal level of economic welfare and subsistence, as well as the opportunity to participate in society. This concept is similar to the central issue in the basic needs-oriented literature, which focuses on access to the goods and services which are essential to human life. These needs include subsistence (potentially including food, shelter, clothing), health care, and primary education. These goods and services make possible life, health, and participation in a changing society, and they may be considered the minimum requirements of human existence.

Satisfaction of basic human needs, or economic human rights, cannot be measured by policy expenditures, or even access to goods and services; it certainly is not reflected by income. It must be represented by a measure of impact. With most measures of actions taken or services provided, there are severe distributional biases.

Goods and services are likely to reach just a few, usually the less needy. Rural population may be excluded altogether. Income statistics are fatally flawed with respect to standards of living, and in general were never intended to reflect quality of life. Beyond the distributional problems of income statistics, are issues of non-comparable monetary units and measures of income and buying power. Financial measures also under-report the non-monetary exchanges which are especially important in the rural sectors of developing states. For these reasons, it is necessary to discuss human rights or basic needs in terms of impact rather than policy output, hospitals built, potable water provided, number of physicians, etc.

In order to measure basic needs satisfaction, I will use Morris' 'Physical Quality of Life Index' (PQLI), which is an additive index of scale of infant mortality, life expectancy at age one, and literacy.[4] This index taps the impact aspect of providing basic needs, rather than simply using policy or output data, whereby the intent substitutes for the impact (as in number of physicians, provision of water, etc.).

Democracy and Quality of Life in Developing Countries

The operational definitions of democracy have been argued about longer than those of economic human rights (see Arat, 1984). Even so, there is little consensus concerning the meaning of democracy, and how to measure it. In one sense, democracy means little more than it meant two hundred years ago: in another sense, it means something totally different. This can be seen in two areas: first, the relevant population of a democracy; and then, the actual instrumental or operational meaning of the term.

The 'relevant population' of democracy is the citizenry, which is legally defined by the requirements of suffrage. Suffrage has expanded tremendously around the world since the United States constitution was written. However, the instrumental meaning of democracy has changed as well. The Greeks saw it as self-government, and for them it was.[5] With the passage of time, and the gradual increase in the size and complexity of societies, such active self-rule was no longer possible. In our time, rather than being a process whereby the citizens create the laws which will shape the good society in which they will live, democracy has become negative, the popular control by the people of their representatives. So, the extent to which a country can be called democratic today matches the extent to which the citizenry (however defined) can hold the government accountable, and force it to protect their rights.

The question arises here as to how democracy and well-being have been related to each other in the past, and how they may be related in developed countries, which score high on measures of democracy and of quality of life. The process of improving standards of living while democracy increased was not smooth or easy, and was briefly referred to above in the discussion of the definition of human rights.

The linked paths of democracy and economic human rights in modern times are first found in the recent industrial revolution in Western Europe, which was accompanied by the growth of capitalism and a market economy, the crumbling of social structures, and disjointed policies of social amelioration. The struggles of this phase of capitalist development led to the broadening of the base of political power, and a mobilization of previously excluded groups into political life. Originally, social policies were enacted as a form of social control. Late nineteenth-century Prussia under Bismarck is one example of this. The poor and the workers were placated by social security measures. The importance of labor improved the political position of the masses, and they gained suffrage and some representation. By the time a level of real prosperity and economic stability had been reached, the less well-off groups were able to demand their share in the wealth of their nations.[6]

The dynamic interaction was between social disruption, political mobilization, and increasing wealth. From this combination, coming to a head in late nineteenth century Europe, social security measures and other policies aimed at protecting economic human rights (and the weakening fabric of social life) were developed, giving rise to the nascent welfare state.

It has been suggested that a certain level of economic development is a prerequisite for democracy (Lipset, 1959). While economic conditions do not necessarily reflect well-being or provision of economic human rights, the relationship suggests that politics and economic conditions are on some level linked, and since economic conditions are likely to be related to well-being, politics will be as well. Other theorists have made similar arguments (e.g. Jackman, 1973). Alternatively, Hewitt (1977) argued that democratic government ensures egalitarian policies, which will in turn lead to benefits for the poor, bringing up the standard of living for the entire population. This argument is echoed in the rural development literature, much of which emphasizes the role of peasant political participation in gaining economic and social objectives. However, on the negative side, Moon and Dixon (1985, p. 670) are not sanguine concerning the potential for democracy to improve the quality of life of a country's population, especially since the existence of 'democracy' does not automatically translate into protection of rights.

The world context within which less developed countries are attempting to develop today is very different from the world of one hundred years ago. While democracy has a potential for strengthening the protection of rights and liberties in developing countries, and therefore support the level of well-being, this potential is not necessarily being fulfilled. (This may in part be attributed to massive social disruption caused by the economic development.) The extent to which this potential is being fulfilled is in part the subject of this study.

DESIGN AND MEASUREMENT

The theoretical arguments, explored in the greater body of development literature, and briefly outlined above, lead to three primary explanations for effective provision of physical well-being, or economic human rights. These are broadly, economic factors, political factors, and policy efforts. I will analyze these factors using causal modeling, regressing the 'Physical Quality of Life Index' or PQLI[7] on the critical hypothesized causal variables, and then estimating internal paths. This will help to distinguish any spurious relationships which might exist.

Underlying this analysis are several assumptions, which should be made explicit. First, while gross national product (GNP) is a poor measure of welfare, and was in fact never intended to represent well-being, some measure of aggregate wealth or productive capacity will be a powerful explanation of well-being. This study will attempt to determine the relative explanatory power of other variables, once the effects of aggregate wealth are controlled. The second assumption is more arguable. I am assuming that wealth and the political system are causally independent. Arguments in the literature go in different directions with respect to causation; clearly the two factors have reciprocal effects which are probably very strong. I suggest, and in fact assume, that one does not cause the other. The third assumption is perhaps the most normative, and therefore problematic. It is that democracy is an extrinsic good, valued because of the good that it can do, and that generally, where democracy is present, the population will be in some way benefited.

Part of the issue being addressed in the model refers to the differential effects of 'manipulable' and 'non-manipulable' variables on economic human rights. A manipulable variable is simply one which can be controlled or changed through human agency; a non-manipulable variable cannot. Economic factors are generally non-manipulable; while they are the subject of action and policy, they are not readily controllable. Nor, for the most part, are political variables, whatever revolutionaries may prefer to believe. Policy expenditures, however, are manipulable, though they are dependent on both economic and political factors. They can be changed via human and political actions. Within the context of these non-manipulable variables, the original question re-emerges; are political or economic factors more important for determining governmental actions?

The context within which I will seek answers to these questions is that of the newly developing states, and the 'third world'. Because of their state of flux, their varying levels of poverty, and their focus on rapid economic development and political stability, developing states are the ideal subject for a study of the relationship of politics to provision of economic human rights. Therefore, the sample which will be used includes only developing countries (LDCs) for which data are generally available.[8] The industrialized market and non-market economies, and the high income oil exporting countries, are excluded on theoretical grounds, and also because of the bias their very high incomes would be likely to cause in the results.

Few if any of the concepts being studied are amenable to easy measurement. The economic variables measure money, or some other tangible factor, and so are less problematic. Economic capacity, or impact on the society, will be measured with two variables. The first is GNP,[9] representing the aggregate wealth or productive capacity of the society. The people live their lives in this economic context, within the structural limitations referenced by GNP, and therefore it must be considered. The other economic variable is likely to have a more direct impact on the lives of the members of the society; i.e. proportion of the labor force which works in the modern sector (industry and service).[10]

The political and policy variables on the other hand, require measurement that is less straightforward. Political factors will be measured with two variables, here called 'democratic institutions' and 'democratic rights and liberties'. Democratic institutions, a structural concept, is measured with an index including the number of parties in the system, form non-party to multi-party, and level of governmental centralization (which indicates whether important powers are held at one or more levels of government; Gastil, 1984, p. 38). The second political measure is much more flexible. Democratic rights and liberties refers not to the structure of the political system, but to the actual liberties available to the people, as well as to the tolerance the government accords to dissent.[11]

The policy variable represents more of a problem in terms of data collection than did the other two variables. This is especially due to the difficulties of collecting any kind of data on the Third World, and the comparability and quality of such data as are available. Information is not systematically collected on policies in developing countries as it is in the West. Furthermore, there are some categories of policies which would be significant for discussions of economic human rights, but which are rare in poor states (for example, welfare, food and rent subsidies, unemployment insurance, old-age pensions). However, there is some information available on policies concerning education and health (Sivard, 1974 and 1983; the figures are for per capita government expenditures). While they do not include all factors which would be significant for well-being (such as rural water and sanitation projects), and they are unclear concerning the impact of external aid, these variables are relevant to my definition of basic needs, and therefore were included in the analysis, as intervening variables channeling the effects of political and economic structural factors.

In conjunction with the effects of political democracy on the provision of economic human rights, this study will address the issue of structural determinism, and the potential for successful policy intervention within the limiting political and economic structures. Essentially, I will estimate the effects of political factors on basic needs provision, controlling for the confounding effects of economic factors.

ANALYSIS

The ordinary least squares estimates are presented below, in Table 10.1. The primary research question concerns the extent to which democracy is positively related to economic human rights, or well-

Table 10.1   Regression of PQLI on political, economic and policy variables
(N = 141)

Variable Name	Parameter Estimate	Standard Error	Standardized Estimate
Democratic institutions	2.31	0.79	.16
Democratic rights, liberties	0.73	0.21	.18
Wealth (ln GNP/c)	8.13	1.87	.38
Modern sector labor	0.38	0.08	.36
Health expenditures per capita	0.40	0.13	.22
Educational expenditure per capita	−0.15	0.05	−.24

$R^2 = .67$
Adjusted $R^2 = .65$

being (and can be inferred to cause it), when the effects of wealth
are controlled. As was expected, wealth (measured by the natural
logarithm of GNP/c) was the most powerful explanatory variable in
the model, with a regression coefficient of 8.13. The other economic
variable, the proportion of the labor force employed in the modern
sector, also had a strong positive effect. However, the economic
variables did not obscure the contributions of the political variables,
which had also had significant positive effects on well-being, independent of the effects of wealth.[12]

To this point, the findings support the theoretical arguments which
suggest that both economic and political factors have a positive impact
on standards of living. In the policy variables however, the relationship
breaks down. On the one hand, health expenditures display a
significant effect on well-being. This finding is logical, and follows
along with the other results. However, government expenditures on
education have an equivalent, negative impact on well-being. This
finding echoes that of Moon and Dixon (1985), when they found a
negative coefficient for the relationship of government expenditures
to well-being,[13] but they had no ready explanation either. However,
having data for specific policy areas, rather than only for total
expenditures, makes substantive interpretation easier. There are two
possible explanations which I can suggest. First, education is a long-
term investment, by its nature, the results of which will not be

immediately evident. This factor might explain in part a negligible coefficient, but not a negative one. However, there is the possibility (even likelihood) that the level of need of the people, and the low development of the human capital (needs which are confirmed by the aggregate indicators of well-being), may spur government programs aimed at rectifying the problems, hence increased expenditures accompanying low levels of well-being would be expected. This implies a non-recursive model, which cannot be estimated with this data set.

While the multiple regression coefficients provide fruitful ground for speculation, more information can be gained by examining the indirect effects, and the internal relationships as well (see Table 10.2). The relationships between the political and policy variables are particularly instructive. 'Democratic institutions' has a significant but not overwhelming effect on democratic rights and liberties, and they both have moderate, similar, significant effects on well-being. However, democratic rights and liberties have a small, negative effect on policy expenditures. Policy, both in education and health, seems to depend more on the level of wealth than on the workings of the

Table 10.2 Causal effects of basic needs model on PQLI (N = 141)

Independent variable	Total association (Pearson R)	Direct effect	Indirect effect	Total causal effect
Democratic institutions	.37**	.16**	.01	.17
Democratic rights, Liberties	.44**	.18**	.02	.20
Wealth	.56**	.38**	.23	.61
Modern sector labor	.70**	.36**	.09	.44
Health per capita	.51**	.22**	—	.22
Education per capita	.47**	−.24**	—	−.24

**significant at the .01 level
$R^2 = .63$

political system. This implies economic prerequisites for policy, if not for democracy. However, the two policy variables cannot be used interchangable; wealth has a much stronger impact on education than on health, while modern sector labor has a smaller impact on education than on health. When their very different effects on well-being are considered, one is left with a confusing picture of the role of policy in the model.

Since economic factors have a strong positive effect on well-being, and a very strong positive effect on policy, it should be expected that there would be at least a moderate, positive effect of policy on well-being. Clearly, there are intervening factors at work; the difference in likely impact lags was mentioned above. Health problems at this level are simply more tractable than education and literacy problems. This in itself would explain much of the differential effects of the two policy variables on well-being. However, it is perhaps more striking that the economic variables affect the two policy variables differently, while 'democratic rights and liberties' have essentially the same effect on both (i.e. −.02 health, and −.08 education). The sign and magnitude of these effects present problems of their own, implying as they do that democracy has little effect, or even a negative effect, on policy expenditures. This strongly contradicts Frank (1977, p. 202), and flies in the face of the theoretical models, and results, of Moon and Dixon (1985, p. 669). However, that contradiction may be rooted in the different samples used. My research did not address the problems of developed states at all; in these states, a very high level of democracy coexists with a very high level of welfare, and highly egalitarian policies. Because of the weight of these figures, the results are biased toward the high scorers, and reflect relationships which may not exist in the developing states. In this study, this bias was avoided. My findings therefore may only serve to emphasize that the Third World is not a reflection of the first, politically or economically. It can be suggested with a high degree of reliability that in the Third World overall (allowing for the possibility of regional differences), political democracy does not have a very strong effect on social policy. However, this is a finding that requires more research.

The different effects of the economic variables on the two policy variables are not attributable to sample anomalies. Wealth (1n GNP) affects educational expenditures more strongly than health expenditures (.67 and .50), but modern sector labor has a stronger impact on health than on education (.26 and .12 respectively). On the one hand, education is generally seen as being a straightforward investment in upgrading labor, or human resources, making available a better educated pool of workers. Health on the other hand, while also necessary for improving human capital, may be viewed more as welfare, which few developing states can afford. Therefore, the state is more likely to expend its resources on education (even though it does not have as good a rate of return). In the case of modern sector labor, the link to government expenditures for health and education is more difficult to explain, in part because it is obviously not the private companies which are determining the expenditures. However, it is possible that some companies require that the government provide infrastructural packages which include basic health services for their workers to complement labor indigenization requirements; alternatively, the relationship may be a function of the level of urbanization of the state. Since health facilities are usually concentrated in urban areas, if in fact more labor is employed in the modern sector in the more highly urbanized states, then the correlation may be spurious, and dependent on this demographic coincidence.

CONCLUSIONS

The essential question addressed above has concerned the effects of democracy on the provision of economic human rights, through the agency of public expenditures on health and education. The findings are mixed, and suggest the need for further, more detailed, research. While political variables have less explanatory power than economic variables, they are still significant, and cannot be excluded from the analysis. It seems likely that democracy, or some channel for representation or accountability, will improve the responsiveness of the government to the needs of the people, but there are likely to be intervening variables which prevent the system from working smoothly. Not all governments have population well-being as a high priority; often the requirements of rapid industrialization come first. This of course will be a greater factor in more authoritarian states. Furthermore, a democratic process does not guarantee a democratic result; questions of state strength and effective implementation become significant, and must be considered. The high level of aggregation may also disguise regional variations within the extremely heterogeneous Third World states.

Clearly, political factors are important in explaining levels of provision of economic human rights. However, specification and measurement of the relevant institutions and influences all require revision in order to develop a more complete understanding of the policy processes in Third World states.

Notes

1. Renteln (1987) has suggested that in the ideas of proportionality and retribution, a basis for some concept of human rights can be found, much farther back, in every cultural context. I am examining a more modern, specific, limited concept of human rights.

2. Karl Polanyi, in *The Great Transformation* (1944), discusses the development of the market system from a system of reciprocity in Great Britain; James Scott, in *The Moral Economy of the Peasant* (1976) refers to a pre-market system still existing today. .

3. See Marshall (1964) for a complete discussion of these kinds of rights.

4. See Morris (1979), especially ch. 5. The PQLI is an index of three measures of well-being. It taps the dimension of impact and the real condition of the population far more accurately than financial measures could.

5. After all, while a minority of the total population ruled the Greek societies, all of the citizens did. Those who were citizens collectively ruled themselves, far more effectively than in any modern society. The definition of citizen has simply expanded dramatically since then.

6. As Polanyi (1944) has suggested, effective political demand followed after industrial development in Great Britain. The problem that Huntington and Nelson have emphasized in developing states today is that effective demand is often increasing faster than the ability of the government to respond, and therefore instability and stunted growth may well result; while this is arguable, the suggestion that economic, social, and political development may not at the outset be mutually compatible goals, and that policymakers would have to deal with difficult choices, had not been addressed previously.

7. The PQLI attempts to address the problem that life and health are not readily translated into dollars, or any other convenient comparative scheme. The indexing system used here is straightforward. Three variables (literacy, infant mortality, life expectancy at age one) are all scaled from zero to one hundred, with zero being the lowest value and one hundred being the highest possible. For literacy this scaling is simple: per cent literate automatically ranges from zero to one hundred. The other two variables are more problematic. For infant mortality, the worst recorded rate since 1950 (Gabon, at 299 deaths per thousand live births) was used as zero. Seven deaths per thousand is the best foreseeable performance in this century (Sweden has eight) and is used as 100. Life expectancy at age one uses a low of thirty-eight (Vietnam, 1950), the lowest reported post-Second World War life expectancy, and a high of seventy-seven, representing the best available estimates of life expectancy by the turn of the century (Sweden is seventy-five).

   While the weightings have been criticized for their arbitrary and atheoretical nature, no scheme is perfect. Furthermore, the correlation coefficients of the PQLI as described above with various alternative weighting schemes was very high (.984–.997), a circumstance which provides at least a surface indication of the robustness of the measure.

For a more in depth discussion of these factors, see Morris (1979), especially ch. 5.

8. I have stratified the universe of cases by aggregate wealth, or Gross National Product (GNP) to exclude the high income oil exporting states and the industrialized market and centrally planned economies. Not only are current development patterns different from the early development of these states, especially considering the changed world context, but the functional form of the relationship of structural and policy variables to provision of economic human rights would be very different. Basic needs are no longer the central, salient social problem for the industrialized states, for the most part. Instead, they are dealing with the not inconsiderable problems of overdevelopment. 'Micro-states' were also deleted. The sample will be augmented by pooling data from two different time points. This will increase the size of the sample, and will smooth out some of the interactions which might be due to historical factors with short-term impacts.

9. Actually, the natural logarithm of GNP per capita. This was employed to reduce some the problems of heteroscedasticity. Unfortunately, the problem of multicollinearity was increased somewhat, though it remained manageable.

10. These two economic variables were selected because of their hypothesized positive impact on well-being. Indexes of industrial production were considered, but were rejected. Theoretically, the relationship of industrialization to well-being is likely to be negative, at least in the short term; the data which I examined supported this hypothesis. The World Bank was the source of both sets of figures.

11. This concept is represented by Arat's (1984) 'Democraticness' index. It includes measures of political participation, competitiveness of the political system, and civil or political liberties (see especially ch. 3). The formula is:

Democraticness = [(effective executive selection
+ (legislative effectiveness * nomination procedure) + 1)
+ (party legitimacy + party competitiveness)]
− government coerciveness.

All data were taken from Banks' *Cross-National Data Archives* (1979).

12. The problem of confounded effects of democracy and GNP has been addressed in part by the use of a sample of developing countries only. The primary reason for the correlation of democracy and wealth is the fact that the wealthiest countries in the world (i.e. the industrialized West) are also democracies. This is no accident, as Lindblom (1977, p. 164) suggested, since polyarchies or democracies were established to protect certain liberties, foremost among them economic liberties, and the arrangements have resulted in highly efficient economic systems. This will therefore bias any results toward them. Leaving them out of the sample allows the unbiased relationship to emerge. A very low, though significant, correlation is present between wealth and the two political variables once the industrialized West is removed.

13. Government expenditures were measured as a percent of GNP, and the

resulting variable was used as a proxy for state strength, or the size of the state apparatus.

References

ARAT, Zehra F. (1984) 'The Viability of Political Democracy in Developing Countries', PhD Dissertation, The State University of New York at Binghamton.

BANKS, A. S. (1979) *Cross-National Time Series Data Archive* (Binghamton, NY: Center for Social Analysis).

BASTER, N. and SCOTT, W. (1969) *Levels of Living and Economic Growth* (Geneva: UN Research Institute for Social Development).

CHENERY, H., AHLUWALIA, M., BELL, C., DULOY, J., JOLLY, R. (eds) (1974) *Redistribution With Growth* (London: Oxford University Press).

CHENERY, H. and SYRQUIN, M. (1975) *Patterns of Development 1950 to 1970* (New York: Oxford University Press).

CRAHAN, M. E. (ed.) (1982) *Human Rights and Basic Needs in the Americas* (Washington, DC: Georgetown University Press).

DONNELLY, Jack (1985) *The Concept of Human Rights* (London: Croom Helm).

DROST, Pieter N. (1951) *Human Rights as Legal Rights* (Leiden: A. W. Sijthoff's Vitgever Smij NV).

FRAKT, P. (1977) 'Democracy, Political Activity, Economic Development and Government Responsiveness', *Comparative Political Studies*, 10, 2 (July): 177–212.

GASTIL, R. (1984) *Freedom in the World* (Westport, Conn.: Greenwood Press).

GILPIN, Robert (1977) 'Economic Interdependence and National Security in Historical Perspective', in K. Knorr and Frank N. Trager (eds), *Economic Issues and National Security*.

HEWITT, C. (1977) 'The Effect of Political Democracy and Social Democracy on Equality in Industrial Societies', *American Sociological Review*, 42 (June): 450–64.

HUNTINGTON, Samuel P. and NELSON, Joan M. (1976) *No Easy Choice* (Cambridge, Mass.: Harvard University Press).

JACKMAN, R. W. (1973) 'On the Relation of Economic Development to Democratic Performance', *American Journal of Sociology*, 17, 3 (August): 611–21.

JACKMAN, R. W. (1974) 'Political Democracy and Social Equality', *American Sociological Review*, 39: 29–45.

KNORR, Klaus and TRAGER, Frank N. (eds) (1977) *Economic Issues and National Security* (Lawrence, Kansas: Regents Press of Kansas).

LEIPZIGER, D. (ed.) (1981) *Basic Needs and Development* (Cambridge, Mass.: Oelgeschlager, Gunn and Huinn).

LEWIS-BECK, M. (1977) 'Relative Importance of Socio-Political and

Economic Variables for Public Policy', *American Political Science Review*, 71 (June): 559–66.

LIPSET, S. M. (1959) 'Some Social Requisites of Democracy: Economic Development of Political Legitimacy', *American Political Science Review*, vol. 153, no. 1 (March 1959): 69–105.

LINDBLOM, C. (1977) *Politics and Markets* (New York: Basic Books).

LITTLE, I. (1982) *Economic Development: Theory, Policy and International Relations* (New York: Basic Books).

MARSHALL, T. H. (1964) *Class, Citizenship and Social Development* (Garden City, New York: Doubleday).

MOON, B. and DIXON, W. (1985) 'Politics, the State, and Basic Human Needs: a cross-national study', *American Journal of Political Science*, (November): 661–94.

MORRIS, M. D. (1979) *Measuring the Condition of the World's Poor* (New York: Pergamon Press).

POLANYI, Karl (1944) *The Great Transformation: The Political and Economic Origins of our times*. Introduction by Robert I. MacIver (Boston: Beacon Press).

RENTELN, A. (1987) 'A Cross-Cultural Approach to Validating International Human Rights'. Paper delivered at the annual meeting of Western Political Science Association.

ROBERTSON, A. H. (1972) *Human Rights in the World* (Manchester: Manchester University Press).

SCOTT, J. C. (1976) *The Moral Economy of the Peasant: Rebellion and Subsistence in Southeast Asia* (New Haven: Yale University Press).

SHUE, Henry (1980) *Basic Rights* (Princeton, NJ: Princeton University Press).

SIVARD, R. L. (1974) *World Military and Social Expenditures 1974* (New York: Institute for World Order).

SIVARD, R. L. (1983) *World Military and Social Expenditures 1983* (Washington, DC: World Priorities).

SPALDING, N. (1987) 'International Obligations and the Nature of the State', paper prepared for presentation at the annual meeting of the Western Political Science Association, Anaheim, Ca., 26–28 March.

WORLD BANK (1983) *World Development Report 1983* (New York: Oxford University Press).

11 Militarization, Human Rights and Basic Needs in the Third World

Robert M. Rosh

According to the Universal Declaration of Human Rights, which has been adopted by the United Nations, human rights include the right to an adequate standard of living and a basic education. Consequently, the developmental policies of states can be analyzed from a human rights perspective as well as an economic perspective.

The effects of Third World militarization on the degree of political rights enjoyed within these countries has often been analyzed. However, Third World military expenditures, like any resource allocation by these states, affects the developmental process as well. Therefore, high military burdens may affect the economic human rights enjoyed by a population.

The debate over how military spending affects the developmental process is especially crucial in a Third World context. In 1978 annual military expenditures by developing countries surpassed $US100 billion; on average they allocate almost 6 per cent of their GNP's to military expenditures (USACDA, 1985). At first glance it would appear that the military allocation policies of many Third World states constitute an extraordinary waste of resources that might otherwise be employed in a effort to provide for the basic needs of their citizenry. For there a few compelling reasons that would lead one to hypothesize that heavy military burdens contribute to a state's ability to provide for the basic needs of its poorest citizens. After all, arms cannot be used to plow fields, immunize children, or prolong life. Large allocations of a country's resources to military expenditures, therefore, might provide for economic growth, but not for development from a basic needs perspective (Streeten, 1979; Morris, 1979). Economic infrastructure and capital accumulation might be generated, but benefits would not necessarily 'trickle down' to a state's neediest. While economic growth is in many respects a necessary condition it is not a sufficient condition in the drive to provide for the basic needs of a populace. The method by which economic growth

190

is attempted affects whether and how quickly policies are designed to provide safe drinking water for the general population, to immunize children against the specific diseases that attack them, to pursue universal literacy, or to provide for minimum daily food requirements.

Economic growth is no longer seen as a panacea with regard to the provision of basic human needs. A 'trickle down' economic rationale has often been employed as a justification for policies that do nothing more than trickle upon the poor and downtrodden. True development, as Goulet (1971) suggests, can only be accomplished when human beings are seen as an ends in themselves and not merely as a means to an end. At the very least, the analysis of Scott (1976) allows one to advance the proposition that the provision of subsistence combined with certain norms of reciprocity are a minimal criteria by which we can judge state policies both empirically and normatively. Policies which advance economic growth, but do nothing to provide for subsistence or reciprical relations between the state and the society are pragmatically unsound and ethically unjust. The allocation of a large percentage of a state's GNP to military expenditures is believed to be such a policy.

Military expenditures obviously have direct opportunity costs in terms of foregone investment and consumption. Given that some portion of these allocations typically are used in the importation and maintenance of advanced weapons systems, a country's balance of payments problems may also be exacerbated. However, military outlays may provide demand in an otherwise slack economy, may cause the creation of backward linkages, and may provide the state with the organized force needed to mobilize or exploit potential resources. In addition, one could argue that threats from regional neighbors or internal turmoil might discourage confidence in production and investment if the state does not allocate the necessary resources to state security.

Nevertheless, countries with high military burdens, this study hypothesizes, typically pursue a top down approach to development because of the need for capital accumulation in order to maintain their military effort, rather than a basic need approach that emphasizes development from the bottom up. Highly militarized countries, it is hypothesized, have experienced growth without development.

PREVIOUS RESEARCH

The 1973 study by Emile Benoit is the point of departure for all subsequent empirical analysis on the effects that military expenditures have on economic growth in Third World countries. Benoit argues that defense expenditures in Third World countries do not have an adverse effect on growth, and, in fact, such expenditures may have an overall positive effect. He found that in forty-four developing countries between 1950–65 defense expenditures as a percentage of national product were positively correlated with their civilian economic growth rates (estimated by subtracting defense from GDP) over this period. Benoit recognized that a high rate of investment from external sources as well as economic aid allowed a number of these states to maintain high defense levels without reducing their investment rates, thus allowing them to achieve high growth rates in spite of the apparent burdens of defense. But even after controlling for these factors Benoit found a positive relationship between high defense burdens and growth rates.

Benoit argued that defense expenditures bring about economic benefits for Third World countries. In particular, he suggests that manpower training may ultimately have a positive effect on the civilian economy. Furthermore, defense programs provide infrastructure such as roads that can be used by the civilian sector of the economy, and defense expenditures may also have a Keynesian effect of stimulating demand. Benoit does not discuss, however, the effect of military expenditures on the provision of basic human needs.

More recently, Ball (1983) argued that Benoit should have used a more inclusive definition of external aid in order to test whether the correlation between economic growth and defense burden was spurious. Benoit simply controlled for direct bilateral economic assistance, and Ball noted that by neglecting to include multilateral and military assistance as well as direct foreign investment the deck was stacked in terms of the correlation between military expenditures and economic growth. Of course, Pye (1962) among others might not see this as a contradiction, and instead might argue that heavy military burdens and increased military participation in the modernization process would positively affect the willingness of First World countries to provide aid thereby spurring economic growth. In this theoretical framework economic and military aid would be an intervening rather than a control variable.

Most of the studies since Benoit's have attempted to refute or support his findings by analyzing different time periods, using different measures, improving statistical techniques, and including additional control variables. For instance, Deger and Smith (1983) found a negative relationship between military expenditures and economic growth using a three-stage least squares model, which was used to estimate average military expenditures and economic growth rates for fifty LDCs during the 1965–73 period. The difficulty of getting data on aid, however, has precluded its incorporation into the model.

Recently there has been one attempt to analyze the consequences of military expenditures on the provision of basic needs as opposed to the attainment of a high rate of economic growth, but this study was not limited to the Third World. Moon and Dixon (1985b) examined the consequences of a state's military burden on the provision of basic needs as measured by the Physical Quality of Life Index (PQLI) developed by Morris (1979). Their model is tested for 116 'contemporary national societies', but it is unclear by what criterion these countries are chosen. Eventually Moon and Dixon find a negative relationship between a country's military burden and its PQLI, but only after developing on overly inclusive model that one must assume suffers terribly from multicollinearity. For instance, Moon and Dixon (1985b) employ state expenditures as a per cent of GNP, military expenditures as a percentage of GNP, and military personnel as a percentage of GNP as three of their independent variables in spite of the fact that all three correlate highly with one another.

Furthermore, Moon and Dixon (1985a, and 1985b) did not include variables that they arguably should have. Surprisingly, they did not test the hypothesis that a country's degree of incorporation or dependence on the world economy affected its ability to provide for the basic needs of its citizens. Apparently, in their search for a model which would demonstrate the negative effects of military burdens on the provision of basic needs they developed a misspecified model. A negative relationship between a country's military burden and its PQLI was produced (1985b). However, a positive relationship between a state's military personnel as a percentage of its total population and its PQLI was also reported. Moon and Dixon claim that this demonstrated that whereas personnel costs had a positive effect on a state's provision of basic needs, expenses on military hardware had a negative effect. One cannot trust these findings, however, because of the statistical problems that plague their model, in particular multicollinearity. This study will attempt to improve on the model and design of Moon and Dixon's study, while testing the relationship between military burdens and the PQLI solely for Third World countries.

RESEARCH DESIGN

Ten cross-sectional models employing three different PQLI scores, for 1970, 1975, and 1980, as the dependent variable are analyzed. The independent variables are lagged up to four years, and are also run simultaneoulsy for 1970 and 1975. The units of analysis are sixty-eight Third World countries for which comprehensive data could be found. It was unclear as to what the appropriate lag period would be given that improvements in the provision of basic needs takes time, while rapid reductions in the physical quality of life can occur if a state reformulates its policy priorities. Therefore, the lags were varied in order to ascertain what if any difference such timing considerations made.

MEASUREMENTS AND HYPOTHESES

It is hypothesized that the greater a country's resource allocations to the military the lower its provision of basic human needs, even after controlling for alternative explanations. The Physical Quality of Life Index (PQLI) is employed as the dependent variable in our model, while the percentage of a country's GNP that is allocated to military expenditures is one of a number of independent variables.

The Physical Quality of Life Index

The introduction of the PQLI as an indicator corresponds with the rise in interest in the basic needs approach to development. The Overseas Development Council (Grant, 1978; and Morris, 1979), have argued that while certain indicators of individual well-being such as health and literacy are correlated with per capita levels of GNP there is a great deal of variation in the provision of basic needs at different levels of development. They set out to establish an indicator that would measure the success of a country in providing for the basic requirements of its populace.

The PQLI was developed to measure certain specific life-serving social characteristics which are readily quantifiable and to utilize raw data which are collected by almost all governments. The council desired an indicator that avoided ethnocentric value judgements, was internationally comparable, and measured results rather than inputs. Basic needs certainly include food, clothing, and shelter, but different societies have different demands depending on the environment.

Therefore, the three data elements used to construct the index were infant mortality, life expectancy at age one, and basic literacy. It is claimed that they meet the criterion outlined, and the Overseas Development Council (ODC) argued that they are good indicators of the results of the total social process. These indicators sum up the combined effects of social relations, nutritional status, public health, and family environment. ODC maintains that the specific factors that account for changes in life expectancy after age one are not the same as those that affect infant mortality, because infants suffer from different diseases and conditions than adults. Literacy rates are included because: increased specialization requires increased literacy, and the achievement of basic literacy increases the potential of the individual to participate in society.

The PQLI is based on a simple index system where each data element is scaled from 0 to 100 (0 representing the worst possible performance imaginable and 100 representing the best performance believed possible) and then averaged so that the PQLI is scaled automatically on an index from 0 to 100. The range for literacy is from 0 to 100 per cent. Infant mortality ranges from 229 to seven deaths per thousand. Life expectancy ranges from thirty-eight to seventy-seven years.

Morris (1979) generated only one PQLI score for the mid-1970s. Using his equations this study has been able to generate scores for 1970 and 1980. Therefore, only three points are employed, because of the difficulty in determining life expectancy after age one as opposed to life expectancy at birth.

Military Burdens

This study attempts to test the consequences of military allocations for the provision of basic needs. Military expenditures as a percentage of gross national product is employed as an independent variable, which Goertz and Diehl (1985) suggest that this is the most widely used indicator of a country's military burden. Gross national product is used rather than gross domestic product because of the desire to analyze the percent of the total resources at a state's command that are allocated to military expenditures. Analyzing total military expenditures was felt to be innappropriate, given that with large variance in the resources of the countries under discussion one needs to control for a country's gross national product. Data on military burdens was obtained from the US Arms Control and Disarmament Agency.

Per Capita Gross National Product

A country's per capita gross national product has long been employed as an indicator of its level of economic development. It represents the total output of a country divided by its total population. While per capita GNP implicitly assumes that resources are fairly distributed, this is often not the case. Third World countries are usually character- ized by severe unequal distributions of resources resulting in the impoverishment of the many and the enrichment of the few. While the Overseas Development Council reported an overall correlation between the PQLI and per capita GNP that was relatively high at .729, when they divided the countries into income categories the relationship was much weaker. Given that this study limits itself to the provision of basic needs in the Third World, it is expected that there will be a positive but not an especially strong relationship between per capita Gross National Product and the PQLI. There are certain 'trickle down' effects from per capita GNP growth over time regardless of whether this growth is inegalitarian, but this process is often an inefficient way of providing basic needs.

Moon and Dixon (1985a) found a very strong relationship between per capita GNP and the PQLI. However, they did not unpack their observations in order to ascertain whether developed states undergo different processes than developing countries. By so doing they could be accused of inadvertently assuming a stages-of-growth argument (Rostow, 1961). The high degree of fit obtained by Moon and Dixon (1985a) resulted from their inclusion of states across all levels of development. Within each subsection a negative relationship might exist, but across each subsection a strongly positive relationship would overwhelm these findings. This study, by including a country's per capita GNP in the model, attempts to analyze the effects of democracy and military burdens on the provision of basic needs after the effects of economic development have been statistically controlled. Annual data for per capita GNP was obtained from Banks (1979) cross-national time-series data archive.

Commodity Concentration

It has long been argued that a country's degree of dependence on the world economy affects its ability to develop. One of the consequences of dependence, it is often argued is the disarticulation of a domestic economy due to its orientation towards production for export. But there is disagreement over whether this ultimately has a positive or negative affect on economic growth and development. According to A. D. Hirschman (1958) the over-development of one sector of the economy may have all sorts of positive trickle down effects, and is, in fact, crucial in order for a country to enjoy its big spurt (which Rostow later termed take-off). Samir Amin (1974), on the other hand, argues that disarticulation serves to dehabilitate an economy. Certainly one can note that the greater the degree to which a country's exports are concentrated in a few commodities the greater its vulnerability to fluctuations in the world market. These market fluctuations negatively affect a state's capacity to plan and implement a developmental program, because state revenue will also vacillate. In addition, Third World countries which are characterized by a high degree of commodity concentration typically specialize in primary products which require little processing. Export enclaves develop which are not closely integrated with the rest of a country's economy, thereby providing few spin-offs and no multiplier effect from the production of these products for export. Therefore, we hypothesize that the greater the degree of a country's exports are characterized by commodity concentration the lower its ability to provide for basic needs as measured by the PQLI. Taylor and Jodice (1983) provide commodity concentration figures for 1970 and 1975, which measure the percentage of a country's commodity exports that are concentrated in one primary product. Their measures are employed in the present study.

Democracy

Certainly the nature of a country's political process can affect the formulation of developmental policy within Third World countries. This study hypothesizes that the greater the extent to which this process is democratic, the more likely it is that policies will be designed to provide for the basic needs of citizens. Policy makers in such a political context are given to concerns about their legitimacy and competitiveness in the political arena, whereas leaders of authoritarian or military regimes may have different priorities. Arat's (1984) democracy index is employed. Her index is closely related to that of Bollen's (1980), but is available for the years under study (1969–78).

Moon and Dixon (1985a) after controlling for per capita GNP reported that Bollen's (1980) indicator of democracy was strongly related to the PQLI. Bollen's democracy index was lagged between ten and fifteen years in Moon and Dixon's model, and while this is probably acceptable in the case of many developed states, Third World countries are much more volatile. While Moon and Dixon (1985a) were analyzing essentially structural variables, structures can decay or develop in ten or fifteen years.

Arms Imports

All military expenditures are not equal, at least with regard to the developmental process. Expenditures on the importation and maintenance of sophisticated weaponry affect the provision of basic needs differently than do expenditures on military personnel. Therefore, this study includes data from the US Arms Control and Disarmament Agency on a developing countries arms imports. The larger the value of these imports the greater the negative effect thay will typically have on a country's balance of payments. The importation of sophisticated weaponry has few positive spin-off effects for an economy, while resulting in very high opportunity costs because of time spent by trained personnel on the maintenance of such equipment. The value of arms imports should provide some sense of the military aid received by a number of countries. In cases where aid is given in the form of grants for military weapons balance of payments problems are less severe; nevertheless spare parts must still be purchased, mechanics trained, and infrastructure provided.

To reiterate, the hypotheses which serve to underlie the model are as follows (see Table 11.1):

1. The greater a country's resource allocations to the military the less it will be able to provide for the basic needs of its citizens.
2. A positive but not an especially strong relationship exists between per capita gross national product and the PQLI.
3. The greater the degree a country's exports are characterized by

Table 11.1   Correlation matrix for 1978

	PQLI	Military burden	GNP/P	Democracy index	Commodity concen- tration	Arms imports
PQLI	1	.15	.15	.44	−.21	.008
Military burden		1	.29	−.15	.16	.55
Per capita GNP			1	−.06	.39	.43
Democracy index				1	−.24	−.11
Commodity concentration					1	.30
Arms imports						1

   commodity concentration the lower its ability to provide for basic
   needs as measured by the PQLI.
4. The greater the value of a country's imports the less it will be able
   to provide for the basic needs of its citizens.
5. The greater the extent to which a country's political process is
   democratic, the more likely policy makers are to establish policies
   designed to provide for the basic needs of their citizens.

FINDINGS

The statistical results suggest that the size of a country's military
burden does not affect a country's provision of basic needs. As Table
11.2 demonstrates, in only two of the ten models is a country's
military burden negatively related to its provision of basic needs with
any degree of strength. In these two instances, when data from 1972
and 1973 were regressed on PQLI scores for 1975, arms imports were
positively correlated with the dependent variable, which is opposite
the relationship hypothesized. In all other years neither variable was
strongly related in either direction to the dependent variable after
controlling for the others. Furthermore, neither arms imports nor
military burdens achieve a statistically significant association with the
PQLI in any of the models. Finally, as Table 11.1 suggests, the
correlations between the independent variables are not of a magnitude
which would suggest that the model suffered from multicollinearity.
   A Third World country's level of democracy as measured by Arat
(1984) is the variable most strongly and consistently related to its

Table 11.2   Results of cross-sectional models

Year	Standardized parameter estimates Unstandardized parameter estimates (level of significance)					R-square of Model
	Military burden	Arms imports	Democracy index	Per capita GNP	Commodity concentration	
1969	.06	−.04	.45	.32	−.14	.39
	39.8	−.001	1.8	.014	−.013	
	(.63)	(.71)	(.0001)	(.001)	(.17)	
1970	.06	−.05	.46	.30	−.13	.37
	42.2	−.0007	1.9	.01	−.01	
	(.59)	(.69)	(.0001)	(.003)	(.20)	
1971	.0009	.05	.46	.27	−.11	.35
	.64	.0008	1.8	.008	−.01	
	(.99)	(.68)	(.0001)	(.01)	(.29)	
1972	−.14	.18	.40	.26	−.15	.33
	6.5	.002	1.6	.006	−.01	
	(.26)	(.13)	(.0006)	(.01)	(.15)	
1973	−.16	.17	.37	.26	−.11	.30
	−89.8	.001	1.6	.005	−.01	
	(.27)	(.23)	(.001)	(.01)	(.30)	
1974	.03	−.0003	.44	.21	−.11	.31
	17	−.000003	1.9	.004	−.01	
	(.84)	(.99)	(.0002)	(.05)	(.3)	
1975	.003	.05	.45	.24	−.20	.33
	2.1	.0005	1.9	.003	−.02	
	(.98)	(.72)	(.0003)	(.04)	(.11)	
1976	−.03	.06	.40	.36	−.32	.34
	−13.8	.0003	1.5	.003	−.02	
	(.82)	(.63)	(.0006)	(.002)	(.01)	
1977	.03	−.04	.39	.37	−.33	.35
	16.4	−.0002	1.4	.004	−.02	
	(.80)	(.74)	(.0006)	(.002)	(.008)	
1978	.04	−.12	.38	.41	−.33	.35
	24.3	−.0006	1.4	.003	−.02	
	(.74)	(.34)	(.001)	(.001)	(.008)	

provision of basic needs even after controlling for per capita GNP. A one standard deviation increase in the democracy index is correlated on average with .4 of a standard deviation increase in a country's PQLI. Political elites who are democratically elected and wish to survive in a democratic political process are more concerned with their political popularity and legitimacy than are regimes which come to power through other means. Legitimacy in Third World countries is closely tied to the provision of basic needs for its citizenry. Hence democratic governments are much more likely to formulate policy programs designed to improve the lives of their populace.

The results also suggest that the greater the degree to which a Third World country's commodities are concentrated in one product the less it is typically able to provide for the basic needs of its population. The existence of export enclaves with their typical lack of backward linkages and multiplier effects, along with the vulnerability that such concentration imposes upon an economy apparently overwhelms any benefit as to be derived from maximising its 'comparative advantage' (Galtung, 1971). The negative relationship between the degree of commodity concentration and the PQLI gets increasingly stronger in the late 1970s, and this may be due in part to the fact that oil exporting economies grew very quickly in size but did not match this growth with a concern for the basic needs of their general population.

Unlike Moon and Dixon (1985a, 1985b) this study did not uncover an extremely strong relationship between per capita gross national product and the PQLI. This is because the investigation was limited to Third World countries, and consequently there was a great less variance in both variables. This also accounts for the relatively weaker fit of the models. Obviously there are a number of factors influencing the provision of basic needs in Third World countries that the models have not captured. This study wished to test the relationship between the PQLI and military burdens after controlling for some obvious alternative explanations, and after the inclusion of only a few such variables the relationship quickly approached zero.

CONCLUSIONS

While statistical relationships which are not significant are not reported as often as they should be, the finding of no relationship in this instance is extremely important and requires a post hoc explanation. The largest single expense of the military is on its personnel, which must be fed, housed, equipped, and trained. The larger a country's military participation ratio, the greater its military burden; indeed, the two indicators are highly correlated with one another. Large-scale military participation may result in an increase in the provisions of basic needs (as captured by the Physical Quality of Life index or PQLI) to a large portion of the adult male population of a country. Ultimately this may have a beneficial effect for their dependents. Military expenditures may also be employed in the Third World context to bolster demand in a slack economy. Highly militarized countries may receive more aid and investment from developed states, which might ultimately serve to improve the lot of the poorest members of a society. All of these possibilities may potentially counteract the negative consequences of high military burdens.

It is also possible, as Luckham (1978) suggests, that military expenditures may not impede economic growth and development in Third World countries, because these allocations may serve to: 1) buttress and reproduce certain conditions of peripheral capitalism necessary for the concentration and accumulation of capital; 2) strengthen state structures and increasing state penetration so as to manage growth; and 3) strengthen ties to international capitalism by providing for the investment conditions favored by both corporations and the core states from which they are located. However, under other structural circumstances such expenditures, Luckham maintains, could be put to much better use. All of these factors may serve to limit the seemingly negative effects of military expenditures.

The relationship between high military burdens and a basic needs approach to development cannot ultimately be answered as of yet with statistical analysis. No strong relationship of any type was found between high military burdens and a country's PQLI. Refinements in the model and the methods may yet uncover a strong negative relationship. Presently, however, the relationship between militarization and development boils down to normative concerns. The limitations of our measures, methods, and results are recognized. Nonetheless, the tremendous allocation of resources to military expenditures by First, Second, and Third World countries certainly threatens a basic human need and a basic human right, that of survival; for weapons and the militaries trained to use them have been developed to kill if need be. Given the nature and working of the interstate system as described by Waltz (1979) among others, or of the demands of the capitalist world economy as maintained by Luckham (1975), developing states may need relatively high military burdens to survive and improve their economic position. In such a context high burdens would not necessarily have a negative effect on their economic development as captured by a basic needs approach. That is to say, however, that the basic needs of the majority of people presently living impoverished lives in the Third World would not be better off in a less militarized world and in less militarized countries.

References

AMIN, Samir (1974) 'Accumulation and Development: A Theoretical Mode', *Review of African Political Economy*, Vol. 4, 1: 9–26.

ARAT, Z. F. (1981) The viability of political democracy in developing countries. Doctoral Dissertation, State University Of New York at Binghamton, 1984.

BALL, N. (1983) 'Defence and development: a critique of the Benoit study', in Helena Tuomi and Raimo Vayryen (eds), *Militarization and Arms Production* (New York: St Martin's Press).

BANKS, A. S. (1979) *Cross-national Time-Series Data Archive* (Binghamton: Center For Social Analysis).

BENOIT, E. (1973) *Defense and Economic Growth in Developing Countries* (Lexington, Mass.: Lexington Books).

BOLLEN, K. (1980) 'Issues in the Comparative Measurement of Political Democracy', *American Sociological Review*, 45, 370–90.

DABELKO, D. and McCORMICK, J. M. (1977) 'Opportunity Costs of Defense: Some Cross-National Evidence', *Journal of Peace Research*, 14, 145–54.

DEGER, S. and SMITH, R. (1983) 'Military Expenditures and Growth in Less Developed Countries', *Journal Of Conflict Resolution*, 27, 335–53.

DIXON, W. J. 'Trade Concentration, Economic Growth, and the Provisions of Basic Human Needs', *Social Science Quarterly*, Vol. 65, 761–74.

FRANK, Andre Gunder (1967) *Capitalism and Underdevelopment in Latin America* (New York: Modern Reader Paperbacks).

GALTUNG, J. (1971) 'A Structural Theory of Imperialism', *Journal of Peace Research*, Vol. 13, 81–94.

GOERTZ, G. and DIEHL, P. F. (1985) Measuring Military Allocations: a Comparison of Different Approaches. Paper presented at the 1985 Annual ISA Conference, Washington DC.

GOULET, Denis (1971) *The Cruel Choice* (New York: Atheneum Press).

GRANT, J. P. (1978) Disparity Reduction Rates in Social Indicators: A Proposal for Measuring and Targeting Progress in Meeting Basic Needs (New York: Overseas Development Council).

HIRSCHMAN, Albert O. (1958) *The Strategy of Economic Development* (New Haven: Yale University Press).

MOON, B. E. and DIXON, W. J. (1985a) 'Politics, The State, and Basic Human Needs: A Cross-National Study' *American Journal of Political Science*, Vol. 29, 661–94.

MOON, B. E. and DIXON, W. J. (1985b) Military Effects on the Provision of basic needs. Paper Presented at The International Studies Association, Washington DC.

MORRIS, M. D. (1979) *Measuring the Condition of the World's Poor: The Physical Quality of Life Index* (New York: Pergamon Press).

PYE, Lucian W. (1962) 'Armies In The Process of Modernization', in John J. Johnson (ed.), *The Role Of The Military In Underdeveloped Countries* (Princeton: Princeton University Press).

ROSTOW, W. W. (1961) *The Stages of Economic Growth: a Non-Communist Manifesto* (Cambridge England: Cambridge University Press).

SCOTT, James C. (1976) *The Moral Economy of The Peasant* (New Haven: Yale University Press).

STREETEN, P. (1979) 'A Basic-Needs Approach to Economic Development', in K. P. Jameson and C. K. Wilber (eds), *Directions in Economic Development* (Notre Dame: University of Notre Dame Press).

TAYLOR, C. L. and D. A. JODICE (1983) World Handbook of Political and Social Indicators (Binghamton, NY: Vail-Ballou).

USACDA UNITED STATES ARMS CONTROL AND DISARMAMENT AGENCY (1985) World Military Expenditures And Arms Transfers (Washington: ACDA Publications).

WALTZ, K. (1979) Theory of International Politics (Reading, Mass.: Addison-Wesley).

12 Abortion, Rights and Public Policy Making in Six Western Democracies

James E. Lennertz

This analysis compares the development of abortion policy in England, France, Ireland, Italy, the United States and West Germany. These policies vary from strong constitutional protection of the woman's autonomous choice in the United States to absolute constitutional protection of the life of the fetus in Ireland. The other nations have moderate policies which generally condition abortion upon defined medical, eugenic, or social circumstances.

The legal and political systems of these countries vary from civil to common law, from traditions with judicial review to traditions without, from federal to unitary structures, and from governments of integrated to governments of separated functions. Though several insitutions were usually involved, institutional emphases were as follows: judicial in the United States and West Germany, parliamentary in England and France, and plebiscitary in Italy and Ireland. Ireland, Italy and France are predominantly Catholic, though with distinctive traditions of belief and practice; England, Germany and the United States are religiously pluralistic with strong Protestant traditions.

The focus of this comparison is not the substance of abortion policies but rather the suitability of the decision making process to the policy problem within the societal context. Abortion, because of both its urgent demands and the diverse nature of changes in law and practice, is an unusually difficult issue, particularly for normally deliberate and incremental policy making institutions. Its intensity and complexity tax 'slack' resources which are necessary for flexible response. Strident rhetoric fuels a confrontational dynamic in which a particular attitude or action becomes a general 'litmus test', whose implications spill over into a broad range of public concerns. Abortion politics, as a variant of 'life-style' regulatory politics, raises nonnegotiable normative issues and stimulates the mobilization of intense, narrowly-defined groups (Tatalovich and Daynes, 1981).

Developments in each nation will be examined with respect to four institutional features critical to effective policy making: (1) a strong theoretical perspective for understanding and responding to the problem; (2) an information-gathering capacity and decisional process appropriate to the generation and organization of the relevant data and argument; (3) effective implementation and feedback capabilities so that the policy can develop responsively over time; and (4) public trust and acceptance of the institution's competence and authority (Carter, 1977).

The abortion issue has been marked by the pervasive and often conflicting use of the concept of rights to characterize the claims of all sides. A distinction should be made between human rights and legal rights. Human rights articulate fundamental values of humanity in community, while legal rights identify individual guarantees against the public power of the state (Friedrich, 1963). Scheingold (1974) identifies the uncritical liberal reliance upon legal rights as the 'myth of rights'. When this perspective dominates abortion developments, harmful polarization of the issues and the society will not only produce extreme policy but also exacerbate antagonisms, complicate compliance and undermine the legitimacy of public institutions and ultimately of the concepts of human and legal rights.

JUDICIAL DECISION: THE UNITED STATES AND WEST GERMANY

While early efforts for liberalization of abortion laws in the United States centered on legislative change in the states, the strategic emphasis shifted in the late 1960s to a national, constitutional rights claim which sought complete autonomy for the woman (Rubin, 1982). In *Roe* v. *Wade* (1973) the US Supreme Court ruled that a woman does have a right, though not an absolute one, to decide to terminate her pregnancy. This right, denoted as 'privacy', was derived from the concept of personal liberty. Although the Court declined to find the fetus to be a 'person' for constitutional purposes, two state interests – medical standards and potential life – were recognized as legitimately qualifying the woman's right. The court, by identifying two temporal points in a normal pregnancy associated with relative medical safety for the mother and viability for the fetus, created a trimester scheme progressing from unrestricted autonomy to state authority, initially for health based regulation and ultimately for general restriction.

There are serious problems with this model as a theoretical perspective. The Court in *Roe* had substantial difficulty relating scientific, moral and philosophical concepts with legal and constitutional concepts. Justice Blackmun's inability to develop a consistent relationship between 'personhood' and the beginning of life and his facile use of maternal mortality data and the concept of viability as constitutional landmarks indicate the weak correspondence between the conceptual systems: 'At present only absurdity seems to result when the abortion issue is placed in a legal context – the Court can (quite literally) do nothing right, so it blunders through like a moralist pretending to be a legislature, snatching feebly at the Constitution in passing' (Newton, 1976–7, p. 250). The litigation strategy required that policy issues be recast in legal language. This vocabulary and grammar of legal rights exacerbated the conflict among persons with deep convictions which were already difficult to reconcile (Frohock, 1983; Schnably, 1984–5). The adversary process polarized these views, accentuating the differences. While abortion would be provocative in any context, consistent opinion data indicate that the majority of Americans prefers a moderate policy and does not consider the issue to be highly salient. Nevertheless, narrow and intense activist groups persist (*The Gallup Report*, 1983; Legge, 1983).

While the clarity of the trimester–autonomy approach appeared to simplify implementation, three features have reduced the effectiveness of the Court's ruling. First, the model prevents a case-by-case or even a categorical balancing of interests; this has forced opponents to contest corollary issues which complicate the analysis without addressing the underlying conflict. Second, viability and medical risk, the factors which mark the periodic breakpoints, are complex and continually changing. Third, implementation within the adversary process after such a 'clear' victory for pro-choice forces changed the focus from fraternal, mobilized solidarity to fragmented, individual disputes (Scheingold, 1974; Schnably, 1984–5). Indeed, the courts have, over the last fourteen years, 'legislated' piecemeal the particulars of an abortion code (Schnably, 1984–5).

The US approach also failed to adequately access the problem of public trust. From the rights perspective *Roe* seemed a logical extension of the liberal activism of the Warren Court. But this mischaracterizes the ruling, which did not open the matter up for reconsideration and reform. Liberal expectations that *Roe* would defuse the potential 'time bomb' and give the society time to adjust to the underlying principle (Rubin, 1982) clearly were not realized. Legislative consideration of moderate abortion models was 'short-circuited' without depoliticizing of the issue (Kommers, 1977). Rather, the politics shifted to non-legislative modes and secondary issues. Unable to proscribe abortions generally or prescribe moderate regulations, pro-life forces have been extremely successful at restricting public funding. This raises a serious equality problem and reinforces a pro-choice view of the pro-life movement as intolerant and insincere, obsessed with abortion as a symbol but unconcerned with civil liberties or other 'pro-life' issues generally (Granberg and Granberg, 1980–1; Schnably, 1984–5).

That is not to say that the *Roe* principles are necessarily inappropriate *per se*. The ultimate effectiveness of a decision is a function not only of what is decided but also of who decides, and how, when and where: 'In spite of the fact that the content of the *Roe* decision was well within the limits of public acceptance, coming as abruptly as it did, with all of the dramatic impact of a major judicial policy pronouncement, it may have accomplished too much too quickly, "like an armoured column that has raced deep into enemy territory, outstripping [its] lines of supply"' (Rubin, 1982, pp. 165–6). Activist court rulings will not destroy public trust if the court articulates a reasoned judgment which integrates public sentiment and interbranch and intergovernmental relations within a model faithful to constitutional values. When, as in *Roe*, the court fails to develop a satisfactory rationale, the decision's authority will only be sustained at the cost of continued challenge and decreased institutional legitimacy (Wardle, 1980).

As of 1970 the German Federal Republic prohibited abortion, although there was a judicially developed exception for health reasons (Gerstein and Lowry, 1976). After extended debate in public and in the Bundestag, a moderate 'indications model' reflective of public opinion appeared to be emerging (Kommers, 1977; Eser, 1986). However, complex parliamentary maneuvers resulted in 1974 in the passage of legislation which sanctioned abortion on demand during the first trimester (Gerstein and Lowry, 1976).

The Constitutional Court, upholding a challenge to the statute by states and legislators, ruled that developing life was a constitutional value which outweighed the woman's autonomy interest and which the state had an affirmative duty to protect. Health and serious social burdens could be taken into account as long as 'the totality of measures designed to protect unborn life [are] appropriate to the significance of the legal value safeguarded by the constitution' (Kommers, 1977, pp. 101–102). Subsequent conforming legislation by the Bundestag was upheld by the European Commission on Human Rights as consistent with human rights (Sealy, 1980). Although public and scholarly debate has continued (Gerstein and Lowry, 1976; Casper, 1979–80), large and strident groups have not been galvanized.

One must not ignore distinctions between the German and US constitutional traditions. There is in Germany a broader sense of participation by the entire legal community in the process of constitutional development. This provides for richer theoretical concepts and models than may develop in the adversary, litigative forum of the United States (Casper, 1979–80). Moreover, while *Roe* characterized the issue in terms of rights, the German Court emphasized competing 'values', tragic human situations, and a balancing of medical, ethical and social 'indications' (Benda, 1977). This expressed a basic difference in emphasis between the constitutional cultures – US individualism versus German communitarianism. Broad participation and communitarian values provide the German Court with a superior perspective for effective institutional response (Kommers, 1977).

Regarding process and implementation, statutes may be considered generally by the Constitutional Court upon petition by legislators and public institutions (Gerstein and Lowry, 1976), rather than according to the American 'cases and controversies' model. Indeed, the Constitutional Court is not part of the normal judicial structure. Its function and tradition has been to arbitrate passionate public conflicts by reconciling law and politics and by admonishing 'the Parliament to fulfill its role as the guardian of the commonwealth against pressure groups and group interests' (Denninger, 1985, p. 1028). Moreover, the Court's guidelines to the Bundestag were clear and consistent with traditional German concern for substantive legislative democracy (Kommers, 1977).

In terms of public trust, it will always be difficult in a pluralistic society for courts to fulfill an educative role with regard to a controversy such as abortion which represents inconsistent views of humanity and society (Frohock, 1983). Yet the German Court, less directly responsive than its US counterpart to the 'felt necessities' of the time (Kommers, 1977), promoted a *modus vivendi* consistent with the legal culture and institutions.

There is a thread in American constitutional analysis which encourages courts to look beyond the formalities of legislative action and act when an informed and concrete analysis indicates that a problem in the political process interfered with appropriate consideration of the constitutional dimension (Carter, 1979). Rather than impose their substantive views upon finding unacceptable legislative consideration, the courts should 'entreat the majority to take a sober second look at the course it has set for the nation' (Funston, 1978, p. 49). Disdaining this approach, US courts have made the abortion controversy a prime example of the 'myth of rights' with its emphasis on symbolic and Olympian struggle and its belief in the efficacy and legitimacy of judicial declarations of legal right which flow from fair, adversarial, rational and apolitical consideration of the issues (Scheingold, 1974). Yet, this approach to abortion has been narrow and incomplete.

> [I]t should come as no surprise that adequate explication and defense of these rights call upon judges to address puzzles that they may have to confess themselves partly powerless to resolve. Nor should we be surprised that full protection of these rights calls upon the rest of us to develop a constitutional discourse that is not constrained by the often narrow boundaries of judicial capacity and competence. For lawmakers, executive officials, scholars, or citizens to deem themselves absolved of the duty to address constitutional rights and concerns that courts have of necessity left imperfectly or incompletely enforced would impoverish our public life and would relegate constitutional discussion to an overly narrow – and, yes, a deliberately unrepresentative – judicial elite (Tribe, 1985, p. 343).

Yet the US tradition posits no substantive vision of the common good but only a procedural model for fairly accommodating competing claims by self-interested individuals (Kommers, 1977). This model of justice as fairness is inadequate for resolving important life-style issues. And it is different from Germany's 'unique but traditional concept of *"Statt"* which has come to mean the community of private individuals who aspire to a higher grade of moral quality than *"Gesellschaft"* or "society"' (Denninger, 1985, p. 1013).

PARLIAMENTARY ENACTMENT: ENGLAND AND FRANCE

Although abortion has been a crime under English law since the nineteenth century, legal opinion considered action to save the mother's life a defense (Potts, Diggory and Peel, 1977). Proponents of liberal change shifted their emphasis from repeal to reform in the 1960s (Francome, 1980). A large Labour majority in the House of Commons, responding to this campaign and to a general liberalization of sexual attitudes, passed the 1967 Abortion Act (Francome, 1978). This law added, as justification, risk of injury to the physical or mental health of the mother or her other children and substantial risk of abnormality in the child (Marsh and Chambers, 1981). There have been since then serious, but unsuccessful, attempts to construct a coalition of Conservatives and Catholic Labour members to substantially tighten the 1967 law. Yet these activities have been more restrained and limited than in the United States (Francome, 1978).

Parliamentary consideration promoted a moderate perspective and language, concentrating on exceptions to a general prohibition that may entitle a medical practitioner to provide abortive treatment. Rights do not constitute the central framework for debate. While this shift in perspective may be too subtle to satisfy the staunchest activists, it does permit development of a more complex evaluation of the morality and acceptability of the statute. This moderation is characteristic of British political culture (Francome, 1980) and exemplifies a consensual rather than a confrontational approach to conflict resolution (Frohock, 1983).

There are four procedural advantages to parliamentary consideration. First, institutional responsibility and accountability are clarified through a conscious concentration of power. This focused the debate upon Parliament and allowed party cohesion and the parliamentary status of the government to support a co-ordinated strategy of compromise. Second, England being a unitary rather than a federal state, legislative reform efforts did not need be diffused over fifty states. Third, since legislative questions were not posed in the 'rarified atmosphere' of the courtroom, parliamentary consideration was legitimately connected with a broader public debate on the matter. Members of Parliament could be informed by public opinion, and public opinion could be informed by the political proceedings. This is constructive regardless of the particulars of the decision (Marsh and Chambers, 1981). Fourth, pragmatic legislative bargaining allowed the decision to be made on second-order rather than first-order notions of right and wrong (Frohock, 1983). In terms of public trust the English commonly look to Parliament and politics rather than the courts for the vindication of their rights (Francome, 1980).

Prior to 1975 abortion was prohibited in France except to safeguard the mother's life (Roujou de Boubee, 1975). After extended public and parliamentary debate, the criminal code was amended to permit abortion during the first ten weeks where pregnancy places the woman in distress and thereafter where there is a threat to the mother's life or health or a risk that the child will suffer a defect. The Constitutional Council upheld the statute in the face of challenge by French legislators (Sealy, 1980).

The law does not speak of rights but rather expands the circumstances that would constitute exceptions to the general prohibition. Indeed, with the decisive support of the feminist Minister of Health came a restrained approach to reform, tolerating abortion under exceptional circumstances as a last recourse (Roujou de Boubee, 1975). Though abortion continues to be a sharp issue in French public affairs, French opinion has been largely supportive (Gallup, 1976) and the law was made permanent in 1979. Despite significant structural and cultural differences, the French experience was quite similar to the English one in terms of institutional characteristics. It was a consensus in practice, though not in fact or morality.

PLEBISCITARY VOTE: ITALY AND IRELAND

Although abortion has been prohibited in Italy since unification in 1861, the Constitutional Court, in a 'highly equivocal' decision in 1975, created an exception for abortions performed to save the mother's life or health (Bognetti, 1984, p. 86; Sealy, 1980). The Court, consistent with its tradition, declined to act as decisively as either the US or German high courts (Bognetti, 1984). Nevertheless, encouraged by this decision and by the 1974 divorce referendum, the feminist movement threatened an abortion referendum and made reform a key parliamentary issue. A developing compromise between the Christian Democrats and Communists stalled when the Catholic church pressured the Christian Democrats. The resulting stalemate brought down the Aldo Moro government. The new Christian Democratic government's abstention from the final vote in 1978 permitted the enactment of new justifications: risk to the mother's life or physical or mental health and 'social circumstances' (Ergas, 1981–2).

In 1980, three groups requested referenda on the new statutory system: (1) extreme conservatives sought to make all abortions criminal; (2) moderate conservatives sought to abrogate certain liberal provisions and reinstate serious maternal life and health risks as the only justifying factors; and (3) radical pro-choice supporters sought to abrogate all limits on the woman's choice. Although each referendum application was procedurally correct, the Constitutional Court, pursuant to Italian law, reviewed the proposals constitutionally. The Court rejected the first proposal because it would, if passed, deprive women of their constitutional rights by denying the maternal life and health justifications. The latter two referendum propositions were certified, though the radical pro-choice proposal was at variance with *dicta* in the 1975 case (Bognetti, 1984).

In May, 1981, both referendum proposals were decisively rejected by Italian voters (Bognetti, 1984). In terms of institutional factors, this was an effective mode of societal decision making. The operative language provided clear choices with respect to an existing policy that had received public, judicial and legislative attention for several years. The process allowed for an authoritative plebiscitary confirmation of the legislative balancing of values and interests tentatively done with the passage of the 1978 law. But the major centrist party had abstained earlier, indicating the dilemma of the Christian Democratic Party caught between its religious and secular bases. The referenda thus allowed the nation to resolve the issue without forcing the Christian Democrats to throw themselves on either horn of the dilemma.

In Ireland the authoritarian relationship between the Irish state and the Catholic church created an unfortunate symbolic conflict where no substantial controversy existed. The text of the existing law, carried forward after independence from an 1861 English codification, absolutely prohibits abortion (Quinlan, 1984; Potts, Diggory and Peel, 1977; Mathews, 1976). Nonetheless, conservative Irish doctors and lawyers became concerned about possible interpretations and applications of the statute for four reasons: (1) the general trend in the western democracies toward liberalization; (2) the absence in the Irish Constitution of explicit protection for the unborn; (3) the articulation by the Irish Supreme Court, relying on US Supreme Court cases on birth control and without explicit Irish constitutional basis, of a right to marital privacy in reproductive matters; and (4) the possibility that the European Convention on Human Rights and Fundamental Freedoms, to which Ireland was a signatory, might be interpreted to require protection of a woman's right to abortion (Quinlan, 1984).

Campaign commitments to bring forward a constitutional amendment to insulate abortion from the possibility of majoritarian change led to decisive majority approval, albeit with a strikingly low turnout, of the amendment in a September 1983 national referendum (Quinlan, 1984). Nevertheless, the effectiveness of this institutional mechanism is seriously suspect. The amendment's language was criticised for its technical ambiguity. Nor did the process allow for an extended public debate. In Ireland, most of the debate centered on the politics of the referendum and the wording of the amendment rather than abortion policy. Final legislative approval depended upon abstention by the major partner of the ruling coalition. Indeed, the Attorney General and the Prime Minister ultimately criticized the ambiguity of the amendment, and the Prime Minister recommended that citizens reject the amendment (Quinlan, 1984). Voters were left merely with intense emotions and religious symbolism. All sides were frustrated and bitter about the course of events. The victorious pro-life supporters worried that the need to resolve ambiguities in the amendment about when 'unborn life' begins and what 'with due regard to the equal right of the mother' means would return the critical decisions to the judiciary, as they had originally feared (Quinlan, 1984). Defeated pro-choice supporters lost confidence in the Catholic majority's capacity for tolerance necessary for movement toward pluralism. Ultimately, the referendum decreased public trust in the process without substantially resolving underlying substantive issues.

CONCLUSIONS

Although it is difficult to reduce these complex and varied developments to a simple evaluation, the experiences of West Germany, England, France and Italy can be distinguished from those of the United States and Ireland. The former group can be described as having had more successful experiences, understanding that a 'solution' is not always possible and that resolution, or even coping, may be the measure of success. Each nation in the first group had an extended period of general public debate which preceded the decisive societal decision. In each of these cases deliberation and decision moved towards a moderate position not dominated in language, perspective or mobilization by irreconcilable extremes. In Italy and the Federal Republic of Germany as well as in England and France, the legislative branch operated critically as an important contributor to the struggle towards a *modus vivendi* which satisfied the center of public opinion as it dissappointed activists. A national, legislative focus was not feasible in the federal United States. Constructive struggle towards a middle ground never occurred in Ireland because the constitutional amendment foreclosed open national debate. Critical to these successes and failure is the relationship between individualistic or communitarian conceptions of society and rights. Rights may protect social and moral values, but they are not identical or even necessarily equivalent: 'A critical doctrine of abortion will necessarily fail if it makes unthinking use of the liberal dichotomies of rights and the Right, politics and morality, public and private. At the same time, however, any effort simply to collapse them would be profoundly misguided' (Schnably, 1984–5, p. 887). In a European tradition which is liberal *and* communitarian, 'right' and 'rights' may be constructively reconciled. In the adversarial and atomistic liberalism of the United States or the religious and authoritarian tradition of Ireland, the mixture is unstable and explosive for pragmatic as well as normative reasons. Rights may require that issues – either frozen in the decisions of an earlier era or vaulted into a premature tomorrow – be reopened and submitted to public dialogue. Rights work worst when they act as 'trump' to pre-empt this vital national seminar (Funston, 1978). Rights work best when they infuse the debate with the fundamental values upon which the community is based. Where this civic pedagogy can take place is where the thorny problem of abortion is best considered.

References

BENDA, E. (1977) 'The Impact of Constitutional Law on the Protection of Unborn Human Life: Some Comparative Remarks', *Human Rights*, 6: 223.

BOGNETTI, Giovanni (1984) 'Italy', in Dennis Campbell (ed.), *Abortion Law and Public Policy*, pp. 83–94 (Dordrecht, The Netherlands: Martinus Nijhoff).

CARTER, L. H. (1979) *Reason in Law* (Boston: Little, Brown).

CARTER, L. H. (1977) 'When Courts Should Make Policy: An Institutional

Approach', in J. A. Gardiner (ed.), *Public Law and Public Policy*, pp. 141–57 (New York: Praeger).

CASPER, G. (1979–80) 'Guardians of the Constitution', *Southern California Law Review*, 53: 773.

DENNINGER, Erhard (1985) 'Judicial Review Revisited: The German Experience', *Tulane Law Review*, 59: 1013.

ERGAS, Y. (1981–2) '1968–79, Feminism and the Italian Party System: Women's Politics in a Decade of Turmoil', *Comparative Politics*, 14: 253.

ESER, Albin (1986) 'Reform of German Abortion Law', *The American Journal of Comparative Law*, 34: 369.

FRANCOME, C. (1980) 'Abortion Politics in the United States', *Political Studies*, 28: 613.

FRANCOME, C. (1978) 'Abortion: Why the Issue Has Not Disappeared', *Political Quarterly* (London), 49: 217.

FRIEDRICH, Carl J. (1963) 'Rights, Liberties, Freedoms: A Reappraisal', *American Political Science Review*, 57: 841.

FROHOCK, F. M. (1983) *Abortion: A Case Study in Law and Morals* (Westport, Connecticut: Greenwood Press).

FUNSTON, R. (1978) *A Vital National Seminar: The Supreme Court in American Political Life* (Palo Alto, Calif.: Mayfield).

GALLUP, G. H. (ed.) (1976) *The Gallup International Public Opinion Polls, France, 1939, 1949–1975* (Westport, Conn.: Greenwood Press).

The Gallup Report (1983) August, 215: 16.

GERSTEIN, H. and LOWRY, D. (1976) 'Abortion, Abstract Norms, and Social Control: The Decision of the West German Federal Constitutional Court', *Emory Law Journal*, 25: 849.

GRANBERG, D. and GRANBERG, B. W. (1980–1) 'Pro-Life Versus Pro-Choice: Another Look at the Abortion Controversy in the US', *Sociology and Social Research*, 65: 424.

KOMMERS, D. P. (1977) 'Abortion and the Constitution: The Cases of the United States and West Germany', in Edward Manier, William Liu and David Solomon (eds), *Abortion: New Direction for Policy Studies*, pp. 83–116 (Notre Dame, Indiana: University of Notre Dame Press).

LEGGE, J. S. Jr. (1983) 'The Determinants of Attitudes Toward Abortion in the American Electorate', *Western Political Quarterly*, 36: 479.

MARSH, D. and CHAMBERS, J. (1981) *Abortion Politics* (London: Junction Books).

MATHEWS, M. (1976) 'Quantitative Interference with the Right to Life: Abortion and Irish Law', *Catholic Lawyer*, 22: 344.

NEWTON, Lisa H. (1976–7) 'Abortion in the Law: An Essay on Absurdity', *Ethics*, 87: 244.

POTTS, M., DIGGORY, P. and PEEL, J. (1977) *Abortion* (Cambridge: Cambridge University Press).

QUINLAN, John A. (1984) 'The Right to Life of the Unborn – Assessment of the Eighth Amendment to the Irish Constitution', *Brigham Young University Law Review*, 1984: 371.

Roe v. Wade (1973) 410 US 113.

ROUJOU DE BOUBEE, G. (1975) 'L'interruption Volontaire de la Grossesse', *Recueil Dalloz Sirey*, October 29, 1975 Chronique, 209.

RUBIN, E. R. (1982) *Abortion, Politics, and the Courts: Roe v. Wade and Its Aftermath* (Westport, Conn.: Greenwood Press).

SCHEINGOLD, S. A. (1974) *The Politics of Rights: Lawyers, Public Policy, and Political Change* (New Haven, Conn.: Yale University Press).

SCHNABLY, Stephen J. (1984–5) 'Normative Judgment, Social Change, and Legal Reasoning in the Context of Abortion and Privacy', *New York University Review of Law and Social Change*, 13: 715.

SEALY, T. R. III (1980) 'Abortion Law Reform in Europe: The European Commission on Human Rights Upholds German Restrictions on Abortion', *Texas International Law Journal*, 15: 162.

TATALOVICH, Raymond and DAYNES, Byron W. (1981) *The Politics of Abortion: A Study of Community Conflict in Public Policy Making* (New York: Praeger).

TRIBE, Laurence H. (1985) 'The Abortion Funding Conundrum: Inalienable Rights, Affirmative Duties, and the Dilemma of Dependence', *Harvard Law Review*, 99: 330.

WARDLE, L. D. (1980) 'The Gap between Law and Moral Order: An Examination of the Legitimacy of the Supreme Court Abortion Decisions', *Brigham Young University Law Review*, 1980: 811.

Part IV

Consequences of Cross-National Variations

13 Can Democracy Survive Where There is a Gap Between Political and Economic Rights?

Zehra F. Arat

Political systems and public policies are strongly linked in a reciprocal cause and effect relationship. If the policies refer to human rights, this relationship appears to be even stronger since the recognition and practices of human rights in a society reflect the nature of the political – or even the social – system. This paper seeks to study the balance among different human rights policies, classifying human rights into two groups, namely civil and political rights and social and economic rights respectively. This paper will also attempt to analyze the impact of these two groups of human rights on the stability of democratic political systems.

A TYPOLOGY FOR HUMAN RIGHTS

Although the concept of human rights is old, its content and scope are still debated. Not interested in resuming such a debate here, the Universal Declaration of Human Rights, accepted by the members of the United Nations, will be employed as the conventional definition of the term. Although each category might have been named differently, human rights are often classified into three groups similar to a typology developed by T. H. Marshall (1964) more than two decades ago:

1. *Civil rights* such as freedom from slavery and servitude, discrimination, torture and inhuman punishment, and arbitrary arrest and imprisonment; freedom of speech, faith, opinion and expression; right to life, security, justice, ownership, and assembly.
2. *Political rights* such as the right to vote, right to nominate for public office, and right to form and join political parties.

221

3. *Social and economic rights* such as the right to education, work,
food, clothing, housing, medical care; in short, the rights ranging
from 'the right to a modicum of economic welfare and security to
the right to share to the full in the social heritage and to live the
life of a civilized being according to the standards prevailing in
the society' (Marshall, 1964, p. 72).

For this study these three categories can be reduced to two by
combining civil rights with political rights. As far as their relationship
to the political system is concerned, the first two categories of human
rights cannot be treated separately since the fulfillment of civil rights
influences the effective utilization of political rights. Both civil and
political rights directly refer to the relationship between the individual
and the state. Social and economic rights refer to the socio-economic
conditions and status of the individual within a society. Thus, human
rights are divided into two groups: civil and political rights and social
and economic rights.

DEMOCRACY AND HUMAN RIGHTS

Overlaps in Definitions

A careful examination of civil and political rights shows they include
the ingredients of a democratic political system. The modern literature
on democracy and contemporary applications of the term indicate
clearly that the meaning attributed to the term 'democracy' has
changed. An early (or the ideal) perception of the term, 'self-
government', has evolved to 'control of government'. According to
Mayo (1960), democracy is a system 'in which public policies are
made, on a majority basis, by representatives subject to effective
popular control at periodic elections which are conducted on the
principle of political equality and under the conditions of political
freedom' (p. 70). This definition, similar to those of MacIver (1947,
p. 198), Schumpeter (1950, p. 284), Dahl (1956, p. 84), Downs (1957,
p. 23), Lipset (1959, p. 71), Sartori (1965, p. 66), and Coulter (1975,
p. 1), shows that this new meaning attributed to 'democracy' makes
it a quality of political systems which varies in degree rather than in
kind. Thus, if democracy is not a have/have not attribute of political
systems, it is necessary to switch from categorical definitions to a
continuum where political systems can be described as 'more' or 'less'

democratic rather than 'democratic' or 'undemocratic'. The place of a political system on such a continuum depends on the extent to which it recognizes and reinforces civil and political rights. Thus, the more strongly civil and political rights are reinforced in a society, the more democratic it becomes.

However, the achievement of a certain level of civil and political rights or a certain level of 'democraticness' does not mean that the level will be sustained.

The Variation in Democraticness

Earlier studies on democracy were mainly interested in explaining the variation in the level of democraticness established in different countries and their findings appeared to agree with the modernization theory. The authors of these studies developed several measures of 'democraticness' and found the economic development level positively related to the democratic performance of a country (Lipset, 1959; Cutright, 1963; Cutright and Wiley, 1969; Smith, 1969; Bollen, 1979). Other scholars further identified the development of democracy as a threshold phenomenon. Their statistical analysis showed that democraticness increased with increases in economic development until a high economic development level was reached; further economic development, however, did not reinforce democraticness (Neubauer, 1967; Jackman, 1973).

The findings by both groups of scholars support an evolutionary thesis of democracy. The thesis suggests that once a highly democratic political system is established, it will be maintained and improved by further economic development. However, this appears to be a false assumption which largely stems from over-reliance on cross-sectional analysis as opposed to longitudinal analysis. The indices or scales of democracy developed by these scholars prevented them from studying the variation in democraticness of a country over time.

An alternative measure of 'democraticness' has been developed by the author (Arat, 1984)[1]. This measure quantifies concepts such as popular control in legislative selection, legislative effectiveness, competitiveness of the nomination procedure, party legitimacy, party competitiveness and government coerciveness. Applied to a group of independent countries for the years 1948 to 1977, this scale of democraticness yields annual scores for 2985 cases (64 to 130 countries for thirty years) from the least democratic to the most democratic respectively.

Annual data on democraticness enable a measure of annual change for this property. The author's study of these scores of annual change displays that the scope of change in democraticness varies considerably (1984, p. 176–201). Some countries manifest extreme change, both up and down the scale, moving from authoritarian to democratic political systems or vice versa. Among the countries studied, Peru displays the greatest positive change, by 15.81 points from 1962 to 1963; and Chile displays the most pronounced decline, with a change score of −16.90 from 1972 to 1973. High increases took place also in Turkey from 1960 to 1961, with a rise of 14.98; in Venezuela from 1958 to 1959, with a rise of 14.88; in Spain from 1976 to 1977, with a rise of 13.27; and in Burma from 1959 to 1960, with a rise of 13.17. Severe declines, on the other hand, are experienced by Uruguay from 1972 to 1973, with a decline of −16.85 points; Greece from 1966 to 1967, with a decline of −16.68 points; Peru from 1967 to 1968, with a decline of −16.04 points; and Burma from 1958 to 1959, with a decline of −15.99 points.

Although these countries with extreme change scores could be placed on the middle of the economic development paradigm, a further analysis of the relationship between economic development and poltical stability is required.

DEMOCRATIC INSTABILITY AND ECONOMIC DEVELOPMENT

A measure of 'instability' in regard to democraticness – based on the index of democraticness discussed above – was developed to identify patterns of vacillation. For each country, the sum of the absolute values of the annual change in democraticness index score was divided by the number of years in the time period covered (which varies for each country according to the date of independence and data availability) to obtain an average score of change in democraticness. This calculation follows the logic that the more frequent and/or larger the shifts a country experiences on the democraticness paradigm, the higher 'democratic instability' score it will get. Out of 127 countries included here, Sudan (3.15), Pakistan (2.67), Burma (2.53), Argentina (2.32), and Peru (2.16) composed the most unstable group; while Austria (0.03), Switzerland (.04), Saudi Arabia (.048), Sweden (.05), and New Zealand (.06) appeared to be the most stable countries – where the mean value for instability is .87 (Table 13.1).

Table 13.1 The list of 127 countries and their instability scores

Austria	.03	Lebanon	.55	Laos	1.08
Switzerland	.04	Ethiopia	.56	Cameroun	1.08
Saudi Arabia	.05	Costa Rica	.57	Germany, Dem. Rep.	1.10
Sweden	.05	Zambia	.57	Cuba	1.10
New Zealand	.06	UK	.58	Panama	1.11
Ireland	.07	Tanzania	.59	El Salvador	1.14
Liberia	.09	Kampuchea	.59	Dominican Rep.	1.15
Belgium	.11	India	.60	Jordon	1.17
Albania	.12	Finland	.60	Philippines	1.19
Japan	.13	Iceland	.61	Uruguay	1.20
Italy	.13	Denmark	.61	Colombia	1.20
Korea, Peoples Rep.	.14	Germany, Fed. Rep.	.62	Vietnam, South	1.22
USSR	.18	Tunisia	.64	Botswana	1.30
Yemen, Arab Rep.	.18	Spain	.65	Madagascar	1.30
Mexico	.19	South Africa	.65	Lesotho	1.30
France	.19	Egypt	.65	Syria	1.36
Bulgaria	.25	Australia	.66	Guyana	1.38
Senegal	.26	Canada	.67	Jamaica	1.40
Mali	.29	Romania	.67	Upper Volta	1.41
Paraguay	.29	Somalia	.69	Brazil	1.41
Libya	.30	Ecuador	.69	Yemen. PDR.	1.46
Niger	.31	Hungary	.73	Korea, Rep.	1.46
Poland	.32	Israel	.74	Chile	1.46
Burundi	.33	Maldives	.75	Barbados	1.47
USA	.36	Morocco	.76	Uganda	1.50
Yugoslavia	.36	Sri Lanka	.79	Nigeria	1.54
Malawi	.38	Ivory Coast	.81	Malaya	1.55
Afghanistan	.38	Mauritius	.81	Indonesia	1.56
Iraq	.39	Portugal	.81	Gambia	1.57
Mongolia	.39	Venezuela	.82	Malta	1.57
Nepal	.40	Czechoslovakia	.83	Guatemala	1.71
Zimbabwe	.40	Nicaragua	.84	Thailand	1.77
Benin	.44	Zaire	.87	Bolivia	1.79
Norway	.45	Vietnam, Peoples Rep.	.88	Turkey	1.81
Rwanda	.46	Haiti	.88	Honduras	1.89
Algeria	.47	Chad	.92	Greece	1.91
Guine	.48	Singapore	.94	Ghana	2.03
China	.48	Congo	.94	Trinidad	2.04
Luxemburg	.48	Central Africa	.96	Peru	2.16
Cyprus	.51	Kuwait	1.00	Argentina	2.32
Iran	.53	Gabon	1.01	Burma	2.53
Netherland	.54	Mauritania	1.03	Pakistan	2.67
				Sudan	3.15

It should be noted that the instability score does not measure political instability, but specifically instability in regard to democraticness. That is, countries ranking high on this scale experience higher rates of change between relatively more authoritarian and democratic systems.

To test the hypothesis that the middle-range developed countries (MDCs) experience higher levels of democratic instability, as opposed to least developed (LDC) and advanced developed (ADC) countries, a regression model which captures the curvi-linearity of the relationship between economic development and instability is used. The instability scores for all of the countries listed on Table 13.1, except Botswana, Lesotho and Maldives (excluded due to lack of information on energy consumption), are regressed on the logarithmic values of their average energy consumption per capita (ENCOM), the commonly used indicator of economic development,[2] and the squared value of this indicator. Logarithmic transformation of average energy consumption values is employed to smooth the data which are highly (positively) skewed.

$$\text{Instability}_i = a + b_1 \, (ln\text{ENCOM})_i + b_2 \, (ln\text{ENCOM})^2_i + u_i$$

In this second degree polynomial model, if the regression coefficient b_1 is positive but b_2 is negative and they are both significant, then a curvi-linear relationship between the instability of the political system and economic development is demonstrated. Economic development appears with democratic instability until a certain level is reached, but further development appears with higher levels of stability in relation to the democraticness of the political system.

The results of this analysis are reported on Table 13.2. The findings display that an evolutionary thesis based on cross-national data for fixed time point is misleading. The findings support the hypothesis that it is the relatively more developed countries (MDCs) which experience more frequent and/or larger shifts between more and less democratic systems. Specifically, if some of the extreme cases seen on Figure 13.1 (which is the plot of instability scores on the logarithmic

Table 13.2   Regression of instability on economic development

Variable	Regression coefficients	
	Model I, N = 124 (including all cases)	Model II, N = 118 (excluding extreme cases)
Intercept	.35*	−.86**
*ln*ENCON	.55*	.76*
*ln*ENCON²	−.05*	−.07*
R^2	.12*	.19*

* Significant at .01 level.
** Significant at .10 level.

values of average energy consumption per capita) are dropped, the model provides a better fit to the data (Table 13.2).

When six cases, Kuwait, Trinidad, Upper Volta, Senegal, Albania and Liberia, are excluded from the analysis, the model explains 19 per cent of the variance in democratic instability scores, which is 7 per cent more than the variance explained with all cases in the group. It is reasonable to drop these cases, since Kuwait and Trinidad have unexpectedly high instability scores for their economic development level. Considering their performance on other socio-economic indicators, it can be argued that these two countries are misplaced on the economic development paradigm by our measure. On the other hand, Upper Volta, as an LDC, experiences unexpectedly high instability. Senegal, Liberia and Albania, as MDCs, experience extremely low level of democratic instability and compose another group of extreme cases which require special treatment.

The analysis shows that establishing of democratic institutions does not guarantee their survival and that the relationship between socio-economic development and democratization is not as smooth as modernization theorists suggest. In fact, the countries which fall

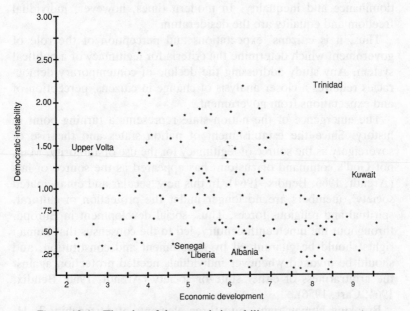

Figure 13.1   The plot of democratic instability scores on economic development level

between the advanced developed countries and the least developed countries tend to experience higher levels of fluctuations between highly democratic and authoritarian systems.

The next question then is 'what problems, common to MDCs, prevent them from maintaining their highly democratic political systems?'

A NEW THEORY OF DEMOCRATIC INSTABILITY

Legitimacy and Human Rights

One common argument advanced to explain the breakdown of highly democratic systems asserts that disintegration tends to take place due to a loss of legitimacy. Legitimacy is defined as the 'degree to which institutions are valued for themselves and considered right and proper' (Lipset, 1959, p. 71).

The crucial point is that the criteria for a legitimate political system will change over time. For example, feudalism was a legitimate political and social system in the past even though it was based on dominance and inequality. In modern times, however, individual freedom and equality are the desideratum.

Thus, it is citizens' expectations and perception of the role of government which determine the criteria for legitimacy of a political system. Any study addressing the decline of contemporary democracies requires a closer analysis of change in citizens' perception of and expectations from government.

The emergence of the nation state represents a turning point in history. Since the establishment of nation states and the rise of sovereignty as the source of legitimacy for the use of authority, Man, not God's command or custom, has appeared as the source of law (Arendt, 1966; Bendix, 1964). In this new 'secular and emancipated society', members are no longer under the protection of cultural, spiritual and religious forces. Thus, social development in Europe, throughout the nineteenth century, led to the consensus that human rights should be guaranteed by government and constitution, and should be invoked whenever individuals needed protection against the arbitrariness of either state or society (Arendt, 1966; Bendix, 1964; Carr, 1956).

Breaking human rights into three elements of citizenship, T. H. Marshall (1964) argues 'it is possible without doing much violence to historical accuracy, to assign the formative period in the life of each to a different century – civil rights to the eighteenth, political to the nineteenth and social to the twentieth. These periods must, of course, be treated with reasonable elasticity, and there is some evident overlap, especially between the last two' (p. 74).

During the twentieth century the role of government has broadened from that of merely maintaining domestic tranquility and protecting the state against foreign attacks. A new obligation appears to be to contribute to the material security of the subjects or the members of society. As Moore states, 'the Nineteenth-Century notion that society bore no responsibility for the welfare of the population, that it was both especially futile and quite immoral to expect the chief of state to take effective action countering threats to popular welfare, now looks like a minor historical aberration' (1978, p. 22).

Thus, in the modern world the extent to which social and economic rights are recognized and reinforced within a society becomes crucial in determining the legitimacy of its political system, especially if it is a highly democratic one.

We have already indicated that civil and political rights are closely related to the nature of political systems and these rights must be recognized by the government in order to maintain a highly democratic political system. The stability of the system, however, is threatened if a highly democratic government cannot reinforce social and economic rights at a comparable level. A conflict arises if social and economic rights draw a declining curve or a constant line while civil and political rights expand over time. This conflict often occurs in young democracies struggling for economic development.

Given low levels of economic development and high levels of economic dependence, a rapid economic growth rate appears to be the major concern of governments in developing countries. Evincing a higher concern about the rate of economic growth, as opposed to an egalitarian distribution of wealth, governments pursue policies which tend to intensify social and economic inequalities (Olson, 1963; Polanyi, 1967; Wright, 1978). Such economic policies, which are either initiated by domestic leadership or imposed by foreign institutions (e.g. the IMF) through high levels of economic dependency and indebtedness, cause the system to be perceived as unresponsive or ineffective, and weaken legitimacy. The continuous neglect of social and economic rights prevents these developing countries from realizing the transformation of 'estate societies' to 'welfare states', which occurred in Western Europe (Bendix, 1964).

Social and economic rights neglected by several elected administrations are likely to weaken citizen confidence in the electoral system. The stagnation of electoral representative systems leads those segments of the society struggling with such problems as unemployment and declining real wages to pursue actions which threaten the foundations of the system of government. Thomas Rose argues that violence is a political resource when the traditional 'bargaining process provides no other alternatives, or at least when some groups perceive no other alternatives' (Rose, 1969, p. 30).

Confronted with high levels of social unrest, governments in developing countries without sufficient economic resources respond with coercive measures. The result is less democratic government. It is common to witness a democratic political elite taking authoritarian measures with a Machiavellian pragmatism while still espousing democracy as the best form of government.

Suppression of social unrest may occur as (a) an incremental policy which gradually curtails civil and political rights at different junctures, or (b) as an absolute transformation of the regime either by the incumbent or the opposition (counter elite). The first strategy, likely to be followed by the incumbent elite, may appear in the form of constitutional amendments, legal codes and governmental sanctions, the second may vary from social revolution to *coup d'etat*. In each case, the 'democraticness' of the system declines. A less democratic government may not be able to meet the demands for increases in social and economic rights, but it will almost certainly be more successful in suppressing them (Bollen, 1979).

Imbalanced Human Rights and Instability

It can be argued that political systems seek a balance between civil and political rights, and social and economic rights. Assuming that both groups of rights are measures on the same scale, a political system would approach a balance and stability when the ratio (RT) of civil and political rights (CIVIPOL) to social and economic rights (SOCIECO) approaches 1.

$$RT = \frac{\text{CIVIPOL}}{\text{SOCIECO}} = 1$$

An imbalance between the two groups of rights would be observed if a system ranks high on one and low on the other, and the ratio is greater or less than 1.

$$RT = \frac{\text{CIVIPOL}}{\text{SOCIECO}} < 1; \quad \text{OR} \quad RT = \frac{\text{CIVIPOL}}{\text{SOCIECO}} > 1;$$

The imbalance in favor of social and economic rights (RT < 1) refers to a condition where the level of democraticness is already low, but social and economic rights policies are effective. We would expect the level of democraticness in such societies to be stable. If the imbalance is in favor of civil and political rights (RT > 1), however, the level of democraticness would tend to decline.

Figure 13.2 refers to the interaction between these two groups of rights and their relation to the level of economic development. According to the argument presented above, the independent nation states which fall into the first three cells are expected to be fairly stable (RT ≤ 1), but the ones in the fourth cell are expected to experience significant levels of democratic instability (RT > 1). The first cell refers to the socialist dictatorships which are economically developed or ranked relatively higher on the scale of social and economic rights and tend to be stable. The second cell includes industrialized, Western democracies which are quite stable in their democratic performance. The third cell includes developing countries under authoritarian rule. Finally, the fourth cell includes developing countries which have failed to improve social and economic rights to the level of their civil and political rights, and appear to be unstable political democracies. These countries tend toward the second cell, but often move back to the third cell. Increasing popularity of democracy as a political system and development of civil rights movements as an ideological force lead some of these MDCs to restore their democratic institutions even if they may not last long. In his discussion of trade-offs between policy goals, Nagel identifies developing countries (MDCs) as the group which experience a higher degree of tension between equality and freedom as opposed to predeveloping/feudal and developed/industrialized societies (Nagel, 1986, p. 99).

In different terms, the growth of negative rights without the support of positive rights tends to bring about a reversal of human rights conditions. Civil and political rights are negative rights in a sense that they generally require non-action by governments. Governments should not torture citizens; should not conduct arbitrary arrests; and

Civil and political rights

	Low	High
High	Socialist dictatorships	Industrialized Western democracies
Low	Authoritarian developing countries	Democratic developing countries

Social and economic rights

Figure 13.2   Balance and imbalance between the two groups of human rights

should not prevent meetings, political participation, freedom of speech. Social and economic rights, on the contrary, are positive rights which require positive action by governments. Governments should maintain a certain quality of life, diminish unemployment, and provide food, shelter, and medical care. Thus, governments, in developing countries which fail to take positive actions to improve social and economic rights risk destabilization by their enfranchised but impoverished citizens.

The Difference between the Old and New Democracies

Since the scope of human rights has expanded in the West, the old democracies have had approximately three centuries to respond to the increasing citizen demands.

According to Lucian Pye (1966), 'the particular pattern of development of any country depends largely upon the sequence in which the crises arise [crises of identity, legitimacy, penetration, participation, integration and distribution] and the ways in which they are resolved' (p. 66). He argues that in England, which is considered to be 'the model of modern democracies', crises arose sequentially and were resolved gradually: 'The English developed a sense of national identity early, the issue of the legitimacy of the monarchy and government was well established before the problem of expanding participation appeared and, finally, serious issues of distribution did not arise until after the political system was relatively well integrated' (p. 66).

In comparison to their counterparts in earlier centuries, however, developing countries today confront more complex and intricate problems. In the wake of emergence as new nation states and facing worldwide pressure to adopt democratic political institutions (McKeon, 1951; Mayo, 1960; Huntington, 1968; Bollen, 1979), the late developers lack the resources and/or willingness to provide material security or a more egalitarian distribution of wealth. Huntington (1968) analyzes the distinction in the historical experience of the late and early developers:

In the modernization of the non-Western parts of the world, however, the problems of the centralization of authority, national integration, social mobilization, economic development, political participation, social welfare have arisen not sequentially but simultaneously. The 'demonstration effect' which the early modernizers have on the later modernizers first intensifies aspirations and then exacerbates frustration (p. 46).

Sequential or gradual social and political change was not unique to the English, but experienced by most of the Western democracies. Even the old human rights (civil and political), which were well received by the emerging economic elite in these countries, were extended to the lower classes gradually. Moreover, the new rights (social and economic) were made possible and maintained in these countries through the Western imperialism. Imperialism enabled an increase in the standard of living for the lower classes without a vast redistribution of wealth at home. The ex-colonies or the developing countries today, however, are not only facing problems which emerge simultaneously, but they also lack the means of exploiting others to satisfy their demanding citizens.

Accordingly, in following strategies which aim at rapid economic growth without an egalitarian distribution of benefits, democratic leaders in developing countries expose themselves to a chain of problems which may eventually result in highly democratic governments being replaced by more authoritarian ones. Olson (1963) also comments on this dilemma: 'It is no doubt true that the underdeveloped countries cannot afford modern welfare measures as well as the advanced nations can. But it is perhaps also true that they need these modern welfare institutions more than advanced countries do' (p. 551).

Notes

1. The data for the components of this measure were obtained from data archives compiled by Arthur Banks and Charles Taylor. These data are documented in Arthur Banks, (1979) *Cross-Polity Time Series Data Archive* (Binghamton, New York: The Center for Social Analysis) and in Charles L. Taylor and Michael C. Hudson (1972) *World Handbook of Political and Social Indicators*, 2nd ed. (New Haven: Yale University Press). Some additional unpublished data for the 1970's were also released by Charles Taylor upon a request by the author.

2. The pitfalls of using a single indicator for a complex concept like socio-economic development or modernization, and the changes in the implications of such indicators over time have been discussed and displayed by Arthur Banks (1981). However, Sofranko, Nolan and Bealer (1975) consider energy consumption per capita as a reliable and valid indicator of modernization, defined by Levy (1966) in terms of the use of inanimate sources of energy. This is a conceptualization which holds valid for a long period of human history. On the basis of their analysis of data from seventy-four countries and for five different commonly used indicators of modernization, Sofranko, Nolan and Bealer (1975) conclude that 'all five societal measures correlate quite highly with each other, and in an empirical sense, are not highly distinct from one another. The overall significance of the findings is that all of the societal measures, whether they are labeled modernization, societal differentiation, human resource development, or economic development are apparently not measuring different aspects of societies, but rather some general underlying dimension. Considering data availability, coverage and accessibility, an argument is presented for use of "energy consumption" as the measure of societal modernity – development' (p. 301).

References

ARAT, Z. F. (1984) The Viability of Political Democracy in Developing Countries. PhD dissertation, The State University of New York at Binghamton.

ARENDT, H. (1966) *The Origins of Totalitarianism*, 3rd edn (New York: Harcourt, Brace & World).

BANKS, A. S. (1981) 'An Index of Socio-Economic Development 1869–1975', *Journal of Politics*, 43(2): 360–411.

BENDIX, R. (1964) *Nation-Building and Citizenship: Studies of Our Changing Social Order* (New York: John Wiley).

BOLLEN, K. (1979) 'Political Democracy and the Timing of Development', *American Sociological Review*, 44(3): 572–87.

CARR, E. H. (1956) *The New Society* (Boston, Mass.: Beacon Press).

COULTER, P. (1975) *Social Mobilization and Liberal Democracy* (Lexington: Lexington Books).

CUTRIGHT, P. (1963) 'National Political Development: It's Measures and Analysis', *American Sociological Review*, 28(2): 253–64.

CUTRIGHT, P. and WILEY, J. A. (1969) 'Modernization and Political Representation, 1927–1966', *Studies in Comparative International Development*, 5(2): 23–41.

DAHL, R. A. (1956) *A Preface to Democratic Theory* (Chicago: University of Chicago Press).

DOWNS, A. (1957) *A Preface to Democratic Theory* (New York: Harper & Row).

HUNTINGTON, S. P. (1968) *Political Order in Changing Societies* (New Haven: Yale University Press).

JACKMAN, R. W. (1973) 'On the Relation of Economic Development to Democratic Performance', *American Journal of Political Science*, 17(3): 611–21.

LEVY, M. J. (1966) *Modernization and the Structure of Societies* (Princeton: Princeton University Press).

LIPSET, S. M. (1959) 'Some Social Requisites of Democracy: Economic Development and Poltical Legitimacy', *American Political Science Review*, 53(1): 69–105.

MacIVER, R. M. (1947) *The Web of Government* (New York: Macmillan).

MARSHALL, T. H. (1964) *Class, Citizenship and Social Development* (Garden City, NY: Doubleday).

MAYO, H. B. (1960) *An Introduction to Democratic Theory* (New York: Oxford University Press).

McKEON, R. (ed.) (1951) *Democracy in a World of Tensions: A Symposium Prepared by UNESCO* (Chicago: University of Chicago Press).

MOORE, B. Jr. (1968) *Injustice: The Social Bases of Obedience and Revolt.* (New York: Pantheon Books).

NAGEL, S. (1984) *Public Policy: Goals, Means, and Methods* (New York: St. Martin's Press).

NEUBAUER, D. E. (1967) 'Some Social Conditions of Democracy', *American Political Science Review*, 61(4): 1002–1009.

OLSON, M. Jr. (1963) 'Rapid Growth as a Destabilizing Force', *Journal of Economic History*, 23(4): 529–53.

POLANYI, K. (1957) *The Great Transformation* (Boston: Beacon Press).

PYE, L. W. (1966) *Aspects of Political Development* (Boston: Little, Brown).

ROSE, T. (1969) 'How Violence Occurs: A Theory and Review of the Literature, in T. Rose (ed.), *Violence in America*, pp. 26–53 (New York: Random House).

SARTORI, G. (1965) *Democratic Theory* (New York: Praeger).

SCHUMPETER, J. A. (1950) *Capitalism, Socialism, and Democracy* (New York: Harper & Brothers).

SMITH, K., Jr. (1969) 'Socioeconomic Development and Political Democracy: A Causal Analysis', *Midwest Journal of Political Science*, 13(1): 95–125.

SOFRANKO, A., NOLAN, M. F. and BEALER, R. C. (1975) 'Energy Use and Alternative Measures of Societal Modernity', *Sociology and Social Research*, 59(4): 301–17.

WRIGHT, C. L. (1978) 'Income Inequality and Economic Growth: Examining the Evidence', *Journal of Developing Areas*, 13(1): 49–66.

14 Human Rights and US Bilateral Aid Allocations to Africa

Thomas E. Pasquarello

Almost fifteen years have passed since the initial efforts of Congress to incorporate human rights concerns in US bilateral aid decisions. During this period new organizations and procedures have been established within the US government to monitor human rights practices abroad, and laws have been passed which specifically link human rights practices to foreign aid decisions. These actions have drawn criticism from both sides of the ideological spectrum. Some liberal critics have argued that human rights concerns have been largely subordinated to economic and national security interests in US aid decisions, while conservatives have often maintained that human rights initiatives have negatively affected US economic and national security interests.

Empirical studies of recent US aid decisions have not resolved the controversy over the effects of human rights initiatives. Carleton and Stohl (1985), Stohl, Carleton and Johnson (1984), Lappé, Collins and Moore (1981), and Chomsky and Herman (1979) have concluded that efforts to link human rights and foreign aid have been, at best, ineffective. However, Cingranelli and Pasquarello (1985), and Schoultz (1981) found more positive effects.

This study examines US bilateral aid decisions toward African nations in Fiscal Year 1982. Its purpose is twofold. Substantively, it focuses on a region that has been largely ignored in empirical studies of human rights and US aid decisions. Methodologically, it addresses issues of measurement and research design that may be responsible for the inconsistent findings of previous evaluations of human rights initiatives.

RESEARCH DESIGN

One of the important differences in research designs among studies of the effect of human rights initiatives on US aid decisions is whether or not they differentiate between the decision to provide aid and the decision of how much aid to provide. Many participants in US foreign aid decisions describe two distinct stages in the allocation process. In the first stage, policy makers perform a function analogous to 'gatekeeping'; some nations are systematically excluded from the aid pool, while others are passed on to the second stage of the process. In the second stage, policy makers decide on the level of assistance to be provided.

With one exception, all of the empirical research to date has focused solely on level decisions, in effect ignoring the fact that different criteria may govern decisions at each stage. However, in Cingranelli and Pasquarello (1985), strong support was found for a two-stage decision process in US aid allocations toward Latin America. Based on this finding, a two-stage model of aid decisions, shown in Figure 14.1, is employed in this study. Should the determinants prove different at each stage of the decision process for Africa as well, the case for two-stage research designs in studies of the effect of human rights initiatives on US aid decisions would be strengthened.

Cingranelli and Pasquarello's work is also the only study of the impact of human rights initiatives on US aid decisions that employs a multivariate research design. If US aid distributions are influenced – as the theoretical literature, aid legislation, and pre-human rights empirical studies of aid allocations suggest they are – not only by human rights concerns, but by a number of factors, then bivariate models can be misleading. Measures of economic and social development and political instability used to model US aid decisions toward Africa in this study are identical with those used in Cingranelli and Pasquarello (1985).

The measure of alternative aid sources used in this study added European bilateral aid and total aid from multilateral sources, while Cingranelli and Pasquarello employed only multilateral aid. This reflects the fact that very little European bilateral aid was distributed to Latin America in the early 1980s, while significant amounts were distributed to Africa during the same period. Similarly, a measure of foreign policy orientation was included in this study, where no measure of this alternative explanation for US aid decisions was used in Cingranelli and Pasquarello (1985). Only one Latin American nation that was a candidate for US bilateral aid in FY 1982 (Nicaragua) had a pro-Soviet foreign policy orientation, while several African candidates had a pro-Soviet orientation. Finally, the measure of

238

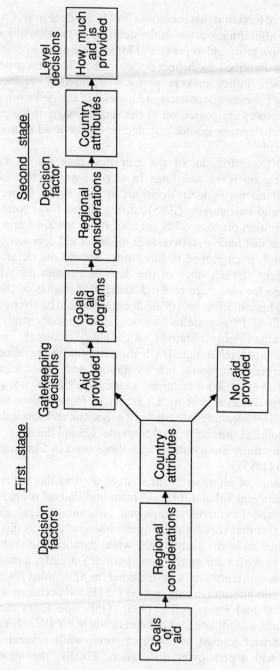

Figure 14.1 A conceptual model of US bilateral aid decisions

geopolitical importance used in Cingranelli and Pasquarello (1985) was clearly inappropriate for a study of US aid decisions toward Africa. Unfortunately, it was not possible to construct a satisfactory substitute for this concept for inclusion in this study. All of the alternative explanations of US aid decisions and their specific indicators are listed in Table 14.1.

Empirical studies of human rights considerations in US aid decisions have been divided between those that combine nations from several regions into a single analysis (e.g. Chomsky and Herman, 1979; Stohl, Carleton and Johnson, 1984; and, Carleton and Stohl, 1985) and those that focus on single regions (e.g. Schoultz, 1981b and 1981c; and, Cingranelli and Pasquarello, 1985). The regional presentation of US bilateral aid programs to Congress, the salience of AID and State Department regional bureaus in the decision process, and the importance of geographic 'spheres of influence' in the international relations literature suggest that the determinants of US aid decisions may be different for differnt regions of the world. To the extent that regional differences in aid decisions do occur, studies that combine nations from different regions into a single sample may obscure relationships that would be significant in separate regional analyses.

This research examines aid decisions for African nations that were candidates for US aid in FY 1982. South Africa was not included as it was not listed as a candidate for assistance in AID's congressional presentation. Chad and Angola were deleted from the analysis due to disclaimers about the accuracy of the available information on their human rights practices. The time period, research design, measures, and methods used in this regional analysis are virtually identical to those used in Cingranelli and Pasquarello (1985) to analyze US aid decisions toward Latin America. This allows for a direct comparison of regional findings and an assessment of the importance of regional research orientations for studies of the impact of human rights on aid decisions.

The specific indicator used to measure US aid levels has varied considerably between empirical studies of the effect of human rights initiatives. Some have combined military and economic assistance into a single measure, while others have examined each type of assistance separately. Since US military and economic aid decisions are governed by different legislation, made by different congressional committees and executive agencies, and generally serve (at least from the donor's point of view) different purposes, it seems appropriate to study each type of aid separately until compelling empirical

Table 14.1 Measures of competing explanations of US foreign aid policies

Variables	Indicators	Hypothesized Relationship
Level of development	Principal components factor, score of per capita gross national product, physicians per capita, primary school enrollment per capita, energy consumption per capita (1980)	Negative
Volume of trade with the US	Total value of goods exported to the US or imported from the US (1979)	Positive
Political instability	Total number of assassinations, general strikes, outbreaks of guerrilla warfare, major government crises, purges, riots, revolutions, anti-government demonstrations, and coups d'etat (1980)	Positive
Population	Population size (1980)	Positive
Level of European and multilateral assistance	Total aid from Western Europe and multilateral agencies (1979)	?
Level of Soviet Bloc assistance	Total aid from USSR and Soviet Bloc nations (1979)	?
Foreign policy orientation	Dummy variable, aligned with communist government coded 0; non-aligned or pro-West coded 1	Positive

Sources: Data on European, multilateral, and Soviet aid was taken from the Organization for Economic Cooperation and Development (1981) *Geographic Distribution of Financial Flows to Developing Countries, 1977/80* (Paris: OECD). Trade data were taken from the United Nations (1981) *1980 Yearbook of International Trade Statistics,* Vol. 1.

Data on Population Size, Level of Development, and Political Stability were taken from Arthur S. Banks, Cross-National Time-Series Data Archive (available from Arthur Banks, University Center at Binghamton, Binghamton, NY 13901).

Data on Foreign Policy Orientation was derived from Arthur S. Banks (1981) *The Political Handbook of the World* (New York, New York: McGraw-Hill).

evidence suggests that the determinants are not significantly different.

Similarly, some studies have standardized aid levels by each nation's population. A priori use of per capita transformations often leads to artificially high or low correlations among sets of variables (Uslaner, 1976). This may explain, in part, why previous studies have reached various conclusions as to the determinants US aid decisions. For this reason, aid levels are standardized by population in this research, but population is included as one of the independent variables in the multivariate models explaining US economic and military aid levels.

Six categories of economic aid are listed in AID's congressional presentation: Development Assistance (DA), Economic Support Funds (ESF), PL 480 Title I Commodities Credits, PL 480 Title II Emergency Food Relief, Peace Corps Programs, and International Narcotics Control Programs. The majority of US economic aid is distributed through the first three programs, and these are added to form the measure of economic assistance used in this study. The last three categories are excluded for a number of reasons.[1]

The measure of US military assistance consists of the combined total of aid distributed under the Military Assistance Program (MAP), direct and guaranteed loans provided under the Foreign Military

Table 14.2 Factor loading for human rights variables on the composite measure of human rights practices

Variables	Factor loading
Use of torture by government	.67
Use of summary executions by government	.52
Harshness of prison conditions	.38
Government-related disappearances	.43
Arbitrary arrest or imprisonment	.80
Fairness of trials	.56
Political prisoners held by government	.72
Government ownership of media	.32
Government interference with free press	.72
Government restricts freedom of assembly	.62
Government restricts union activity	.47
Government harasses religious groups	.46
Government restricts domestic travel	.45
Government restricts foreign travel	.67
Government restricts emigration	.52

242

Table 14.3 Human rights factor scores, foreign policy orientation and US economic and military assistance levels for African nations, 1980

Country	Score	Foreign policy orientation (0 = aligned with communist government) (1 = pro-West or non-aligned)	US economic assistance ($US millions)	US military assistance ($US millions)
Benin	-1.2	1*	0.0	0.0
Botswana	1.50	1	11.0	0.6
Burundi	-0.65	0	5.0	0.0
Cameroun	-1.20	1*	15.3	1.5
Cape Verde	0.86	1*	3.5	0.0
Central African Republic	1.30	1	1.0	0.0
Comoro Islands	-0.79	1	0.0	0.0
Congo Republic	0.58	0	3.0	0.0
Djibouti	0.80	1*	2.0	0.1
Equatorial Guinea	0.73	0	1.0	0.0
Ethiopia	-2.60	0	0.0	0.0
Gabon	0.72	1	0.0	0.0
Gambia	1.50	1*	0.0	2.7
Ghana	1.20	1*	1.2	0.0
Guinea	-0.90	1	8.4	0.3
Guinea-Bissau	0.17	0	6.1	0.0
Ivory Coast	0.47	1	2.4	0.0
Kenya	0.47	1*	53.9	33.1
Lesotho	-0.07	1*	10.2	0.0

Liberia	12.6	62.0	1	−0.82
Madagascar	0.0	5.0	0	−0.37
Malawi	0.1	7.7	1*	−0.50
Mauritania	0.0	6.3	1*	−0.13
Mauritius	1.5	5.5	1*	1.50
Mozambique	0.0	0.0	0	−1.00
Niger	2.4	13.0	1*	−0.02
Nigeria	0.0	0.0	1*	1.20
Rwanda	0.0	6.5	0	−0.44
Seychelles	0.0	2.0	1*	0.37
Sierra Leone	0.0	6.1	1	0.88
Somalia	25.4	48.9	1*	−1.70
Sudan	101.2	149.2	1*	−0.22
Swaziland	0.0	8.7	1*	0.15
Tanzania	0.0	15.6	1*	0.05
Togo	0.0	3.4	1*	−0.60
Uganda	0.0	7.0	1	−0.12
Upper Volta	0.1	11.2	1	0.97
Zaire	10.7	20.3	1*	−1.00
Zambia	0.0	27.0	1*	−1.40
Zimbabwe	0.1	75.0	1*	1.30

* Non-aligned nation.

Sales Program (FMS), and aid provided under the International Military Education and Training Program (IMET). The amount of economic assistance and military aid distributed to each African nation is listed in Table 14.3.

No matter how closely this study models US bilateral aid decisions, the findings are only as reliable as the operational measure of African nations human rights practices. Information about the human rights practices of African nations was gathered through a content analysis of the *Country Reports on Human Rights Practices* (US State Department, 1981). This information was combined into a single measure of human rights practices using principal components factor analysis.[2] The factor loadings and scores are listed in Tables 14.2 and 14.3.

Valid measures of comparative human rights practices are difficult to construct, because there is disagreement over what rights are fundamental and what constitutes the denial of a fundamental right (see for example, Donnelly, 1982; Thompson 1978; Van Dyke, 1973), and over the objectivity, consistency, and accuracy of sources of information on human rights practices. The most common language used by Congress to describe phenomena that should trigger actions in defense of human rights is 'a consistent pattern of gross violations of internationally recognized human rights', and the most important source of internationally recognized human rights is the United Nations' Universal Declaration of Human Rights. The individual variables listed in Table 14.2 cover most of the specific violations of human rights specified by the Universal Declaration of Human Rights, except for those dealing with economic rights.[3]

The accuracy and consistency of the measures is enhanced by the procedures used to gather information for the *Country Reports*. The State Department gathers information about the human rights practices of other nations through an annual questionnaire sent to each US embassy, a review of reports issued by US intelligence agencies, a review of human rights articles from the print media, and a review of reports issued by human rights organizations issued by human rights agencies such as Amnesty International. Initial drafts are prepared by the embassies, and subsequent drafts are edited by appropriate area experts within the State Department, in consultation with the embassy and the State Department's Bureau of Human Rights.

Even with this series of checks and balances, the information in the *Country Reports* is the subject of some controversy, and there are those who would claim that the information is fabricated to support the views of the administration (cf. Carleton and Stohl, 1985, p. 218). An examination of the reports provides evidence to the contrary. The reports contain harsh criticisms of nations which have traditionally been friendly toward the US, and of nations which have been singled out by particular administrations to receive large amounts of aid. In the 1980 *Country Reports* the Philippines, South Korea, and China, are examples of nations in the former category, and El Salvador is an example of a nation in the latter category. In addition, in a random sample of 100 countries, Amnesty International's annual report and the *Country Reports* agreed 81 and 77 per cent of the time, respectively, on the two items of human rights information – whether or not the government practiced torture, and whether or not the government arbitrarily arrested and imprisoned its citizens – covered in both documents.[4]

No source of information of human rights practices is seen as unbiased by all parties concerned with US foreign policy, but the *Country Reports* receive bipartisan support from members of relevant congressional committees and their staffs. Given the focus of this research, this support may be more important in evaluating the effectiveness of the measures used here than any attempt to establish the *Country Reports* as a completely accurate source of information on human rights practices.

FINDINGS

Gatekeeping Decisions

Table 14.4 presents the results of a logistic multiple regression explaining whether or not each African nation was the recipient of US bilateral economic and military assistance in FY 1982. The 't' values roughly indicate the magnitude and direction of the relationship between each of the theoretically relevant explanatory variables and the decision to provide each type of assistance, statistically controlling for the effects of the other variables in the analysis.[5]

In the economic assistance gatekeeping model, a nation's level of respect for human rights was the most important determinant in whether or not it received US aid. All things being equal, nations with African poor human rights records were less likely to receive economic assistance, while nations with better human rights records

Table 14.4 Logistic regression results explaining the decision by the United States to provide economic and military aid to African nations in FY 1982 (N = 40; 0 = no aid, 1 = aid)

Independent variable	Economic aid		Independent variable	Military aid	
	Coefficient	t value		Coefficient	t value
Respect for human rights	2.01	2.05	Respect for human rights	.16	.39
Level of economic development	−1.11	−1.43	Foreign policy orientation	8.8	15.85
Aid from European and multilateral sources	0.009	1.34	Volume of trade with US	.0000001	.35
Political instability	0.45	0.72	Level of economic development	.06	.11
Foreign policy orientation	0.43	0.37	Political instability	.34	1.2
Constant	0.58		Constant	−9.31	

were likely to receive at least some aid. The level of economic and social development was negatively related to the likelihood that African nations received economic assistance, i.e. nations with relatively high levels of development tended not to receive any economic aid. Nations that received higher combined levels of bilateral aid from European nations and multilateral agencies were more likely to receive at least some economic assistance from the United States. Finally, the level of political instability and foreign policy orientations proved relatively unimportant in predicting decisions to provide aid.

For the military assistance gatekeeping model, African nation's foreign policy orientation was by far the most important predictor of whether or not they received US aid. Human rights and all of the other hypothetically relevant factors were relatively unimportant in explaining whether or not US military assistance was provided to African nations.

Tables 14.5 and 14.6 further illustrate the role played by the most important determinants of military and economic aid gatekeeping decisions. One-third of the African nations with poor human rights

Table 14.5   Relationship between the human rights practices of African nations and the decision to provide or withhold economic aid in FY 1982 (N = 40)

Economic aid provided	Human rights practices		
	Poor	*Average*	*Good*
Yes	8	13	13
No	4	1	1

Somers D = .17

Table 14.6   Relationship between African nations foreign policy orientation and the US decision to provide or withhold military aid in FY 1982 (N = 43)

Military aid provided	Foreign policy orientation	
	Aligned with communist government(s)	*Non-aligned or pro-West*
Yes	0	16
No	8	19

Somers D = .46

records received no economic assistance from the US, while only one-fourteenth of nations with average and good human rights records were excluded. For military assistance and foreign policy orientation the relationship was even clearer; no nation that was aligned with the communist bloc received any US aid in FY 1982.

Level of Assistance Decisions

A different pattern of relationships emerges for levels of US economic and military assistance provided to African nations. Table 14.7 shows

Table 14.7   Results of (OLS) multiple regression models explaining levels of US economic and military assistance to African nations in FY 1982

Independent variable	*Dependent variable: level of economic aid* *coefficient of determination: 62* *N = 31*		
	b	Standard error	Standard beta
Intercept	6.45	5.93	
Respect for human rights	−0.76	4.26	−0.02
Aid from Soviet Union	10.11	2.17	0.63
Aid from European and multilateral sources	0.05	0.03	0.25

Independent variable	*Dependent variable: level of military aid* *coefficient of determination: 92* *N = 14*		
	b	Standard error	Standard beta
Intercept	−3.16	5.54	
Respect for human rights	−1.11	2.85	−0.04
Aid from Soviet Union	6.96	1.21	0.72
Aid from European and multilateral sources	0.05	0.02	0.30

the results of multiple regression analyses for factors hypothesized to influence these decisions. Human rights factors are not an important factor in predicting economic or military aid levels. In both cases the direction of the relationship is negative, indicating that African nations with poor human rights records tend to receive slightly more of both types of US aid.

Combined levels of European bilateral aid and aid from multilateral organizations were the best predictors of US economic and military aid. African nations that received higher levels of aid from these sources were more likely to receive high levels of aid from the United States. None of the other theoretically relevant variables were strongly associated with economic or military aid levels in the bivariate correlations or in preliminary multiple regression analyses, and they were dropped from the final models to minimize problems of missing data.

US Aid Allocations to Sudan

While US aid allocations to Sudan have not received anywhere near the attention that has been directed toward aid allocated to El Salvador, a closer examination shows that Sudan enjoyed a most favored status among African aid recipients in FY 1982 similar to the one afforded El Salvador in Latin America. Sudan received only slightly less total bilateral assistance from the US – $US 252 million to El Salvador's $US 268 million – and nearly as large a per cent of the regional total – 24 per cent to El Salvador's 27 per cent – making each a significant outlier in their respective regions.

Table 14.8   US and Soviet aid levels for selected African nations ($US millions)

Country	US economic aid	US military aid	Soviet aid
Sudan	149.0	101.2	10.6
Madagascar	5.0	0.0	2.0
Mali	9.6	0.1	1.0
Guinea	6.1	0.0	0.3
Congo	3.0	0.0	0.2
Tanzania	15.6	0.0	0.2
Uganda	7.0	0.0	0.1
Zambia	27.0	0.0	0.1
Ghana	8.4	0.0	0.1
Kenya	53.0	33.0	0.0
Zaire	20.3	10.7	0.0
Niger	13.0	2.4	0.0
Cameroun	15.3	1.5	0.0
Liberia	62.0	12.6	0.0
Somali Republic	49.0	25.4	0.0

Table 14.8 shows that Sudan also received a large amount of Soviet assistance relative to other African nations. This suggests that the standard beta coefficients for Soviet aid levels, and the magnitude of the coefficients of determination for the models explaining US aid levels are inordinately influenced by Sudan, and that a more general pattern of relationships may emerge if Sudan is removed from the analysis. Table 14.9 shows the effects of removing Sudan from the multiple regression models. The goodness of fit of the models is significantly reduced, and the effect of higher Soviet bloc aid levels on US aid levels changes from positive to negative for both types of assistance. The effect of higher combined levels of European bilateral aid and aid from multilateral sources remains positive, and its relative importance (as indicated by the standard betas) is increased in both models, while higher levels of respect for human rights continue to predict lower levels of US military and economic assistance.

Table 14.9　Results of (OLS) multiple regression models explaining levels of US economic and military assistance to African nations in FY 1982 (Sudan excluded)

Independent variable	Dependent variable: level of economic aid coefficient of determination: .18		
	b	Standard error	Standard beta
Intercept	6.45	5.93	
Respect for human rights	−0.76	4.26	−0.02
Aid from the Soviet Union	10.11	2.17	0.63
Aid from European and multilateral sources	0.05	0.03	0.25

Independent variable	Dependent variable: level of military aid coefficient of determination: .45 N = 14		
	b	Standard error	Standard beta
Intercept	−3.17	5.72	
Respect for human rights	−0.50	3.11	−0.05
Aid from the Soviet Union	−54.31	101.59	0.13
Aid from European and multilateral sources	0.05	0.02	0.62

CONCLUSIONS

The empirical findings provide evidence of a role for human rights in the US aid decisions that is considerably more complex than the one described by critics on either side of the ideological spectrum. The results show that human rights concerns have had a positive impact on US aid decisions. Even though human rights were a factor only in gatekeeping decisions for economic aid, they were by far the most consistent predictor of whether or not African nations received this type of assistance. Less comforting to those who favor a strong role for human rights concerns in US foreign policy is the finding that there were weak negative relationships between the degree of respect for human rights and levels of economic and military assistance allocated to African nations in FY 1982.

However, it is obvious that human rights considerations were not the sole factor governing US aid decisions toward Africa. In gatekeeping decisions for military assistance it appears that the primary concern of policy makers awas to inhibit the spread of communist influence in the region, as no African nation aligned with the communist world received any US military assistance in FY 1982. In level decisions, availability of aid from alternative sources was a much more important factor than level of respect for human rights in determining US economic and military aid allocations.

The latter findings show that competition for influence, not concern for human rights, was the dominant motive in US policy toward Africa. When Sudan was removed from the analyses of level decisions competition remained the dominant motive, but the emphasis was changed. For most of Africa it was not east–west competition, but competition with European nations that motivated US aid decisions.

Since the research design, measures, and time period are identical with those used to study US aid decisions toward Latin America in Cingranelli and Pasquarello (1985), a comparison of findings provides insight into the proper models and measures to use in subsequent studies of these decisions.

As in Cingranelli and Pasquarello, different patterns characterize gatekeeping and aid level decisions. The two-stage model of aid decisions has been described as a 'significant contribution to existing work on the issue' (Carleton and Stohl, 1986, p. 3) by two of the most active researchers in the field, and the findings of this research provide additional support for this model.

In contrast to Cingranelli and Pasquarello (1985), the determinants of US military and economic aid levels for African nations were similar. However, the determinants of military and economic gate-keeping decisions were again very different. These findings suggest that prudent researchers should examine military and economic aid decisions separately, at least in the initial phases of their research.

Neither study provides any support for standardizing aid levels by population. As in Latin America, population was unrelated to military and economic aid levels for African nations in the bivariate correlations, and it was never an important predictor of aid levels in the preliminary multiple regression analyses.

This research and Cingranelli and Pasquarello (1985) provide the first empirical evidence that regional studies of aid decisions are more appropriate than studies which combine nations from different regions into a single sample. The structure of aid determinants was decidedly different for Latin America and Africa in FY 1982, even though the models and measures were the same. Combining these regions into a single sample would have diminished statistical relationships that were important in predicting aid decisions in the separate regional analysis.

Notes

1. PL 480 II funds were excluded for two reasons. First, legislation governing the distribution of economic assistance allows aid to be provided to repressive governments if it will directly benefit needy people. PL 480 II relief is provided in cases of national emergencies such as earthquakes, crop failures, etc. None of the participants in the foreign aid process interviewed for this study could recall a single instance where emergency food assistance had been denied on the basis of poor human rights records. In addition, PL 480 II food relief is distributed via multilateral agencies, and this study is focused on bilateral aid allocations. Peace Corps funds are excluded because they also meet the 'basic needs' criteria outlined above. International Narcotics Control Funds are excluded because they are clearly designed to achieve different policy goals than other kinds of economic aid.
2. For detailed information on the coding procedures and factor analyses used in this study see Cingranelli and Pasquarello (1985).
3. The lack of information on economic rights in the *Country Reports* is not critical in this instance as these rights have not been an important consideration in the debate among US policy makers over the disbursement of foreign aid.
4. It is difficult to make comparisons of the human rights reports produced

by different organizations because of the differing formats, definitions, and time periods used in the reports. An independent coder was employed to compare the Amnesty International and State Department reports for calendar year 1980.
5. Logistic regression is more appropriate for estimating dichotomous dependent variables than ordinary least squares. For a comparison of these two procedures see King (1986).

References

CARLETON, D. and M. STOHL (1985) 'The Foreign Policy of Human Rights: Rhetoric and Reality from Jimmy Carter to Ronald Reagan', *Human Rights Quarterly*, 7: 205–29.

CARLETON, D. and STOHL, M. (1986) 'The Role of Human Rights in US Foreign Assistance Policy: A Critique and Re-appraisal'. Unpublished manuscript, Department of Political Science, Purdue University.

CHOMSKY, N. and HERMAN, E. (1979) *The Political Economy of Human Rights: Washington Connection and Third World Fascism* (Boston: South End Press).

CINGRANELLI, D. L. and PASQUARELLO, T. (1985) 'Human Rights Practices and the Distribution of U.S. Foreign Aid to Latin American Countries', *American Journal of Political Science*, 29 (August): 540–63.

DONNELLY, J. (1982) 'Human Rights and Foreign Policy', *World Politics*, 34 (July): 574–95.

KING, G. (1986) 'How Not to Lie With Statistics: Avoiding Common Mistakes in Quantitative Political Science', *American Journal of Political Science*, 30: 666–87.

LAPPE, F. M., COLLINS, J. and KINLEY, D. (1981) *Aid as Obstacle* (San Francisco: Institute for Food and Development Policy).

SCHOULTZ, L. (1981a) *Human Rights and US Policy Toward Latin America* (Princeton: Princeton University Press).

SCHOULTZ, L. (1981b) 'US Foreign Policy and Human Rights', *Comparative Politics*, 13 (January): 149–70.

SCHOULTZ, L. (1981c) 'US Policy Toward Human Rights in Latin America: A Comparative Analysis of Two Administrations', in Ved P. Nanda, James R. Scarritt, and George W. Shepherd, Jr. (eds), *Global Human Rights: Public Policies, Comparative Measures and NGO Strategies*, pp. 77–91 (Boulder, Co.: Westview Press).

STOHL, M., CARLETON, D. and JOHNSON, S. E. (1984) 'Human Rights and U.S. Foreign Assistance from Nixon to Carter', *Journal of Peace Research*, 21: 215–26.

THOMPSON, Kenneth (1978) 'New Reflections on Ethics and Foreign Policy: The Problem of Human Rights', *Journal of Politics*, 40 (November): 984–1010.

US STATE DEPARTMENT (1981) *Country Reports on Human Rights Practices* (Washington, DC: US Government Printing Office).
VAN DYKE, V. (1973) 'Human Rights Without Discrimination', *American Political Science Review*, 67 (December): 1267–90.

Index